Thomas Chatterton, Thomas Tyrwhitt

Poems, Supposed to Have Been Written at Bristol

Thomas Chatterton, Thomas Tyrwhitt

Poems, Supposed to Have Been Written at Bristol

ISBN/EAN: 9783744711296

Printed in Europe, USA, Canada, Australia, Japan

Cover: Foto ©Thomas Meinert / pixelio.de

More available books at **www.hansebooks.com**

P O E M S,

SUPPOSED TO HAVE BEEN WRITTEN AT BRISTOL,

BY THOMAS ROWLEY, AND OTHERS,

IN THE FIFTEENTH CENTURY.

THE THIRD EDITION;

TO WHICH IS ADDED

AN APPENDIX,

CONTAINING SOME OBSERVATIONS UPON THE
LANGUAGE OF THESE POEMS;

TENDING TO PROVE,

THAT THEY WERE WRITTEN, NOT BY ANY ANCIENT
AUTHOR,

BUT ENTIRELY BY THOMAS CHATTERTON.

[iii]

THE

C O N T E N T S

O F   T H I S   V O L U M E.

2   Epiftle

iv CONTENTS.

PREFACE.

THE Poems, which make the principal part of this Collection, have for some time excited much curiofity, as the fuppofed productions of THOMAS ROWLEY, a prieft of Briftol, in the reigns of Henry VI. and Edward IV. They are here faithfully printed from the moft authentic MSS that could be procured; of which a particular defcription is given in the *Introductory account of the feveral pieces contained in this volume*, fubjoined to this Preface. Nothing more therefore feems neceffary at prefent, than to inform the Reader fhortly of the manner in which thefe Poems were firft brought to light, and of the authority upon which they are afcribed to the perfons whofe names they bear.

This

This cannot be done fo fatisfactorily as in the words of Mr. George Catcott of Briftol, to whofe very laudable zeal the Publick is indebted for the moft confiderable part of the following collection. His account of the matter is this : " The firft difcovery of cer-
" tain MSS having been depofited in Red-
" clift church, above three centuries ago, was
" made in the year 1768, at the time of
" opening the new bridge at Briftol, and was
" owing to a publication in *Farley's Weekly*
" *Journal*, 1 October 1768, containing an
" *Account of the ceremonies obferved at the*
" *opening of the old bridge*, taken, as it was
" faid, from a very antient MS. This ex-
" cited the curiofity of fome perfons to en-
" quire after the original. The printer,
" Mr. Farley, could give no account of it,
" or of the perfon who brought the copy;
" but after much enquiry it was difcovered,
" that

" that the perfon who brought the copy
" was a youth, between 15 and 16 years of
" age, whofe name was Thomas Chatterton,
" and whofe family had been fextons of
" Redclift church for near 150 years.   His
" father, who was now dead, had alfo been
" mafter of the free-fchool in Pile-ftreet.
" The young man was at firft very unwilling
" to difcover from whence he had the ori-
" ginal; but, after many promifes made to
" him, he was at laft prevailed on to ac-
" knowledge, that he had received this, *toge-*
" *ther with many other MSS*, from his father,
" who had found them in a large cheft in
" an upper room over the chapel on the
" north fide of Redclift church."

   Soon after this Mr. Catcott commenced his
acquaintance with young Chatterton *, and,
partly

---

   * The hiftory of this youth is fo intimately connected with
that of the poems now publifhed, that the Reader cannot be
too early apprized of the principal circumftances of his fhort

life.

partly as prefents partly as purchafes, procured from him copies of many of his MSS.

in

life. He was born on the 20th of November 1752, and
educated at a charity-fchool. on St. Auguftin's Back, where
nothing more was taught than reading, writing, and accounts.
At the age of fourteen, he was articled clerk to an attorney,
with whom he continued till he left Briftol in April 1770.

Though his education was thus confined, he difcovered an
early turn towards poetry and Englifh antiquities, particularly
heraldry. How foon he began to be an author is not known.
In the *Town and Country Magazine* for March 1769, are two
letters, probably, from him, as they are dated at Briftol, and
fubfcribed with his ufual fignature, D. B. The firft contains
fhort extracts from two MSS, " *written three hundred years
ago by one Rowley, a Monk,*" concerning drefs in the age of
Henry II. ; the other, " ETHELGAR, *a Saxon poem,*" in bom-
baft profe. In the fame Magazine for May 1769, are three
communications from Briftol, with the fame fignature, D. B.
viz. CERDICK, *tranflated from the Saxon* (in the fame ftyle
with ETHELGAR), p. 233.—*Obfervations upon Saxon heraldry,*
with drawings of *Saxon atchievements,* &c. p. 245.—ELINOURE
and JUGA, *written three hundred years ago by* T. ROWLEY, *a
fecular prieft,* p. 273. This laft poem is reprinted in this volume, p. 19. In the fubfequent months of 1769 and 1770
there are feveral other pieces in the fame Magazine, which are
undoubtedly of his compofition.

In April 1770, he left Briftol and came to London, in
hopes of advancing his fortune by his talents for writing, of
which, by this time, he had conceived a very high opinion.

In

in profe and verfe. Other copies were difpofed of, in the fame way, to Mr. William Barrett,

In the profecution of this fcheme, he appears to have almoft entirely depended upon the patronage of a fet of gentlemen, whom an eminent author long ago pointed out, as *not the very worft judges or rewarders of merit*, the bookfellers of this great city. At his firft arrival indeed he was fo unlucky as to find two of his expected Mæcenafes, the one in the King's Bench, and the other in Newgate. But this little difappointment was alleviated by the encouragement which he received from other quarters; and on the 14th of May he writes to his mother, in high fpirits upon the change in his fituation, with the following farcaftic reflection upon his former patrons at Briftol. "*As to Mr. ——, Mr. ——, Mr. ——, &c. &c. they rate literary lumber fo low, that I believe an author, in their eftimation, muft be poor indeed! But here matters are otherwife. Had* Rowley *been a* Londoner *inftead of a* Briftowyan, *I could have lived by copying his works.*"

In a letter to his fifter, dated 30 May, he informs her, that he is to be employed "*in writing a voluminous hiftory of* London, *to appear in numbers the beginning of next winter.*" In the mean time, he had written fomething in praife of the Lord Mayor (Beckford), which had procured him the honour of being prefented to his lordfhip. In the letter juft mentioned he gives the following account of his reception, with fome curious obfervations upon political writing: "The Lord Mayor received me as politely as a citizen could. But the devil of the matter is, there is no money to be got of this fide of the

queftion.

Barrett, an eminent furgeon at Briftol,
who has long been engaged in writing
the hiftory of that city. Mr. Barrett alfo
procured from him feveral fragments, fome

queftion.—But he is a poor author who cannot write on both
fides.—Effays on the patriotic fide will fetch no more than
what the copy is fold for. As the patriots themfelves are
fearching for a place, they have no gratuity to fpare.—On
the other hand, unpopular effays will not even be accepted;
and you muft pay to have them printed : but then you feldom
lofe by it, as courtiers are fo fenfible of their deficiency in
merit, that they generoufly reward all who know how to
dawb them with the appearance of it."

   Notwithftanding his employment on the Hiftory of London,
he continued to write inceffantly in various periodical publi-
cations. On the 11th of July he tells his fifter that he had
pieces laft month in the *Gofpel Magazine*; the *Town and Country, viz.* Maria Friendlefs; Falfe Step; Hunter of Oddities;
To Mifs Bufh, &c. *Court and City*; *London*; *Political Regifter*, &c. But all thefe exertions of his genius brought in
fo little profit, that he was foon reduced to real indigence;
from which he was relieved by death (in what manner is not
certainly known), on the 24th of Auguft, or thereabout, when
he wanted near three months to complete his eighteenth year.
The floor of his chamber was covered with written papers,
which he had torn into fmall pieces; but there was no appearance (as the Editor has been credibly informed) of any writings
on parchment or vellum,

                                  of

of a confiderable length, written upon vellum *, which he afferted to be part of his original MSS. In fhort, in the fpace of about eighteen months, from October 1768 to April 1770, befides the Poems now publifhed, he produced as many compofitions, in profe and verfe, under the names of Rowley, Canynge, &c. as would nearly fill fuch another volume.

In April 1770 Chatterton went to London, and died there in the Auguft follow-

* One of thefe fragments, by Mr. Barrett's permiffion, has been copied in the manner of a *Fac fimile*, by that ingenious artift Mr. Strutt, and an engraving of it is inferted at p. 288. Two other fmall fragments of Poetry are printed in p. 277, 8, 9. See the *Introductory Account*. The fragments in profe, which are confiderably larger, Mr. Barrett intends to publifh in his Hiftory of Briftol, which, the Editor has the fatisfaction to inform the Publick, is very far advanced. In the fame work will be inferted *A Difcorfe on Briftowe*, and the other hiftorical pieces in profe, which Chatterton at different times delivered out, as copied from Rowley's MSS.; with fuch remarks by Mr. Barrett, as he of all men living is beft qualified to make, from his accurate refearches into the Antiquities of Briftol.

ing; fo that the whole hiftory of this very extraordinary tranfaction cannot now probably be known with any certainty. Whatever may have been his part in it; whether he was the author, or only the copier (as he conftantly afferted) of all thefe productions; he appears to have kept the fecret entirely to himfelf, and not to have put it in the power of any other perfon, to bear certain teftimony either to his fraud or to his veracity.

The queftion therefore concerning the authenticity of thefe Poems muft now be decided by an examination of the fragments upon vellum, which Mr. Barrett received from Chatterton as part of his original MSS., and by the internal evidence which the feveral pieces afford. If the Fragments fhall be judged to be genuine, it will ftill remain to be determined, how far their ge-

nuinenefs

nuineneſs ſhould ſerve to authenticate the reſt of the collection, of which no copies, older than thoſe made by Chatterton, have ever been produced. On the other hand, if the writing of the Fragments ſhall be judged to be counterfeit and forged by Chatterton, it will not of neceſſity follow, that the matter of them was alſo forged by him, and ſtill leſs, that all the other compoſitions, which he profeſſed to have copied from antient MSS., were merely inventions of his own. In either caſe, the deciſion muſt finally depend upon the internal evidence.

It may be expected perhaps, that the Editor ſhould give an opinion upon this. important queſtion ; but he rather chooſes, for many reaſons, to leave it to the determination of the unprejudiced and intelligent Reader. He had long been deſirous

that

that thefe Poems fhould be printed; and therefore readily undertook the charge of fuperintending the edition. This he has executed in the manner, which feemed to him beft fuited to fuch a publication; and here he means that his tafk fhould end. Whether the Poems be really antient, or modern; the compofitions of Rowley, or the forgeries of Chatterton; they muft always be confidered as a moft fingular literary curiofity.

INTRO-

INTRODUCTORY ACCOUNT

OF THE

SEVERAL PIECES

CONTAINED IN THIS VOLUME.

Thefe three Eclogues are printed from a MS. furnifhed by Mr. Catcott, in the hand-writing of Thomas Chatterton. It is a thin copy-book in 4to. with the following title in the firft page. "*Eclogues and other Poems by* Thomas Rowley, *with a Gloffary and Annotations by* Thomas Chatterton."

There is only one other Poem in this book, viz. the fragment of "*Goddwyn, a Tragedie*," which fee below, p. 173.

This Poem is reprinted from the *Town and Country Magazine* for May 1769, p. 273. It is there entitled, "*Elinoure and*

and Juga. Written three hundred years ago by T. Rowley a secular prieft." And it has the following fubfcription; " D. B. Briftol, May, 1769." Chatterton foon after told Mr. Cat- cott, that he (Chatterton) inferted it in the Magazine.

The prefent Editor has taken the liberty to fupply [between hooks] the names of the fpeakers, at ver. 22 and 29, which had probably been omitted by fome accident in the firft publi- cation; as the nature of the compofition feems to require, that the dialogue fhould proceed by alternate ftanzas.

VERSES TO LYDGATE.   p. 23
SONGE TO ÆLLA.   Ibid·
LYDGATE'S ANSWER.   26

Thefe three fmall Poems are printed from a copy in Mr. Catcott's hand-writing. Since they were printed off, the Editor has had an opportunity of comparing them with a copy made by Mr. Barrett from the piece of vellum, which Chat- terton formerly gave to him as the original MS. The varia- tions of importance (exclufive of many in the fpelling) are fet down below *.

                                     T H E

● *Verfes to Lydgate.*
   In the title for *Ladgate,* r. *Lydgate.*
   ver. 2.   r. *Thatt I and thee* .
        3. for *bee,* r. *goe.*
        7. for *fyghte,* r. *wryte.*

                                     Songe

This Poem is printed from a copy made by Mr. Catcott, from one in Chatterton's hand-writing.

Songe to Ælla.

The title in the vellum MS. was fimply " *Songe toe Ælle*," with a fmall mark of reference to a note below, containing the following words—" *Lorde of the caftelle of Bryftowe ynne daies of yore.*" It may be proper alfo to take notice, that the whole fong was there written like profe, without any breaks, or divifions into verfes.

 ver. 6. for *braftynge*, r. *burftynge*.
  11. for *valyante*, r. *burlie*.
  23. for *dyfmall*, r. *honore*.
Lydgate's anfwer.
No title in the vellum MS.
 ver. 3. for *varfes*, r. *pene*.
 antep. for *Lendes*, r. *Sendes*.
 ult. for *lyne*, r. *thynge*.

Mr. Barrett had alfo a copy of thefe Poems by Chatterton, which differed from that, which Chatterton afterwards produced as the original, in the following particulars, among others.

In the title of the *Verfes to Lydgate.*
  Orig. *Lydgate* —— Chat. *Ladgate.*
 ver. 3. Orig. *goe.* —— Chat. *doe.*
  7. Orig. *wryte.* —— Chat. *fyghte.*
 Songe to Ælla.
 ver. 5. Orig. *Dacyane.* — Chat. *Dacya's.*
  Orig. *whofe lockes* — Chat. *whofe hayres.*
  11. Orig. *burlie.* —— Chat. *branded.*
  22. Orig. *kennft.* —— Chat. *hearft.*
  23. Orig. *honore.* —— Chat. *dyfmall.*
  26. Orig. *Yprauncynge* — Chat. *Ifrayning.*
  30. Orig. *gloue.* —— Chat. *glare.*

         Sit

Sir Simon de Bourton, the hero of this poem, is fuppofed to have been the firft founder of a church dedicated to *oure Ladie,* in the place where the church of St. Mary Ratcliffe now ftands.   Mr. Barrett has a fmall leaf of vellum (given to him by Chatterton as one of Rowley's original MSS.), entitled, " *Vita de Simon de Bourton,*" in which Sir Simon is faid, as in the poem, to have begun his foundation in confequence of a vow made at a tournament.

THE DETHE OF SYR CHARLES BAWDIN.   p. 44

This Poem is reprinted from the copy printed at London in 1772, with a few corrections from a copy made by Mr. Catcott, from one in Chatterton's hand-writing.

The perfon here celebrated, under the name of *Syr Charles Bawdin,* was probably *Sir Baldewyn Fulford,* Knt. a zealous Lancaftrian, who was executed at Briftol in the latter end of 1461, the firft year of Edward the Fourth.   He was attainted, with many others, in the general act of Attainder, 1 Edw. IV. but he feems to have been executed under a fpecial commiffion for the trial of treafons, &c. within the town of Briftol.   The fragment of the old chronicle, publifhed by Hearne at the end of *Sprotti Chronica,* p. 289. fays only ; " Item *the fame yere* (1 Edw. IV.) *was takin Sir Baldewine Fulford and behedid att Briftow.*"   But the matter is more fully ftated in the act which paffed in 7 Edw. IV. for the reftitution in blood and eftate of

Thomas

Thomas Fulford, Knt. eldeft fon of Baldewyn Fulford, late
of Fulford, in the county of Devonfhire, Knt. *Rot. Pat.*
8 Edw. IV. p 1. m. 13. The preamble of this act, after
ftating the attainder by the act 1 Edw. IV. goes on thus :
" And alfo the faid Baldewyn, the faid firft yere of your noble
reign, at Briftowe in the fhere of Briftowe, before Henry Erle
of Effex William Haftyngs of Haftyngs Knt. Richard Chock
William Canyng Maire of the faid towne of Briftowe and
Thomas Yong, by force of your letters patentes to theym and
other directe to here and determine all treefons &c. doon withyn
the faid towne of Briftowe before the vth day of September the
firft yere of your faid reign, was atteynt of dyvers trefons by
him doon ayenft your Highnes &c." If the commiffion fate
foon after the vth of September, as is moft probable, King
Edward might very poffibly be at Briftol at the time of Sir
Baldewyn's execution ; for, in the interval between his coro-
nation and the parliament which met in November, he made
a progrefs (as the Continuator of Stowe informs us, p. 416.)
by the South coaft into the Weft, and was (among other
places) at Briftol. Indeed there is a circumftance which might
lead us to believe, that he was actually a fpectator of the execution from the minfter-window, as defcribed in the poem.
In an old accompt of the Procurators of St. Ewin's church,
which was then the minfter, from xx March in the 1 Edward
IV. to 1 April in the year next enfuing, is the following article,

cle, according to a copy made by Mr. Catcott from the original book.

> " Item *for wafhynge the church payven ageyns* } iiij d. ob.
> *Kynge Edward 4th is comynge.*

ÆLLA, a tragycal enterlude.   p. 65

This Poem, with the *Epiftle, Letter,* and *Entroductionne,* is printed from a folio MS. furnifhed by Mr. Catcott, in the beginning of which he has written, " Chatterton's tranfcript. 1769." The whole tranfcript is of Chatterton's hand-writing.

GODDWYN, a Tragedie.   p. 173

This Fragment is printed from the MS. mentioned above, p. xv. in Chatterton's hand-writing.

ENGLYSH METAMORPHOSIS.   p. 196

This Poem is printed from a fingle fheet in Chatterton's hand-writting, communicated by Mr. Barrett, who received it from Chatterton.

BALADE OF CHARITIE.   p. 203

This Poem is alfo printed from a fingle fheet in Chatterton's hand-writing. It was fent to the Printer of the *Town and Country Magazine,* with the following letter prefixed :

" To

"*. To the Printer of the Town and Country Magazine.

SIR,

If the Glossary annexed to the following piece will make the language intelligible; the Sentiment, Description, and Versification, are highly deserving the attention of the literati.

July 4, 1770.   D. B."

In printing the first of these poems two copies have been made use of, both taken from copies of Chatterton's hand-writing, the one by Mr. Catcott, and the other by Mr. Barrett. The principal difference between them is at the end, where the latter has fourteen lines from ver. 550, which are wanting in the former. The second poem is printed from a single copy, made by Mr. Barrett from one in Chatterton's hand-writing.

It should be observed, that the Poem marked Nº 1, was given to Mr. Barrett by Chatterton with the following title; "*Battle of Hastings, wrote by Turgot the Monk, a Saxon, in the tenth century, and translated by Thomas Rowlie, parish preeste of St. Johns in the city of Bristol, in the year 1465.—The remainder of the poem I have not been happy enough to meet with.*" Being afterwards prest by Mr. Barrett to produce any part of this poem in the original hand-writing, he at last said, that he wrote this poem himself for a friend; but that he had another,

c   the

the copy of an original by Rowley : and being then defired to produce that other poem, he, after a confiderable interval of time, brought to Mr. Barrett the poem marked N° 2, as far as ver. 530 incl. with the following title; " *Battle of Haftyngs by Turgotus, tranflated by Roulie for W. Canynge Efq.*" The lines from ver. 531 incl. were brought fome time after, in confequence of Mr. Barrett's repeated follicitations for the conclufion of the poem,

The firft of thefe Poems is printed from a copy made by Mr. Catcott, from one in Chatterton's hand-writing.

The other is taken from a MS. in Chatterton's hand-writing, furnifhed by Mr. Catcott, entitled, " *A Difcorfe on Briftowe, by Thomas Rowlie.*" See the Preface, p. xi. n. *,

This is one of the fragments of vellum, given by Chatterton to Mr. Barrett, as part of his original MSS.

The 34 firft lines of this poem are extant upon another of the vellum-fragments, given by Chatterton to Mr. Barrett.

The

The remainder is printed from a copy furnifhed by Mr. Cat-cott, with fome corrections from another copy, made by Mr. Barrett from one in Chatterton's hand-writing. This poem makes part of a profe-work, attributed to Rowley, giving an account of *Painters, Carvellers, Poets,* and other eminent natives of Briftol, from the earlieft times to his own. The whole will be publifhed by Mr. Barrett, with remarks, and large additions; among which we may expect a complete and authentic hiftory of that diftinguifhed citizen of Briftol, Mr. William Canynge. In the mean time, the Reader may fee feveral particulars relating to him in *Cambden's Britannia,* Somerfet'. Col. 95.—*Rymer's Fœdera,* &c. ann. 1449 & 1450.—*Tanner's Not. Monaft.* Art. BRISTOL and WESTBURY.—*Dugdale's Warwickfhire,* p. 634.

It may be proper juft to remark here, that Mr. Canynge's brother, mentioned in ver. 129, who was lord mayor of London in 1456, is called *Thomas* by Stowe in his Lift of Mayors, &c.

The tranfaction alluded to in the laft Stanza is related at large in fome Profe Memoirs of Rowley, of which a very incorrect copy has been printed in the *Town and Country Magazine* for November 1775. It is there faid, that Mr. Canynge went into orders, to avoid a marriage, propofed by King Edward, between him and a lady of the Widdevile family. It is certain, from the Regifter of the Bifhop of Worcefter, that Mr. Canynge was ordained *Acolythe* by Bifhop Carpenter on

19 September 1467, and received the higher orders of *Subdeacon, Deacon,* and *Prieſt,* on the 12th of March, 1467, O. S. the 2d and 16th of April, 1468, reſpectively.

ON HAPPIENESSE, by William Canynge. p. 286
ONNE JOHNE A DALBENIE, by the ſame. Ibid.
THE GOULER'S REQUIEM, by the ſame.   287
THE ACCOUNTE OF W. CANYNGE'S FEASTE. 288

Of theſe four Poems attributed to Mr. Canynge, the three firſt are printed from Mr. Catcott's copies. The laſt is taken from a fragment of vellum, which Chatterton gave to Mr. Barrett as an original. The Editor has doubts about the reading of the ſecond word in ver. 7, but he has printed it *keene,* as he found it ſo in other copies. The Reader may judge for himſelf, by examining the *Fac ſimile* in the oppoſite page.

With reſpect to the three friends of Mr. Canynge mentioned in the laſt line, the name of *Rowley* is ſufficiently known from the preceding poems. *Iſcamm* appears as an actor in the tragedy of *Ælla,* p. 66. and in that of *Goddwyn,* p. 174.; and a poem, aſcribed to him, entitled " *The merry Tricks of Laymington,*" is inſerted in the " *Diſcorſe of Briſtowe.*" Sir *Theobald Gorges* was a knight of an antient family ſeated at Wraxhall, within a few miles of Briſtol [See *Rot. Parl.* 3 H. VI. n. 28. *Leland's Itin.* vol. VII. p. 98.]. He has alſo appeared above as an actor in both the tragedies, and as the author of one of the *Mynstrelles songes* in *Ælla*, p. 91. His connexion with Mr. Canynge is verified by a deed of the latter, dated 20 October, 1467, in which he gives to truftees, in part of a benefaction of £.500 to the Church of St. Mary Redcliffe, " *certain jewells of* Sir *Theobald Gorges* Knt." which had been pawned to him for £.160.

ADVER-

ADVERTISEMENT.

THE Reader is defired to obferve, that the notes at the bottom of the feveral pages, throughout the following part of this book, are all copied from MSS. in the hand-writing of Thomas Chatterton.

POEMS,

P O E M S, &c.

ECLOGUE THE FIRST.

WHANNE Englonde, fmeethynge [1] from her
  lethal [2] wounde,

From her galled necke dyd twytte [3] the chayne
  awaie,

Kennynge her legeful fonnes falle all arounde,

(Myghtie theie fell, 'twas Honoure ledde the fraie,)

Thanne inne a dale, bie eve's dark furcote [4] graie,   5

Twayne lonelie fhepfterres [5] dyd abrodden [6] flie,

(The roftlyng liff doth theyr whytte hartes affraie [7],)

And wythe the owlette trembled and dyd crie;

Firfte Roberte Neatherde hys fore boefom ftroke,

Then fellen on the grounde and thus yfpoke.   10

---

[1] *Smething*, fmoking; in fome copies *bletheynge*, but in the oral as
above.   [2] deadly.   [3] pluck or pull.   [4] *Surcote*, a cloke, or mantel,
which hid all the other drefs.   [5] fhepherds.   [6] abruptly, fo Chaucer,
Syke he abredden dyd attourne.   [7] affright.

ROBERTE.

Ah, Raufe! gif thos the howres do comme alonge,

Gif thos wee flie in chafe of farther woe,

Oure fote wylle fayle, albeytte wee bee ftronge,

Ne wylle oure pace fwefte as oure danger goe.

To oure grete wronges we have enheped [8] moe,   15

The Baronnes warre! oh! woe and well-a-daie!

I haveth lyff, bott have efcaped foe,

That lyff ytfel mie Senfes doe affraie.

Oh Raufe, comme lyfte, and hear mie dernie [9] tale,

Comme heare the balefull [10] dome of Robynne of the

Dale.   20

RAUFE.

Saie to mee nete; I kenne thie woe in myne;

O! I've a tale that Sabalus [11] mote [12] telle.

Swote [13] flouretts, mantled meedows, foreftes

dygne [14];

Gravots [15] far-kend [16] arounde the Errmiets [17] cell;

---

[8] Added. [9] fad. [10] woeful, lamentable. [11] the Devil. [12] might.
[13] fweet. [14] good, neat, genteel. [15] groves, fometimes ufed for a
coppice. [16] far-feen. [17] Hermit.

The

The fwote ribible [18] dynning [19] yn the dell;   25
The joyous daunceynge ynn the hoaftrie [20] courte;
Eke [21] the highe fonge and everych joie farewell,
Farewell the verie fhade of fayre dyfporte [22]:
Impeftering [23] trobble onn mie heade doe comme,
Ne on kynde Seynéte to warde [24] the aye [25] encreafynge
     dome.   30

ROBERTE.

Oh! I coulde waile mie kynge-coppe-decked mees [26],
Mie fpreedynge flockes of fhepe of lillie white,
Mie tendre applynges [27], and embodyde [28] trees,
Mie Parker's Grange [29], far fpreedynge to the fyghte,
Mie cuyen [30] kyne [31], mie bullockes ftringe [32] yn
     fyghte,   35
Mie gorne [33] emblaunched [34] with the comfreie [35]
     plante,
Mie floure [36] Seynéte Marie fhotteyng wythe the lyghte,
Mie ftore of all the bleffynges Heaven can grant.

---

[18] violin. [19] founding. [20] inn, or public-houfe. [21] alfo. [22] pleafure. [23] annoying. [24] to keep off. [25] ever, always. [26] meadows.
[27] grafted trees. [28] thick, ftout. [29] liberty of pafture given to the
Parker. [30] tender. [31] cows. [32] ftrong. [33] garden. [34] whitened.
[35] cumfrey, a favourite difh at that time. [36] marygold.

I amm dureſſed [37] unto ſorrowes blowe,
Ihanten'd [38] to the peyne, will lette ne ſalte teare flowe. 40

RAUFE.

Here I wille obaie [39] untylle Dethe doe 'pere,
Here lyche a foule empoyſoned leathel [40] tree,
Whyche ſleaeth [41] everichone that commeth nere,
Soe wille I fyxed unto thys place gre [42].
I to bement [43] haveth moe cauſe than thee ;   45
Sleene in the warre mie boolie [44] fadre lies ;
Oh ! joieous I hys mortherer would ſlea,
And bie hys ſyde for aie encloſe myne eies.
Calked [45] from everych joie, heere wylle I blede ;
Fell ys the Cullys-yatte [46] of mie hartes caſtle ſtede. 50

ROBERTE.

Oure woes alyche, alyche our dome [47] ſhal bee.
Mie ſonne, mie ſonne alleyn [48], yſtorven [49] ys ;

[37] hardened. [38] accuſtomed. [39] abide. This line is alſo wrote,
" Here wyll I obaie untill dethe appere" but this is modernized.
[40] deadly. [41] deſtroyeth, killeth. [42] grow. [43] lament. [44] much-
loved, beloved. [45] caſt out, ejected. [46] alluding to the portcullis,
which guarded the gate, on which often depended the caſtle. [47] fate.
[48] my only ſon. [49] dead.

Here

Here wylle I ftaie, and end mie lyff with thee;

A lyff lyche myn a borden ys ywis.

Now from een logges 5º fledden is felynefs 5¹,   55

Mynfterres 5² alleyn 5³ can boafte the hallie 54 Seyncte,

Now doeth Englonde weare a bloudie dreffe

And wyth her champyonnes gore her face depeyncte;

Peace fledde, diforder fheweth her dark rode 55,

And thorow ayre doth flie, yn garments fteyned with
     bloude.

5º cottages.   5¹ happinefs.   5² monafterys.   5³ only.   54 holy.
55 complexion.

ECLOGUE THE SECOND.

SPRYTES[1] of the blefte, the pious Nygelle fed,
Poure owte yer pleafaunce [2] onn mie fadres hedde.

Rycharde of Lyons harte to fyghte is gon,
Uponne the brede [3] fea doe the banners gleme [4];
The amenufed [5] nationnes be afton [6],   5
To ken [7] fyke [8] large a flete, fyke fyne, fyke breme [9].
The barkis heafods [10] coupe [11] the lymed [12] ftreme;
Oundes [13] fynkeynge oundes upon the hard ake [14]
     riefe;
The water flughornes [15] wythe a fwotye [16] cleme [17]
Conteke [18] the dynnynge [19] ayre, and reche the fkies. 10
Sprytes of the blefte, on gouldyn trones [20] aftedde [21],
Poure owte yer pleafaunce onn mie fadres hedde.

[1] Spirits, fouls. [2] pleafure. [3] broad. [4] fhine, glimmer. [5] diminifhed, leffened. [6] aftonifhed, confounded. [7] fee, difcover, know. [8] fuch, fo. [9] ftrong. [10] heads. [11] cut. [12] glaffy, reflecting. [13] waves, billows. [14] oak. [15] a mufical inftrument, not unlike a hautboy. [16] fweet. [17] found. [18] confufe, contend with. [19] founding. [20] thrones. [21] feated.

The

The gule [22] depeyncted [23] oares from the black tyde,
Decorn [24] wyth fonnes [25] rare, doe fhemrynge [26] ryfe;
Upfwalynge [27] doe heie [28] fhewe ynne drierie pryde, 15
Lyche gore-red eftells [29] in the eve [30] merk [31] fkyes;
The nome-depeyncted [32] fhields, the fperes aryfe,
Alyche [33] talle rofhes on the water fyde;
Alenge [34] from bark to bark the bryghte fheene [35]
    flyes;
Sweft-kerv'd [36] delyghtes doe on the water glyde.   20
Sprites of the blefte, and everich Seyncte ydedde,
Poure owte youre pleafaunce on mie fadres hedde.

The Sarafen lokes owte: he doethe feere,
That Englondes brondeous [37] fonnes do cotte the waie.
Lyke honted bockes, theye reineth [38] here and there, 25
Onknowlachynge [39] inne whatte place to obaie [40].
The banner glefters on the beme of daie;
The mitte [41] croffe Jerufalim ys feene;

[22] red. [23] painted. [24] carved. [25] devices. [26] glimmering.
[27] rifing high, fwelling up. [28] they. [29] a corruption of *eftoile*, Fr. a
ftar. [30] evening. [31] dark. [32] rebus'd fhields; a herald term, when
the charge of the fhield implies the name of the bearer. [33] like.
[34] along. [35] fhine. [36] fhort-lived. [37] furious. [38] runneth. [39] not
knowing. [40] abide. [41] mighty.

Dhereof

Dhereof the fyghte yer corrage doe affraie [42],
In balefull [43] dole their faces be ywreene [44].   30
Sprytes of the blefte, and everich Seynéte ydedde,
Poure owte your pleafaunce on mie fadres hedde.

The bollengers [45] and cottes [45], foe fwyfte yn fyghte,
Upon the fydes of everich bark appere ;
Foorthe to his offyce lepethe everych knyghte,   35
Eftfoones [46] hys fquyer, with hys fhielde and fpere.
The jynynge fhieldes doe fhemre and moke glare [47] ;
The dofheynge oare doe make gemoted [48] dynne ;
The reynyng [49] foemen [50], thynckeynge gif [51] to dare,
Boun [52] the merk [53] fwerde, theie feche to fraie [54],
     theie blyn [55].   40
Sprytes of the blefte, and everyche Seynéte ydedde,
Powre oute yer pleafaunce onne mie fadres hedde.

Now comm the warrynge Sarafyns to fyghte ;
Kynge Rycharde, lyche a lyoncel [56] of warre,

---

[42] affright. [43] woeful. [44] covered. [45] different kinds of boats.
[46] full foon, prefently. [47] glitter. [48] united, affembled. [49] running.
[50] foes. [51] if. [52] make ready. [53] dark. [54] engage. [55] ceafe, ftand
ftill. [56] a young lion.

Inne

Inne fheenynge goulde, lyke feerie [57] gronfers [58],
   dyghtes [59],   45
Shaketh alofe hys honde, and feene afarre.
Syke haveth I efpyde a greter ftarre
Amenge the drybblett [60] ons to fheene fulle bryghte;
Syke funnys wayne [61] wyth amayl'd beames doe barr
The blaunchie [63] mone or eftells [64] to gev lyghte.   50
Sprytes of the blefte, and everich Seyncte ydedde,
Poure owte your pleafaunce on mie fadres hedde.

Diftraughte [65] affraie [66], wythe lockes of blodde-red
   die,
Terroure, emburled [67] yn the thonders rage,
Deathe, lynked to difmaie, dothe ugfomme [68] flie, 55
Enchafynge [69] echone champyonne war to wage.
Speeres bevyle [70] fperes; fwerdes upon fwerdes en-
   gage;
Armoure on armoure dynn [71], fhielde upon fhielde;

---

[57] flaming. [58] a meteor, from *gron*, a fen, and *fer*, a corruption
of fire; that is, a fire exhaled from a fen. [59] deckt. [60] fmall, infig-
nificant. [61] carr. [62] enameled. [63] white, filver. [64] ftars. [65] diftracting. [66] affright. [67] armed. [68] terribly. [69] encouraging, heat-
ing. [70] break, a herald term, fignifying a fpear broken in tilting.
[71] founds.

Ne dethe of thofandes can the warre affuage,
Botte falleynge nombers fable 72 all the feelde.   60
Sprytes of the blefte, and everych Seynête ydedde,
Poure owte youre pleafaunce on mie fadres hedde.

The foemen fal arounde ; the crofs reles 73 hye ;
Steyned ynne goere, the harte of warre ys feen ;
Kyng Rycharde, thorough everyche trope dothe flie, 65
And beereth meynte 74 of Turkes onto the greene ;
Bie hymm the floure of Afies menn ys fleene 75 ;
The waylynge 76 mone doth fade before hys fonne ;
Bie hym hys knyghtes bee formed to actions deene 77,
Doeynge fyke marvels 78, ftrongers be afton 79.   70
Sprytes of the blefte, and everych Seynête ydedde,
Poure owte your pleafaunce onn mie fadres hedde.

The fyghte ys wonne ; Kynge Rycharde mafter is ;
The Englonde bannerr kiffeth the hie ayre ;
Full of pure joie the armie is iwys 80,   75
And everych one haveth it onne his bayre 81 ;

72 blacken.   73 waves.   74 many, great numbers.   75 flain.
76 decreafing.   77 glorious, worthy.   78 wonders.   7 aftonifhed.
80 certainly.   81 brow.

Agayne

Agayne to Englonde comme, and worfchepped there,
Twyghte [82] into lovynge armes, and feafted eft [83];
In everych eyne aredynge nete of wyere [84],
Of all remembrance of paft peyne berefte   80
Sprites of the blefte, and everich Seyncte ydedde,
Syke pleafures powre upon mie fadres hedde.

Syke Nigel fed, whan from the bluie fea
The upfwol [85] fayle dyd daunce before his eyne;
Swefte as the wifhe, hee toe the beeche dyd flee, 85
And founde his fadre fteppeynge from the bryne.
Lette thyffen menne, who haveth fprite of loove,
Bethyncke untoe hemfelves how mote the meetynge
proove.

[82] plucked, pulled.   [83] often.   [84] grief, trouble.   [85] fwollen.

ECLOGUE

WOULDST thou kenn nature in her better
     parte ?
Goe, ferche the logges [1] and bordels [2] of the hynde [3];
Gyff [4] theie have anie, itte ys roughe-made arte,
Inne hem [5] you fee the blakied [6] forme of kynde [7]. .
Haveth your mynde a lycheynge [8] of a mynde ?   5
Woulde it kenne everich thynge, as it mote [9] bee ?
Woulde ytte here phrafe of the vulgar from the
    hynde,
Withoute wifeegger [10] wordes and knowlache [11] free ?
Gyf foe, rede thys, whyche Iche dyfporteynge [12]
    pende;
Gif nete befyde, yttes rhyme maie ytte commende.   10

[1] lodges, huts.   [2] cottages.   [3] fervant, flave, peafant.   [4] if.
[5] a contraction of *them*.   [6] naked, original.   [7] nature.   [8] liking.
[9] might. The fenfe of this line is, Would you fee every thing in its
primæval ftate.   [10] wife-egger, a philofopher.   [11] knowledge
[12] fporting.

MANNE.

M A N N E.

Botte whether, fayre mayde, do ye goe?
  O where do ye bende yer waie?
I wille knowe whether you goe,
  I wylle not bee affeled [13] naie.

W O M A N N E.

To Robyn and Nell, all downe in the delle,   15
  To hele [14] hem at makeynge of haie.

M A N N E.

Syr Roggerre, the parfone, hav hyred mee there,
  Comme, comme, lett us tryppe ytte awaie,
We'lle wurke [15] and we'lle fynge, and wylle drenche [16]
  of ftronge beer
  As longe as the merrie fommers daie.   20

W O M A N N E.

How harde ys mie dome to wurch!
  Moke is mie woe.

[13] anfwered.   [14] aid, or help.   [15] work.   [16] drink.

Dame

Dame Agnes, whoe lies ynne the Chyrche
    With birlette [17] golde,
Wythe gelten [18] aumeres [19] ſtronge ontolde,   25
What was ſhee moe than me, to be ſoe?

M A N N E.

I kenne Syr Roger from afar
    Tryppynge over the lea;
Ich aſk whie the loverds [20] ſon
    Is moe than mee.   30

S Y R R O G E R R E.

The ſweltrie [21] ſonne dothe hie apace hys wayne [22],
From everich beme a ſeme [23] of lyfe doe falle;
Swythyn [24] ſcille [25] oppe the haie uponne the playne;
Methynckes the cockes begynneth to gre [26] talle.
Thys ys alyche oure doome [27]; the great, the ſmalle, 35
Moſte withe [28] and bee forwyned [29] by deathis darte.
See! the ſwote [30] flourette [31] hathe noe ſwote at alle;
Itte wythe the ranke wede bereth evalle [32] parte.

---

[17] a hood, or covering for the back part of the head. [18] guilded.
[19] borders of gold and ſilver, on which was laid thin plates of either
metal counterchanged, not unlike the preſent ſpangled laces. [20] lord.
[21] ſultry. [22] car. [23] feed. [24] quickly, preſently. [25] gather.
[26] grow. [27] fate. [28] a contraction of wither. [29] dried. [30] ſweet.
[31] flower. [32] equal.

The

The cravent [33], warrioure, and the wyfe be blente [34],
Alyche to drie awaie wythe thofe theie dyd bemente [35]. 40

MANNE.

All-a-boon [36], Syr Prieft, all-a-boon,
  Bye yer preeftfchype nowe faye unto mee ;
Syr Gaufryd the knyghte, who lyvethe harde bie,
  Whie fhoulde hee than mee
       Bee more greate,   45
Inne honnoure, knyghtchoode and eftate ?

SYR ROGERRE.

Attourne [37] thine eyne arounde thys haied mee,
Tentyflie [38] loke arounde the chaper [39] delle [40];
An anfwere to thie barganette [41] here fee,
Thys welked [42] flourette wylle a lefon telle : 50
Arift [43] it blew [44], itte florifhed, and dyd welle,
Lokeynge afcaunce [45] upon the naighboure greene ;
Yet with the deigned [46] greene yttes rennome [47] felle,
Eftfoones [48] ytte fhronke upon the daie-brente [49] playne,

---

[33] coward. [34] ceafed, dead, no more. [35] lament. [36] a manner of afking a favour. [37] turn. [38] carefully, with circumfpection. [39] dry, fun-burnt. [40] valley. [41] a fong, or ballad. [42] withered. [43] arifen, or arofe. [44] bloffomed. [45] difdainfully. [46] difdained. [47] glory. [48] quickly. [49] burnt.

Didde not yttes loke, whileſt ytte there dyd ſtonde, 55
To croppe ytte in the bodde move ſomme dred honde.

Syke 59 ys the waie of lyffe; the loverds 51 ente 52
Mooveth the robber hym therfor to flea 53;
Gyf thou has ethe 54, the ſhadowe of contente,
Beleive the trothe 55, theres none moe haile 56 yan
    thee.   60
Thou wurcheſt 57; welle, canne thatte a trobble bꬱe?
Slothe moe wulde jade thee than the rougheſt daie.
Couldeſt thou the kivercled 58 of ſoughlys 59 fee,
Thou wouldſt eftſoones 60 fee trothe ynne whatte I
    faie;
Botte lette me heere thie waie of lyffe, and thenne 65
Heare thou from me the lyffes of odher menne.

M A N N E.

I ryſe wythe the ſonne,
Lyche hym to dryve the wayne 61,
And eere mie wurche is don
I fynge a fonge or twayne 62.   70

50 ſuch. 51 lord's. 52 a purſe or bag. 53 flay. 54 eaſe. 55 truth.
56 happy. 57 workeſt. 58 the hidden or ſecret part of. 59 fouls.
60 full ſoon, or preſently. 61 car. 62 two.

                                                  I followe

I followe the plough-tayle,
Wythe a longe jubb ⁶³ of ale.
  Botte of the maydens, oh!
Itte lacketh notte to telle;
Syre Preefte mote notte crie woe,   75
Culde hys bull do as welle.
I daunce the befte heiedeygnes ⁶⁴,
And foile ⁶⁵ the wyfeft feygnes ⁶⁶.
  On everych Seynctes hie daie
Wythe the mynftrelle ⁶⁷ am I feene,   80
All a footeygne it awaie,
Wythe maydens on the greene.
But oh! I wyfhe to be moe greate,
In rennome, tenure, and eftate.

SYR ROGERRE.

Has thou ne feene a tree uponne a hylle,   85
Whofe unlifte ⁶⁸ braunces ⁶⁹ rechen far toe fyghte;
Whan fuired ⁷⁰ unwers ⁷¹ doe the heaven fylle,
Itte fhaketh deere ⁷² yn dole ⁷³ and moke affryghte.

---

⁶³ a bottle. ⁶⁴ a country dance, ftill practifed in the North.
⁶⁵ baffle. ⁶⁶ a corruption of *feints*. ⁶⁷ a minftrel is a mufician.
⁶⁸ unbounded. ⁶⁹ branches. ⁷⁰ furious. ⁷¹ tempefts, ftorms.
⁷² dire. ⁷³ difmay.

C   Whyleft

Whyleft the congeon 74 flowrette abeffie 75 dyghte 76,

Stondethe unhurte, unquaced 77 bie the ftorme :   90

Syke is a picte 78 of lyffe : the manne of myghte

Is tempeft-chaft 79, hys woe greate as hys forme,

Thiefelfe a flowrette of a fmall accounte,

Wouldft harder felle the wynde, as hygher thee dydfte

mounte.

74 dwarf.   75 humility.   76 decked.   77 unhurt.   78 picture.
79 tempeft-beaten.

ELINOURE

ELINOURE and JUGA.

ONNE Ruddeborne [1] bank twa pynynge May-
    dens fate,

Theire teares fafte dryppeynge to the waterre cleere;

Echone bementynge [2] for her abfente mate,

Who atte Seyn* te Albonns fhouke the morthynge [3]
    fpeare.

The nottebrowne Elinoure to Juga fayre   5

Dydde fpeke acroole [4], wythe languifhment of eyne,

Lyche droppes of pearlie dew, lemed [5] the quyvryng
    brine.

ELINOURE.

O gentle Juga! heare mie dernie [6] plainte,

To fyghte for Yorke mie love ys dyghte [7] in ftele;

O maie ne fanguen fteine the whyte rofe peyn* te,   10

Maie good Sene* te Cuthberte watche Syrre Roberte
    wele.

Moke moe thanne deathe in phantafie I feele;

[1] Rudborne (in Saxon, red-water), a River near Saint Albans, famous for the battles there fought between the Houfes of Lancafter and
York. [2] lamenting. [3] murdering. [4] faintly. [5] gliftened.
[6] fad complaint. [7] arrayed, or cafed.

See! fee! upon the grounde he bleedynge lies;
Inhild 8 fome joice 9 of lyfe, or elfe mie deare love dies.

J U G A.

Syfters in forrowe, on thys daife-ey'd banke,   15
Where melancholych broods, we wyll lamente;
Be wette wythe mornynge dewe and evene danke;
Lyche levynde 10 okes in eche the odher bente,
Or lyche forlettenn 11 halles of merriemente,
Whofe gaftlie mitches 12 holde the traine of fryghte 13,20
Where lethale 14 ravens bark, and owlets wake the
        nyghte.

[E L I N O U R E.]

No moe the mifkynette 15 fhall wake the morne,
The minftrelle daunce, good cheere, and morryce plaie;
No moe the amblynge palfrie and the horne
Shall from the leffel 16 rouze the foxe awaie;   25
I'll feke the forefte alle the lyve-longe daie;

8 infufe.   9 juice.   10 blafted.   11 forfaken.   12 ruins.
13 fear.   14 deadly or deathboding.   15 a fmall bagpipe.
16 in a confined fenfe, a bufh or hedge, though fometimes ufed as a
forefl.

                                            Alle

Alle nete amenge the gravde chyrche [17] glebe wyll
.   goe,
And to the paſſante Spryghtes lecture [18] mie tale of woe.

[J   U   G   A.]

Whan mokie [19] cloudis do hange upon the leme
Of leden [20] Moon, ynn ſylver mantels dyghte ;   30
The tryppeynge Faeries weve the golden dreme
Of Selyneſs [21], whyche flyethe wythe the nyghte ;
· Thenne (botte the Seynctes forbydde !) gif to a
      ſpryte
Syrr Rychardes forme ys lyped, I'll holde dyſtraughte
Hys bledeynge claie-colde corſe, and die eche daie ynn
'   -   thoughte.   45

E L I N O U R E.

Ah woe bementynge wordes; what wordes can ſhewe!
Thou limed [22] ryver, on thie linche [23] maie bleede
Champyons, whoſe bloude wylle wythe thie waterres
      flowe,
And Rudborne ſtreeme be Rudborne ſtreeme indeede!
Haſte, gentle Juga, tryppe ytte oere the meade,   40

[17] church-yard.   [18] relate.   [19] black.   [20] decreaſing.   [21] happineſs.
[22] glaſſy.   [23] bank.

To

'To knowe, or wheder we mufte waile agayne,

Or wythe oure fallen knyghtes be menged onne the
    plain.

Soe fayinge, lyke twa levyn-blafted trees,

Or twayne of cloudes that holdeth ftormie rayne;

Theie moved gentle oere the dewie mees²⁴,   45

To where Seyncte Albons holie fhrynes remayne.

There dyd theye fynde that bothe their knyghtes were
    flayne,

Diftraughte ²⁵ theie wandered to fwollen Rudbornes
    fyde,

Yelled theyre leathalle knelle, fonke ynn the waves, and
    dyde.

²⁴ meeds.   ²⁴ diftracted.

To JOHNE LADGATE.

[Sent with the following *Songe to Ælla.*]

WELL thanne, goode Johne, fythe ytt muft needes
  be foe,
Thatt thou & I a bowtynge matche muft have,
Lette ytt ne breakynge of oulde friendfhyppe bee,
Thys ys the onelie all-a-boone I crave.

Rememberr Stowe, the Bryghtftowe Carmalyte,
Who whanne Johne Clarkynge, one of myckle lore,
Dydd throwe hys gauntlette-penne, wyth hym to fyghte,
Hee fhowd fmalle wytte, and fhowd hys weakneffe more.

Thys ys mie formance, whyche I nowe have wrytte,
The beft performance of mie lyttel wytte.

SONGE to ÆLLA, Lorde of the castel of
Brystowe ynne daies of yore.

Oh thou, orr what remaynes of thee,
 Ælla, the darlynge of futurity,
Lett thys mie fonge bolde as thie courage be,
 As everlaftynge to pofteritye.

Whanne Dacya's fonnes, whofe hayres of bloude-redde
 hue
Lyche kynge-cuppes braftynge wythe the morning due,
 Arraung'd ynne dreare arraie,
 Upponne the lethale daie,
Spredde farre and wyde onne Watchets fhore ;
 Than dyddft thou furioufe ftande,
 And bie thie valyante hande
Beefprengedd all the mees wythe gore.

 Drawne bie thyne anlace felle,
 Downe to the depthe of helle
 Thoufandes of Dacyanns went ;
 Bryftowannes, menne of myghte,
 Ydar'd the bloudie fyghte,
 And actedd deeds full quent.

 Oh thou, whereer (thie bones att refte)
 Thye Spryte to haunte delyghteth befte,
Whetherr upponne the bloude-embrewedd pleyne,
 Orr whare thou kennft fromm farre
 The dyfmall crye of warre,
Orr feeft fomme mountayne made of corfe of fleyne ;

'Orr feeft the hatchedd ftede,
Ypraunceynge o'er the mede,
And neighe to be amenged the poynctedd fpeeres;
    Orr ynne blacke armoure ftaulke arounde
    Embattel'd Bryftowe, once thie grounde,
And glowe ardurous onn the Caftle fteeres;

    Orr fierye round the mynfterr glare;
    Lette Bryftowe ftylle be made thie care;
Guarde ytt fromme foemenne & confumynge fyre;
    Lyche Avones ftreme enfyrke ytte rounde,
    Ne lette a flame enharme the grounde,
Tylle ynne one flame all the whole worlde expyre.

The underwritten Lines were compofed by JOHN
LADGATE, a Prieft in London, and fent to
ROWLIE, as an Anfwer to the preceding *Songe*
of Ælla.

HAVYNGE wythe mouche attentyonn redde
    Whatt you dydd to mee fende,
Admyre the varfes mouche I dydd,
    And thus an anfwerr lende.

Amongs the Greeces Homer was
    A Poett mouche renownde,
Amongs the Latyns Vyrgilius
    Was befte of Poets founde.

The Brytifh Merlyn oftenne hanne
    The gyfte of infpyration,
And Afled to the Sexonne menne
    Dydd fynge wythe elocation.

Ynne Norman tymes, Turgotus and
    Goode Chaucer dydd excelle,
Thenn Stowe, the Bryghtftowe Carmelyte,
    Dydd bare awaie the belle.

Nowe

Nowe Rowlie ynne thefe mokïe dayes
  Lendes owte hys fheenynge lyghtes,
And Turgotus and Chaucer lyves
  Ynne ev'ry lyne he wrytes.

EHE

THE TOURNAMENT.

AN INTERLUDE.

ENTER AN HERAWDE.

THE Tournament begynnes; the hammerrs
    founde;
The courferrs lyffe [1] about the menfuredd [2] fielde;
The fhemrynge armoure throws the fheene arounde;
Quayntyffed [3] fons [4] depictedd   onn eche fheelde.
The feerie [5] heaulmets, wythe the wreathes amielde [6], 5
Supportes the rampynge lyoncell [7] orr beare,
Wythe ftraunge depyctures [8], Nature maie nott
    yeelde,
Unfeemelie to all orderr doe appere,
Yett yatte [9] to menne, who thyncke and have a
    fpryte [10],
Makes knowen thatt the phantafies unryghte.   10

---

[1] fport, or play.   [2] bounded, or meafured.   [3] curioufly devifed.
[3] fancys or devices.   [4] painted, or difplayed.   [5] fiery.
[6] ornamented, enameled.   [7] a young lion.   [8] drawings paint-
ings.   [9] that.   [10] foul.

I, Sonne

I, Sonne of Honnoure, fpencer [11] of her joies,
Muft fwythen [12] goe to yeve [13] the fpeeres arounde,
Wythe advantayle [14] & borne [15] I meynte [16] emploie,
Who withoute mee woulde fall untoe the grounde.
Soe the tall oake the ivie twyfteth rounde; 15
Soe the nefhe [17] flowerr grees [18] ynne the woodeland
    fhade.
The worlde bie diffraunce ys ynne orderr founde;
Wydoute unlikeneffe nothynge could bee made.
As ynn the bowke [19] nete [20] alleyn [21] cann bee donne,
Syke [22] ynn the weal of kynde all thynges are partes of
    onne. 20

Enterr SYRR SYMONNE DE BOURTONNE.

Herawde [23], bie heavenne thefe tylterrs ftaie too long.
Mie phantafie ys dyinge forr the fyghte.
The mynftrelles have begonne the thyrde warr fonge,
Yett notte a fpeere of hemm [24] hath grete mie fyghte.
. I feere there be ne manne wordhie mie myghte. 25
I lacke a Guid [25], a Wyllyamm [26] to entylte.

[11] difpenfer. [12] quickly. [13] give. [14] armer. [15] burnifh.
[16] many. [17] young, weak, tender. [18] grows. [19] body. [20] nothing.
[21] alone. [22] fo. [23] herald. [24] a contraction of *them*.
[25] *Guie de Sancto Egidio,* the moft famous tilter of his age.
[26] William Rufus.

To reine [27] anente [28] a fele [29] embodiedd knyghte,
Ytt gettes ne rennome [30] gyff hys blodde þee fpylte.
Bie heavenne & Marie ytt ys tyme they're here ;
I lyche nott unthylle [31] thus to wielde the fpeare.   30

HERAWDE.

Methynckes I heare yer flugghornes [32] dynn [33] fromm
farre.

BOURTONNE.

Ah ! fwythenn [34] mie fhielde & tyltynge launce bee
bounde [35].
Eftfoones [36] behefte [37] mie Squyerr to the warre.
I flie before to clayme a challenge grownde.

[Goeth oute.

HERAWDE.

Thie valourous actes woulde meinte [38] of menne
aftounde ;

Harde bee yer fhappe [39] encontrynge thee ynn fyghte ;

---

[27] run.   [28] againft.   [29] feeble.   [30] honour, glory.   [31] ufelefs.
[32] a kind of claryon.   [33] found.   [34] quickly.   [35] ready.   [36] foon.
[37] command.   [38] moft.   [39] fate, or doom.

Anenſt ⁴⁰ all menne thou bereſt to the grounde,
Lyche the hard häyle dothe the tall roſhes pyghte ⁴¹.
As whanne the mornynge ſonne ydronks the dew,
Syche nothe thie valourous aĉtes drocke ⁴² eche
    knyghte's hue.   40

THE LYSTES. THE KYNGE. SYRR SYMONNE DE
BOURTONNE, SYRR HUGO FERRARIS, SYRR RA-
NULPH NEVILLE, SYRR LODOVICK DE CLYNTON,
SYRR JOHAN DE BERGHAMME, AND ODHERR
KNYGHTES, HERAWDES, MYNSTRELLES, AND
SERVYTOURS ⁴³.

KYNGE.

The barganette ⁴³; yee mynſtrelles tune the ſtrynge,
Somme aĉtyonn dyre of auntyante kynges now ſynge.

MYNSTRELLES.

Wyllyamm, the Normannes floure botte Englondes
    thorne,
The manne whoſe myghte delievretie ⁴⁴ hadd knite ⁴⁵,

⁴⁰ againſt   ⁴¹ pitched, or bent down.   ⁴² drink.
⁴³ ſervants, attendants.   ⁴³ ſong, or ballad.   ⁴⁴ aĉtivity.   ⁴⁵ .

Snett

Snett [46] oppe hys long ftrunge bowe and fheelde
 aborne [47],   45
Behefteynge [48] all hys hommageres [45] to fyghte.
Goe, rouze the lyonn fromm hys hyfted [50] denne,
Lett thie floes [51] drenche the blodde of anie thynge bott
 menue.

Ynn the treed forrefte doe the knyghtes appere;
Wyllyamm wythe myghte hys bowe enyronn'd [52]
 plies [53];   50
Loude dynns [54] the arrowe ynn the wolfynn's eare;
Hee ryfeth battent [55], roares, he panctes, hee dyes.
Forflagenn att thie feete lett wolvynns bee,
Lett thie floes drenche theyre blodde, bott do ne bre-
 drenn flea.

Throwe the merke [56] fhade of twiftynde trees hee
 rydes;   55
The flemed [57] owlett [58] flapps herr eve-fpeckte [59] wynge;
The lordynge [60] toade ynn all hys paffes bides;
The berten [61] neders [62] att hymm darte the ftynge;

[46] bent. [47] burnifhed. [48] commanding. [49] fervants. [50] hidden.
[51] arrows. [52] worked with iron. [53] bends. [54] founds. [55] loudly.
[56] dark, or gloome. [57] & [58] frighted owl. [59] marked with evening dew.
[60] ftanding on their hind legs. [61] venomous. [62] adders.

The

Styll, ftylle, hee paffes onn, hys ftede aftrodde,

Nee hedes the daungerous waie gyff leadynge untoe
    bloodde. 60

The lyoncel, fromme fweltrie [61] countries braughte,

Coucheynge binethe the fheltre of the brierr,

Att commyng dynn [64] doth rayfe hymfelfe dif-
    traughte [65],

He loketh wythe an eie of flames of fyre.

Goe, fticke the lyonn to hys hyltren denne, 65

Lette thie floes [66] drenche the blood of anie thynge
    botte menn.

Wythe paffent [67] fteppe the lyonn mov'th alonge;

Wyllyamm hys ironne-woven bowe hee bendes,

Wythe myghte alyche the roghlynge [68] thonderr
    ftronge;

The lyonn ynn a roare hys fpryte foorthe fendes. 70

Goe, flea the lyonn ynn hys blodde-fteyn'd denne,

Botte bee thie takelle [69] drie fromm blodde of odherr
    menne.

Swefte froom the thyckett ftarks the ftagge awaie;

The couraciers [70] as fwefte doe afterr flie.

[61] hot, fultry.   [64] found, noife.   [65] diftracted.   [66] arrows.
[67] walking leifurely.   [68] rolling.   [69] arrow.   [70] horfe courfers.

                                  Hee

Hee lepethe hie, hee ftondes, hee kepes att baie, 75
Botte metés the arrowe, and eftfoones 7¹ doth die.
Forflagenn atte thie fote lette wylde beaftes bee,
Lett thie floes drenche yer blodde, yett do ne bredrenn
    flee.

Wythe murtherr tyredd, hee fleynges hys bowe
    alyne 7².
The ftagge ys ouch'd 7³ wythe crownes of lillie
    flowerrs.   80
Arounde theire heaulmes theie greene verte doe en-
    twyne ;
Joying and rev'lous ynn the grene wode bowerrs.
Forflagenn wyth thie floe lette wylde beaftes bee,
Fcefte thee upponne theire flefhe, doe ne thie bredrenn
    flee.

K Y N G E.

Nowe to the Tourneie 74; who wylle fyrfte
    affraie 75 ?   85

7¹ full foon.   7² acrofs his fhoulders.   7³ garlands of flowers being
put round the neck of the game, it was faid to be *ouch'd*, from *ouch*, a
chain, worn by earls round their necks.   74 Turnament.   75 fight, or
encounter.

H E-

HERAULDE.

Nevylle, a baronne, bee yatte [76] honnoure thyne.

BOURTONNE.

I clayme the paffage.

NEVYLLE.

I contake [77] thie waie.

BOURTONNE.

Thenn there's mie gauntlette [78] onn mie gaberdyne [79].

HEREHAULDE.

A leegefull [80] challenge, knyghtes & champyonns
    dygne [81],
A leegefull challenge, lette the flugghorne founde. 90
        [Syrr Symonne *and* Nevylle *tylte.*
Nevylle ys goeynge, manne and horfe, toe grounde.
              [Nevylle *falls.*
Loverdes, how doughtilie [82] the tylterrs joyne!

---

[76] that. [77] difpute. [78] glove. [79] a piece of armour. [80] lawful.
[81] worthy. [82] furioufly.

Yee champyonnes, heere Symonne de Bourtonne
  fyghtes,
Onne hee hathe quacedd [83], affayle [84] hymm, yee
  knyghtes.

FERRARIS.

I wylle anente [85] hymm goe; mie fquierr, mie fhielde; 95
Orr onne orr odherr wyll doe myckle [86] fcethe [87]
Before I doe departe the liffedd [88] fielde,
Miefelfe orr Bourtonne hereupponn wyll blethe [89].
  Mie fhielde.

BOURTONNE.

Comme onne, & fitte thie tylte-launce ethe [90].
Whanne Bourtonn fyghtes, hee metes a doughtie
  foe.   100
        [*Theie tylte.* Ferraris *falleth.*
Hee falleth ; nowe bie heavenne thie woundes doe
  fmethe [91] ;
I feere mee, I have wroughte thee myckle woe [92].

---

[83] vanquifhed.   [84] oppofe.   [85] againft.   [86] much.
[87] damage, mifchief.   [88] bounded.   [89] bleed.   [90] eafy.   [91] fmoke.
[92] hurt, or damage.

                                                    H E-

HERAWDE.

Bourtonne hys feconde beereth to the feelde.
Comme onn, yee knyghtes, and wynn the honnour'd
fheeld.

BERGHAMME.

I take the challenge; fquyre, mie launce and ftede. 105
I, Bourtonne, take the gauntlette; forr mee ftaie.
Botte, gyff thou fyghtefte mee, thou fhalt have mede 93;
Somme odherr I wylle champyonn toe affraie 94;
Perchaunce fromme hemm I maie poffefe the daie,
Thenn I fchalle bee a foemanne forr thie fpere.   120
Herehawde, toe the bankes of Knyghtys faie,
De Berghamme wayteth forr a foemann heere.

CLINTON.

Botte longe thou fchalte ne tende 95; I doe thee fie 96.
Lyche forreying 97 levynn 98, fchalle mie tylte-launce
flie.

    [Berghamme & Clinton *tylte.* Clinton *fallethe.*

93 reward.   94 fight or engage.   95 attend or wait.   96 defy.
97 & 98 deftroying lightening.

BERGHAMME.

Nowe, nowe, Syrr Knyghte, attoure [99] thie beeveredd [100]
    eyne.   115

I have borne downe, and efte [101] doe gauntlette thee.

Swythenne [102] begynne, and wrynn [103] thie fhappe [104]
    orr myne ;

Gyff thou dyfcomfytte, ytt wylle dobblie bee.

    [Bourtonne & Burghamm *tylteth*. Berghamme *falls*.

HERAWDE.

Symonne de Bourtonne haveth borne downe three,

And bie the thyrd hathe honnoure of a fourthe.   120

Lett hymm bee fett afyde, tylle hee doth fee

A tyltynge forr a knyghte of gentle wourthe.

Heere commethe ftraunge knyghtes ; gyff corteous [105]
    heie [106],

Ytt welle befeies [107] to yeve [108] hemm ryghte of
    fraie [109].

---

[99] turn.   [100] beaver'd.   [101] again.   [102] quickly.   [103] declare.
[104] fate.   [105] worthy.   [106] they.   [107] becomes.   [108] give.   [109] fyght.

FIRST

FIRST KNYGHTE.

Straungerrs wee bee, and homblie doe wee clayme 125
The rennome [110] ynn thys Tourneie [111] forr to tylte ;
Dherbie to proove fromm cravents [112] owre goode
    name,
Bewrynnynge [113] thatt wee gentile blodde have fpylte.

HEREHAWDE.

Yee knyghtes of cortefie, thefe ftraungerrs, faie,
Bee you fulle wyllynge forr to yeve hemm fraie? 130
   [*Fyve Knyghtes tylteth wythe the ftraunge Knyghte,*
   and bee everichone [114] overthrowne.

BOURTONNE.

Nowe bie Seynéte Marie, gyff onn all the fielde
Ycrafedd [115] fperes and helmetts bee befprente [116],
Gyff everyche knyghte dydd houlde a piercedd [117]
    fheeld,
Gyff all the feelde wythe champyonne blodde bee
    ftente [118],

[110] honour.   [111] Tournament.   [112] cowards.   [113] declaring.
[114] every one.   [115] broken, fpilt.   [116] fcatter'd.
[117] broken, or pierced through with darts.   [118] ftained.

Yett toe encounterr hymm I bee contente.   135

Annodherr launce, Marſhalle, anodherr launce.

Albeyttee hee wythe lowes ¹¹⁹ of fyre ybrente ¹²⁰,

Yett Bourtonne woulde agenſte hys val ¹²¹ advance.

Fyve haveth fallenn downe anethe ¹²² hys ſpeere,

Botte hee ſchalle bee the next thatt falleth heere. 140

Bie thee, Seynĉte Marie, and thy Sonne I ſweare,

Thatt ynn whatte place yonn doughtie knyghte ſhall
fall

Anethe ¹²³ the ſtronge puſh of mie ſtraught ¹²⁴ out
ſpeere,

There ſchalle aryſe a hallie ¹²⁵ chyrches walle,

The whyche, ynn honnoure, I wylle Marye calle, 145

Wythe pillars large, and ſpyre full hyghe and rounde.

And thys I faifullie ¹²⁶ wylle ſtonde to all,

Gyff yonderr ſtraungerr falleth to the grounde.

Straungerr, bee boune ¹²⁷; I champyonn ¹²⁸ you to
warre.

Sounde, founde the flughorncs, to bee hearde fromm
farre.   150

[Bourtonne & the Straungerr *tylt.* Straunger *falleth.*

¹¹⁹ flames.   ¹²⁰ burnt.   ¹²¹ healm.   ¹²² beneath.   ¹²³ againſt.
¹²⁴ ſtretched out.   ¹²⁵ holy.   ¹²⁶ faithfully.   ¹²⁷ ready.   ¹²⁸ challenge.

KYNGE,

KYNGE.

The Mornynge Tyltes now ceafe.

HERAWDE.

Bourtonne ys kynge.

Dyfplaie the Englyfhe bannorre onn the tente;

Rounde hymm, yee mynftrelles, fongs of achments [129]
    fynge;

Yee Herawdes, getherr upp the fpeeres be-
    fprente [130];

To Kynge of Tourney-tylte bee all knees bente. 155

Dames faire and gentle, forr youre loves hee foughte;

Forr you the longe tylte-launce, the fwerde hee
    fhente [131];

Hee jouftedd, alleine [132] havynge you ynn thoughte.

Comme, mynftrelles, found the ftrynge, goe onn eche
    fyde,

Whyleft hee untoe the Kynge ynn ftate doe ryde. 160

---

[129] atchievements, glorious actions.   [130] broken fpears.
[131] broke, deftroyed.   [132] only, alone.

MYN-

MYNSTRELLES.

Whann Battayle, fmethynge [133] wythe new quickenn'd
    gore,

Bendynge wythe fpoiles, and bloddie droppynge
    hedde,

Dydd the merke [134] woode of ethe [135] and reft explore,

Seekeynge to lie onn Pleafures downie bedde,

    Pleafure, dauncyng fromm her wode,   165

    Wreathedd wythe floures of aiglintine,

    Fromm hys vyfage wafhedd the bloude,

    Hylte [136] hys fwerde and gaberdyne.

Wythe fyke an eyne fhee fwotelie [137] hymm dydd
    view,

Dydd foe ycorvenn [138] everrie fhape to joie,   170

Hys fpryte dydd chaunge untoe anodherr hue,

Hys armes, ne fpoyles, mote anie thoughts emploie.

    All delyghtfomme and contente,

    Fyre enfhotynge [139] fromm hys eyne,

    Ynn hys arms hee dydd herr hente [140],   175

    Lyche the merk [141]-plante doe entwyne.

[133] fmoaking, fteaming.   [134] dark, gloomy.   [135] eafe.
[136] hid, fecreted. [137] fweetly. [138] moulded. [139] fhooting, darting.
[140] grafp, hold.   [141] night-fhade.

Soe, gyff thou loveſt Pleaſure and herr trayne,
Onknowlachynge [141] ynn whatt place herr to fynde,
Thys rule yſpende [143], and ynn thie mynde retayne;
Seeke Honnoure fyrſte, and Pleaſaunce lies be-
    hynde.   180

      [141] ignorant, unknowing.   [143] conſider.

BRISTOWE

BRISTOWE TRAGEDIE:

OR THE DETHE OF

SYR CHARLES BAWDIN.

THE featherd fongfter chaunticleer
  Han wounde hys bugle horne,
And tolde the earlie villager
  The commynge of the morne:

Kynge EDWARDE fawe the ruddie ftreakes   5
  Of lyghte eclypfe the greie;
And herde the raven's crokynge throte
  Proclayme the fated daie.

" Thou'rt ryght," quod hee, " for, by the Godde
  " That fyttes enthron'd on hyghe!   10
" CHARLES BAWDIN, and hys fellowes twaine,
  " To-daie fhall furelie die."

            Thenne

Thenne wythe a jugge of nappy ale
    Hys Knyghtes dydd onne hymm waite;
" Goe tell the traytour, thatt to-daie   15
    " Hee leaves thys mortall ſtate."

Syr CANTERLONE thenne bendedd lowe,
    Wythe harte brymm-fulle of woe;
Hee journey'd to the caſtle-gate,
    And to Syr CHARLES dydd goe.   20

Butt whenne hee came, hys children twaine,
    And eke hys lovynge wyfe,
Wythe brinie tears dydd wett the floore,
    For goode Syr CHARLESES lyfe.

" O goode Syr CHARLES!" ſayd CANTERLONE, 25
    " Badde tydyngs I doe brynge."
" Speke boldlie, manne," ſayd brave Syr CHARLES,
    " Whatte ſays thie traytor kynge?"

" I greeve to telle, before yonne ſonne
    " Does fromme the welkinn flye,   30
" Hee hath uponne hys honour ſworne,
    " Thatt thou ſhalt ſurelie die."

                   " Wee

" Wee all muft die," quod brave Syr CHARLES;
　" Of thatte I'm not affearde;
" Whatte bootes to lyve a little fpace?　　　35
　" Thanke JESU, I'm prepar'd:

" Butt telle thye kynge, for myne hee's not,
　" I'de fooner die to-daie
" Thanne lyve hys flave, as manie are,
　" Tho' I fhoulde lyve for aie."　　　40

Thenne CANTERLONE hee dydd goe out,
　To telle the maior ftraite
To gett all thynges ynne reddynefs
　For goode Syr CHARLESES fate.

Thenne Maifterr CANYNGE faughte the kynge,　45
　And felle down onne hys knee;
" I'm come," quod hee, " unto your grace
　" To move your clemencye."

Thenne quod the kynge," " Youre tale fpeke out,
　" You have been much oure friende;　　50
" Whatever youre requeft may bee,
　" Wee wylle to ytte attende."
　　　　　　　　　　　　" My

" My nobile liege ! alle my requeſt
    " Ys for a nobile knyghte,
" Who, tho' may hap hee has donne wronge,   55
    " He thoghte ytte ſtylle was ryghte :

" Hee has a ſpouſe and children twaine,
    " Alle rewyn'd are for aie ;
" Yff thatt you are reſolv'd to lett
    " CHARLES BAWDIN die to-daie."   60

" Speke nott of ſuch a traytour vile,"
    " The kynge ynne furie ſayde ;
" Before the evening ſtarre doth ſheene,
    " BAWDIN ſhall looſe hys hedde :

" Juſtice does loudlie for hym calle,   65
    " And hee ſhalle have hys meede :
" Speke, Maiſter CANYNGE ! Whatte thynge elſe
    " Att preſent doe you neede ?"

" My nobile leige !" goode CANYNGE ſayde,
    " Leave juſtice to our Godde.   70
" And laye the yronne rule aſyde ;
    " Be thyne the olyve rodde.

                           " Was

" Was Godde to ferche our hertes and reines,
    " The beft were fynners grete ;
" Christ's vycarr only knowes ne fynne,   75
    " Ynne alle thys mortall ftate.

" Lett mercie rule thyne infante reigne,
    " 'Twylle fafte thye crowne fulle fure ;
" From race to race thy familie
    " Alle fov'reigns fhall endure :

" Butt yff wythe bloode and flaughter thou
    " Beginne thy infante reigne,
" Thy crowne uponne thy childrennes brows
    " Wylle never long remayne."

" Canynge, awaie ! thys traytour vile   85
    " Has fcorn'd my power and mee ;
" Howe canft thou thenne for fuch a manne
    " Intreate my clemencye ?"

" My nobile liege ! the trulie brave
    " Wylle val'rous actions prize,   90
" Refpect a brave and nobile mynde,
    " Altho' ynne enemies."

7   " Canynge,

" Canynge, awaie ! By Godde ynne Heav'n
  " Thatt dydd mee beinge gyve,
" I wylle nott tafte a bitt of breade   95
  " Whilft thys Syr Charles dothe lyve.

" By Marie, and alle Seinctes ynne Heav'n,
  " Thys funne fhall be hys lafte."
Thenne Canynge dropt a brinie teare,
  And from the prefence pafte.   100

Wyth herte brymm-fulle of gnawynge grief,
  Hee to Syr Charles dydd goe,
And fatt hymm downe uponne a ftoole,
  And teares beganne to flowe.

" Wee all muft die," quod brave Syr Charles; 105
  " Whatte bootes ytte howe or whenne ;
" Dethe ys the fure, the certaine fate
  " Of all wee mortall menne.

" Saye why, my friend, thie honeft foul
  " Runns overr att thyne eye ;   110
" Is ytte for my moft welcome doome
  " Thatt thou doft child-lyke crye ?"

                    E   Quod

Quod godlie CANYNGE, " I doe weepe,
    " Thatt thou foe foone muſt dye,
" And leave thy fonnes and helpleſs wyfe;   115
    " 'Tys thys thatt wettes myne eye."

" Thenne drie the tears thatt out thyne eye
    " From godlie fountaines fprynge;
" Dethe I defpife, and alle the power
    " Of EDWARDE, traytor kynge.   120

" Whan throgh the tyrant's welcom means
    " I ſhall refigne my lyfe,
" The Godde I ferve wylle foone provyde
    " For bothe mye fonnes and wyfe.

" Before I fawe the lyghtfome funne,   125
    " Thys was appointed mee;
" Shall mortal manne repyne or grudge
    " Whatt Godde ordeynes to bee?

" Howe oft ynne battaile have I ſtoode,
    " Whan thoufands dy'd arounde;   130
" Whan fmokynge ſtreemes of crimfon bloode
    " Imbrew'd the fatten'd grounde:

                              " Howe

" How dydd I knowe thatt ev'ry darte,
   " Thatt cutte the airie waie,
" Myghte nott fynde paſſage toe my harte,   135
   " And cloſe myne eyes for aie ?

" And ſhall I nowe, forr feere of dethe,
   " Looke wanne and bee dyſmayde ?
" Ne! fromm my herte flie childyſhe feere,
   " Bee alle the manne diſplay'd.   140

" Ah, goddelyke HENRIE ! Godde forefende,
   " And guarde thee and thye ſonne,
" Yff 'tis hys wylle; but yff 'tis nott,
   " Why thenne hys wylle bee donne.

" My honeſt friende, my faulte has beene   145
   " To ſerve Godde and mye prynce ;
" And thatt I no tyme-ſerver am,
   " My dethe wylle ſoone convynce.

" Ynne Londonne citye was I borne,
   " Of parents of grete note;   150
" My fadre dydd a nobile armes
   " Emblazon onne hys cote :

       E 2   I make

" I make ne doubte butt hee ys gone
     " Where foone I hope to goe;
" Where wee for ever fhall bee bleft,   155
     " From oute the reech of woe :

" Hee taughte mee juftice and the laws
     " Wyth pitie to unite;
" And eke hee taughte mee howe to knowe
     " The wronge caufe fromm the ryghte: 160

" Hee taughte mee wythe a prudent hande
     " To feede the hungrie poore,
" Ne lett mye fervants dryve awaie
     " The hungrie fromme my doore :

" And none can faye, butt alle mye lyfe   165
     " I have hys wordyes kept;
" And fumm'd the actyonns of the daie
     " Eche nyghte before I flept.

" I have a fpoufe, goe afke of her,
     " Yff I defyl'd her bedde ?
" I have a kynge, and none can laie
     " Blacke treafon onne my hedde.

                    6   " Ynne.

" Ynne Lent, and onne the holie eve,
  " Fromm flefhe I dydd refrayne ;
" Whie fhould I thenne appeare difmay'd   175
  " To leave thys worlde of payne ?

" Ne ! haplefs HENRIE ! I rejoyce,
  " I fhalle ne fee thye dethe ;
" Mofte willynglie ynne thye juft caufe
  " Doe I refign my brethe.   180

" Oh, fickle people ! rewyn'd londe !
  " Thou wylt kenne peace ne moe ;
" Whyle RICHARD's fonnes exalt themfelves,
  " Thye brookes wythe bloude wylle flowe.

" Saie, were ye tyr'd of godlie peace,   185
  " And godlie HENRIE's reigne,
" Thatt you dydd choppe youre eafie daies
  " For thofe of bloude and peyne ?

" Whatte tho' I onne a fledde bee drawne,
  " And mangled by a hynde,   190
" I doe defye the traytor's pow'r,
  " Hee can ne harm my mynde ;

    E 3   " Whatte

" Whatte tho', uphoifted onne a pole,
  " Mye lymbes fhall rotte ynne ayre,
" And ne ryche monument of braffe   195
    " CHARLES BAWDIN's name fhall bear;

" Yett ynne the holie booke above,
  " Whyche tyme can't eate awaie,
" There wythe the fervants of the Lorde
  " Mye name fhall lyve for aie.   200

" Thenne welcome dethe! for lyfe eterne
  " I leave thys mortall lyfe:
" Farewell, vayne worlde, and alle that's deare,
  " Mye fonnes and lovynge wyfe!

" Nowe dethe as welcome to mee comes,   205
  " As e'er the moneth of Maie;
" Nor woulde I even wyfhe to lyve,
  " Wyth my dere wyfe to ftaie."

Quod CANYNGE, " 'Tys a goodlie thynge
  " To bee prepar'd to die;   210
" And from thys world of peyne and grefe
  " To Godde ynne Heav'n to flie."

                                            And

And nowe the bell beganne to tolle,
 And claryonnes to founde;
Syr CHARLES hee herde the horfes feete 215
 A·prauncyng onne the grounde :

And juft before the officers,
 His lovynge wyfe came ynne,
Weepynge unfeigned teeres of woe,
 Wythe loude and dyfmalle dynne. 220

" Sweet FLORENCE ! nowe I praie forbere,
 " Ynne quiet lett mee die;
" Praie Godde, thatt ev'ry Chriftian foule
 " Maye looke onne dethe as I.

" Sweet FLORENCE! why thefe brinie teeres ? 225
 " Theye wafhe my foule awaie,
" And almoft make mee wyfhe for lyfe,
 " Wyth thee, fweete dame, to ftaie.

" 'Tys butt a journie I fhalle goe
 " Untoe the lande of blyffe; 230
" Nowe, as a proofe of hufbande's love,
 " Receive thys holie kyffe."

    E 4   Thenne

Thenne FLORENCE, fault'ring ynne her faie,
   Tremblynge thefe wordyes fpoke,
" Ah, cruele EDWARDE! bloudie kynge!   235
   " My herte ys welle nyghe broke:

" Ah, fweete Syr CHARLES! why wylt thou goe,
   " Wythoute thye lovynge wyfe?
" The cruelle axe thatt cuttes thye necke,
   " Ytte eke fhall ende mye lyfe."   240

And nowe the officers came ynne
   To brynge Syr CHARLES awaie,
Whoe turnedd toe his lovynge wyfe,
   And thus toe her dydd faie:

" I goe to lyfe, and nott to dethe;   245
   " Trufte thou ynne Godde above,
" And teache thye fonnes to feare the Lorde,
   " And ynne theyre hertes hym love:

" Teache them to runne the nobile race
   " Thatt I theyre fader runne: 250
" FLORENCE! fhou'd dethe thee take—adieu!
   " Yee officers, leade onne."
                Thenne

Thenne FLORENCE rav'd as anie madde,
    And dydd her treffes tere ;
" Oh! ftaie, mye hufbande! lorde! and lyfe!"—255
    Syr CHARLES thenne dropt a teare.

'Tyll tyredd oute wythe ravynge loud,
    Shee fellen onne the flore ;
Syr CHARLES exerted alle hys myghte,
    And march'd fromm oute the dore.   260

Uponne a fledde hee mounted thenne,
    Wythe lookes fulle brave and fwete ;
Lookes, thatt enfhone ne moe concern
    Thanne anie ynne the ftrete.

Before hym went the council-menne,   265
    Ynne fcarlett robes and golde,
And taffils fpanglynge ynne the funne,
    Muche glorious to beholde :

The Freers of Seincte AUGUSTYNE next
    Appeared to the fyghte,   270
Alle cladd ynne homelie ruffett weedes,
    Of godlie monkyfh plyghte :

                        Ynne

Ynne diffraunt partes a godlie pſaume
    Moſte ſweetlie theye dydd chaunt;
Behynde theyre backes ſyx mynſtrelles came,   275
    Who tun'd the ſtrunge bataunt.

Thenne fyve-and-twentye archers came;
    Echone the bowe dydd bende,
From reſcue of kynge HENRIES friends
    Syr CHARLES forr to defend.   280

Bolde as a lyon came Syr CHARLES,
    Drawne onne a clothe-layde ſledde,
Bye two blacke ſtedes ynne trappynges white,
    Wyth plumes uponne theyre hedde :

Behynde hym fyve-and-twentye moe   285
    Of archers ſtronge and ſtoute,
Wyth bended bowe echone ynne hande,
    Marched ynne goodlie route :

Seincte JAMESES Freers marched next,
    Echone hys parte dydd chaunt;   290
Behynde theyre backs ſyx mynſtrelles came,
    Who tun'd the ſtrunge bataunt :

                        Thenne

Thenne came the maior and eldermenne,
    Ynne clothe of fcarlett deck't ;
And theyre attendyng menne echone,   295
    Lyke Eafterne princes trickt :

And after them a multitude
    Of citizenns dydd thronge ;
The wyndowes were alle fulle of heddes,
    As hee dydd paffe alonge.   300

And whenne hee came to the hyghe croffe,
    Syr CHARLES dydd turne and faie,
" O Thou, thatt faveft manne fromme fynne,
  " Wafhe mye foule clean thys daie !"

Att the grete mynfterr wyndowe fat   305
    The kynge ynne mycle ftate,
To fee CHARLES BAWDIN goe alonge
    To hys moft welcom fate.

Soone as the fledde drewe nyghe enowe,
    Thatt EDWARDE hee myghte heare,   310
The brave Syr CHARLES hee dydd ftande uppe,
    And thus hys wordes declare :

                                       " Thou

" Thou feeſt mee, EDWARDE! traytour vile!
 " Expos'd to infamie;
" Butt bee aſſur'd, diſloyall manne! 315
 " I'm greaterr nowe thanne thee.

" Bye foule proceedyngs, murdre, bloude,
 " Thou weareſt nowe a crowne;
·" And haſt appoynted mee to dye,
 " By power nott thyne owne. 320

" Thou thynkeſt I ſhall dye to-daie;
 " I have beene dede 'till nowe,
" And ſoone ſhall lyve to weare a crowne
 " For aie uponne my browe:

" Whylſt thou, perhapps, for ſom few yeares, 325
 " Shalt rule thys fickle lande,
" To lett them knowe howe wyde the rule
 " 'Twixt kynge and tyrant hande:

" Thye pow'r unjuſt, thou traytour ſlave!
 " Shall falle onne thye owne hedde"— 330
Fromm out of hearyng of the kynge
 Departed thenne the ſledde.

       Kynge

Kynge EDWARDE's foule rush'd to hys face,
    Hee turn'd hys hedde awaie,
And to hys broder GLOUCESTER   335
    Hee thus dydd speke and saie :

" To hym that foe-much-dreaded dethe
    " Ne ghaftlie terrors brynge,
" Beholde the manne ! hee spake the truthe,
    " Hee's greater thanne a kynge !   340

" Soe lett hym die !" Duke RICHARD sayde ;
    " And maye echone oure foes
" Bende downe theyre neckes to bloudie axe,
    " And feede the carryon crowes."

And nowe the horfes gentlie drewe   345
    Syr CHARLES uppe the hyghe hylle ;
The axe dydd glyfterr ynne the funne,
    Hys pretious bloude to spylle.

Sytr CHARLES dydd uppe the scaffold goe,
    As uppe a gilded carre   350
Of victorye, bye val'rous chiefs
    Gayn'd ynne the bloudie warre :

                         And

And to the people hee dydd faie,
    " Beholde you fee mee dye,
" For fervynge loyally mye kynge,   355
    " Mye kynge moft rightfullie.

" As longe as EDWARDE rules thys lande,
    " Ne quiet you wylle knowe ;
" Youre fonnes and hufbandes fhalle bee flayne,
    " And brookes wythe bloude fhalle flowe. 360

" You leave youre goode and lawfulle kynge,
    " Whenne ynne adverfitye ;
" Lyke mee, untoe the true caufe ftycke,
    " And for the true caufe dye."

Thenne hee, wyth preeftes, uponne hys knees, 365
    A pray'r to Godde dydd make,
Befeechynge hym unto hymfelfe
    Hys partynge foule to take.

Thenne, kneelynge downe, hee layd hys heede
    Moft feemlie onne the blocke ;   370
Whyche fromme hys bodie fayre at once
    The able heddes-manne ftroke :

5   And

And oute the bloude beganne to flowe,
 And rounde the fcaffolde twyne;
And teares, enow to wafhe't awaie,   375
 Dydd flowe fromme each mann's eyne.

The bloudie axe hys bodie fayre
 Ynnto foure parties cutte;
And ev'rye parte, and eke hys hedde,
 Uponne a pole was putte.   380

One parte dydd rotte onne Kynwulph-hylle,
 One onne the mynfter-tower,
And one from off the caftle-gate
 The crowen dydd devoure:

The other onne Seyncte Powle's goode gate, 385
 A dreery fpectacle;
Hys hedde was plac'd onne the hyghe croffe,
 Ynne hyghe-ftreete moft nobile.

Thus was the ende of BAWDIN's fate:
 Godde profper longe oure kynge, 390
And grante hee maye, wyth BAWDIN's foule,
 Ynne heav'n Godd's mercie fynge!

       ÆLLA:

ÆLLA:

A

TRAGYCAL ENTERLUDE,

OR

DISCOORSEYNGE TRAGEDIE,

WROTENN BIE

THOMAS ROWLEIE;

PLAIEDD BEFORE

Mastre CANYNGE, atte hys howse nempte
the Rodde Lodge;

[alsoe before the Duke of Norfolck, JOHAN
HOWARD.]

F

PERSONNES REPRESENTEDD.

ÆLLA,   bie *Thomas Rowleie*, Preeſte, the Aucthoure.

CELMONDE,   *Johan Iſcamm*, Preeſte.

HURRA,   Syrr *Thybbotte Gorges*, Knyghte.

BIRTHA,   Maſtre *Edwarde Canynge*.

Odherr Partes bie *Knyghtes Mynſtrelles*.

EPISTLE TO MASTRE CANYNGE ON ÆLLA.

TYS fonge bie mynftrelles, thatte yn auntyent
tym,

Whan Reafonn hylt [1] herfelfe in cloudes of nyghte,

The preefte delyvered alle the lege [2] yn rhym ;

Lyche peyncted [3] tyltynge fpeares to pleafe the fyghte,

The whyche yn yttes felle ufe doe make moke [4]
dere [5],   5

Syke dyd theire auncyante lee deftlie [6] delyghte the eare.

Perchaunce yn Vyrtues gare [7] rhym mote bee thenne,

Butte efte [8] nowe flyeth to the odher fyde ;

In hallie [9] preefte apperes the ribaudes [10] penne,

Inne lithie [11] moncke apperes the barronnes pryde : 10

But rhym wythe fomme, as nedere [12] widhout teethe,

Make pleafaunce to the fenfe, botte maie do lyttel
fcathe [13].

---

[1] hid, concealed. [2] law. [3] painted. [4] much. [5] hurt, damage.
[6] fweetly. [7] caufe. [8] oft. [9] holy. [10] rake, lewd perfon.
[11] humble. [12] adder. [13] hurt, damage.

F 2   Syr

Syr Johne, a knyghte, who hath a barne of lore [14],

Kenns [15] Latyn att fyrſt fyghte from Frenche or Greke

Pyghtethe [16] hys knowlachynge [17] ten yeres or more, 1

To rynge upon the Latynne worde to ſpeke.

Whoever ſpekethe Englyſch ys deſpyſed,

The Englyſch hym to pleaſe moſte fyrſte be latynized.

Vevyan, a moncke, a good requiem [18] ſynges ;

Can preache ſo wele, eche hynde [19] hys meneyng
 knowes ;

Albeytte theſe gode guyfts awaie he flynges,

Bceynge aꞇ badde yn vearſe as goode yn proſe.

Hee ſynges of ſeynctes who dyed for yer Godde,

Everych wynter nyghte afreſche he ſheddes theyr blodc

To maydens, huſwyfes, and unlored [20] dames,

Hee redes hys tales of merryment & woe.

Loughe [21] loudlie dynneth [22] from the dolte
 adrames [24] ;

He ſwelles on laudes of fooles, tho' kennes [25] hem

[14] learning.   [15] knows.   [16] plucks or tortures.   [17] knowl
[18] a ſervice uſed ofer the dead.   [19] peaſant.   [20] unlearned.   [21] la
[22] ſounds.   [23] ſcorn.   [24] churls.   [25] knows.

Sommetyme at tragedie theie laughe and fynge,
It merrie yaped ²⁶ fage ²⁷ fomme hard-drayned water
brynge.   30

Yette Vevyan ys ne foole, beyinde ²⁸ hys lynes.
Geofroie makes vearfe, as handycraftes theyr ware ;
Wordes wythoute fenfe fulle groffyngelye ²⁹ he twynes,
Cotteynge hys ftorie off as wythe a fheere ;
Waytes monthes on nothynge, & hys ftorie donne, 35
Ne moe you from ytte kenn, than gyf ³⁰ you neere be-
gonne.

Enowe of odhers ; of miefelfe to write,
Requyrynge whatt I doe notte nowe poffefs,
To you I leave the tafke ; I kenne your myghte
Wyll make mie faultes, mie meynte ³¹ of faultes, be
lefs.   40
ÆLLA wythe thys I fende, and hope that you
Wylle from ytte cafte awaie, whatte lynes maie be un-
true.

²⁶ laughable.   ²⁷ tale, jeft.   ²⁸ beyond.   ²⁹ foolifhly.   ³⁰ if.
³¹ many.

Playes made from hallie ¹² tales I holde unmeete ;

Lette fomme greate ftorie of a manne be fonge ;

Whanne, as a manne, we Godde and Jefus treate, 45

In mie pore mynde, we doe the Godhedde wronge.

Botte lette ne wordes, whyche droorie ¹³ mote ne heare,

Bee placed yn the fame.   Adieu untylle anere ¹⁴.

THOMAS ROWLEIE

¹² holy.   ¹³ ftrange perverfion of words. *Droorie* in its antien
fignification ftood for *modefty*.   ¹⁴ another.

LETTER TO THE DYGNE MASTRE CANYNGE.

STRAUNGE dome ytte ys, that, yn thefe daies of
    oures,

Nete [15] butte a bare recytalle can hav place ;

Nowe fhapelie poefie haft lofte yttes powers,

And pynant hyftorie ys onlie grace ;

Heie [16] pycke up wolfome weedes, ynftedde of flowers, 5

And famylies, ynftedde of wytte, theie trace ;

Nowe poefie canne meete wythe ne regrate [17],

Whylfte profe, & herehaughtrie [18], ryfe yn eftate.

Lette kynges, & rulers, whan heie gayne a throne,

Shewe whatt theyre grandfieres, & great granfieres
    bore,   10

Emarfchalled armes, yatte, ne before theyre owne,

Now raung'd wythe whatt yeir fadres han before ;

Lette trades, & toune folck, lett fyke [19] thynges alone,

Ne fyghte for fable yn a fielde of aure ;

[15] nought.   [16] they.   [17] efteem.   [18] heraldry.   [19] fuch.

F 4   Seldomm,

Seldomm, or never, are armes vyrtues mede,   15
Shee nillynge 40 to take myckle 41 aie dothe hede.

A man afcaunfe upponn a piece maye looke,
And fhake hys hedde to ftyrre hys rede 42 aboute;
Quod he, gyf I afkaunted oere thys booke,
Schulde fynde thereyn that trouthe ys left wythoute; 20
Eke, gyf 43 ynto a vew percafe 44 I tooke
The long beade-rolle of al the wrytynge route,
Afferius, Ingolphus, Torgotte, Bedde,
Thorow hem 45 al nete lyche ytte I coulde rede.—

Pardon, yee Graiebarbes 46, gyff I faie, onwife   25
Yee are, to ftycke fo clofe & byfmarelie 47
To hyftorie; you doe ytte tooe moche pryze,
Whyche amenufed 48 thoughtes of poefie;
Somme drybblette 49 fhare you fhoulde to yatte 50 alyfe 51,
Nott makynge everyche thynge bee hyftorie;   30
Inftedde of mountynge onn a wynged horfe,
You onn a rouncy 51 dryve yn dolefull courfe.

40 unwilling. 41 much. 42 wifdom, council. 43 if. 44 perchance.
45 them. 46 Greybeards. 47 curioufly. 48 leffened. 49 fmall.
50 that. 51 allow. 52 cart-horfe.

Cannynge

Cannynge & I·from common courſe dyſſente;

Wee ryde the·ſtede, botte yev to hym the reene;

Ne wylle betweene craſed molterynge bookes be pente, 35

Botte ſoare on hyghe, & yn the ſonne-bemes ſheene;

And where ·wee kenn ſomme iſhad 53 floures beſprente,

We take ytte, & from oulde rouſte doe ytte clene;

Wee wylle ne cheynedd to one paſture bee,

Botte ſometymes ſoare 'bove trouthe of hyſtorie.   40

Saie, Canynge, whatt was vearſe yn daies of yore?

Fyne thoughtes, and couplettes ſetyvelie 54 bewryen 55,

Notte ſyke as doe annoie thys age ſo ſore,

A keppened poyntelle 56 reſtynge at eche lyne.

Vearſe maie be goode, botte poeſie wantes more,   45

An onliſt 57 lecturn 58, and a ſonge adygne 59;

Accordynge to the rule I have thys wroughte,

Gyff ytt pleaſe Canynge, I care notte a groate.

The thynge ytts moſte bee yttes owne defenſe;

Som metre maie notte pleaſe a womannes ear.   50

---

53 broken.   54 elegantly.   55 declared, expreſſed.

56. a pen, uſed metaphorically, as a muſe or genius.   57 boundleſs.

58 ſubject.   59 nervous, worthy of praiſe

Canynge

Canynge lookes notte for poefie, botte fenfe ;
And dygne, & wordie thoughtes, ys all hys care.
Canynge, adieu ! I do you greete from hence ;
Full foone I hope to tafte of your good cheere ;
Goode Byfhoppe Carpynter dyd byd mee faie,   55
Hee wyfche you healthe & felineffe for aie.

T. ROWLEIE,

ENTRO-

ENTRODUCTIONNE.

SOMME cherifaunei [60] 'tys to gentle mynde,
    Whan heie have chevyced [61] theyre londe from
       bayne [62],
Whan theie ar dedd, theie leave yer name behynde,
And theyre goode deedes doe on the earthe remayne;
Downe yn the grave wee ynhyme [63] everych fteyne,   5
Whyleft al her gentleneffe ys made to fheene,
Lyche fetyve baubels [64] geafonne [65] to be feene.

ÆLLA, the wardenne of thys [66] caftell [67] ftede,
Whyleft Saxons dyd the Englyfche fceptre fwaie,
Who made whole troopes of Dacyan men to blede,   10
Then feel'd [68] hys eyne, and feeled hys eyne for aie,
Wee rowze hym uppe before the judgment daie,
To faie what he, as clergyond [69], can kenne,
And howe hee fojourned in the vale of men.

[60] comfort.   [61] preferved.   [62] ruin.   [63] inter.   [64] jewels.   [65] rare.
[66] Briftol.   [67] caftle.   [68] clofed.   [69] taught.

ÆLLA.

Æ L L A.

C E L M O N D E, att B R Y S T O W E.

BEFORE yonne roddie fonne has droove hys
    wayne
Throwe halfe hys joornie, dyghte yn gites [1] of goulde,
Mee, happelefs mee, hee wylle a wretche behoulde,
Miefelfe, and al that's myne, bounde ynne myfchaunces
    chayne.

Ah ! Birtha, whie, dydde Nature frame thee fayre ? 5
Whie art thou all thatt poyntelle [2] canne bewreene [3] ?
Whie art thou nott as coarfe as odhers are ?—
Botte thenn thie foughle woulde throwe thy vyfage
    fheene,
Yatt fhemres onn thie comelie femlykeene [4],
Lyche nottebrowne cloudes, whann bie the fonne
    made redde, 10

[1] robes, mantels. [2] a pen. [3] exprefs. [4] countenance.

Orr

Orr fcarlette, wythe waylde lynnen clothe ywreene 5,

Syke 6 woulde thie fpryte upponn thie vyfage fpredde.

Thys daie brave Ælla dothe thyne honde & harte

Clayme as hys owne to be, whyche nee ftomm hys mofte

   parte.

And cann I lyve to fee herr wythe anere 7 !   15

Ytt cannotte, mufte notte, naie, ytt fhalle not bee.

Thys nyghte I'll putte ftronge poyfonn ynn the beere,

And hymm, herr, and myfelfe, attenes 8 wyll flea.

Affyft mee, Helle ! lett Devylles rounde mee tende,

To flea miefelfe, mie love, & eke mie doughtie 9 friende.20

ÆLLA, BIRTHA.

ÆLLA.

Notte, whanne the hallie priefte dyd make me knyghte,

Bleffynge the weaponne, tellynge future dede,

Howe bie mie honde the prevyd 10 Dane fhoulde blede,

Howe I fchulde often bee, and often wynne, ynn fyghte;

---

5 covered.   6 fuch.   7 another.   8 at once.   9 mighty.
10 hardy, valorous.

Notte, whann I fyrſte behelde thie beauteous hue, 25
Whyche ſtrooke mie mynde, & rouzed mie ſofter ſoule;
Nott, whann from the barbed horſe yn fyghte dyd
    viewe
The flying Dacians oere the wyde playne roule,
Whan all the troopes of Denmarque made grete dole,
Dydd I fele joie wyth ſyke reddoure [11] as nowe,   30
Whann hallie preeſt, the lechemanne of the ſoule,
Dydd knytte us both ynn a caytyſnede [12] vowe:
Now hallie Ælla's ſelyneſſe ys grate;
Shap [13] haveth nowe ymade hys woes for to emmate [14].

B I R T H A.

Mie lorde, & huſbande, ſyke a joie ys myne;   35
Botte mayden modeſtie moſte ne ſoe faie,
Albeytte thou mayeſt rede ytt ynn myne eyne,
Or ynn myne harte, where thou ſhalte be for aie;
Inne ſothe, I have botte meeded oute thie faie [15];
For twelve tymes twelve the mone hathe bin
    yblente [16],   40

---

[11] violence. [12] binding, enforcing. [13] fate. [14] leſſen, decreaſe.
[15] faith. [16] blinded.

As manie tymes hathe vyed the Godde of daie,
And on the graffe her lemes [17] of fylverr fente,
Sythe thou dydft cheefe mee for thie fwote to bee,
Enactynge ynn the fame mofte faiefullie to mee.

Ofte have I feene thee atte the none-daie feafte,   45
Whanne deyfde bie thiefelfe, for wante of pheeres [18],
Awhylft thie merryemen dydde laughe and jeafte,
Onn mee thou femeft all eyne, to mee all eares.
Thou wardeft mee as gyff ynn hondred feeres,
Aleft a daygnous [19] looke to thee be fente,   50
And offrendes [20] made mee, moe thann yie compheeres,
Offe fcarpes [21] of fcarlette, & fyne paramente [22];
All thie yntente to pleafe was lyffed [23] to mee,
I faie ytt, I mofte ftreve thatt you ameded bee.

Æ L L A.

Mie lyttel kyndneffes whyche I dydd doe,   55
  Thie gentlenefs doth corven them foe grete,
Lyche bawfyn [24] olyphauntes [25] mie gnattes doe
    fhewe ;
  Thou doeft mie thoughtes of paying love amate [26].

[17] lights, rays.   [18] fellows, equals.   [19] difdainful.
[20] prefents, offerings.   [21] fcarfs.   [22] robes of fcarlet.   [23] bounded.
[24] large.   [25] elephants.   [26] deftroy.

Botte

Botte hann mie actyonns ſtraughte²⁷ the rolle of fate,

Pyghte thee fromm Hell, or broughte Heaven down

    to thee,   60

Layde the whol worlde a falldſtole atte thie feete,

On ſmyle woulde be ſuffycyll mede for mee.

I amm Loves borro'r, & canne never paie,

Bott be hys borrower ſtylle, & thyne, mie ſwete, for aie.

BIRTHA.

Love, doe notte rate your achevmentes ²⁸ ſoe ſmalle;65

As I to you, ſyke love untoe mee beare;

For nothynge paſte wille Birtha ever call,

Ne on a foode from Heaven thynke to cheere.

As farr as thys frayle brutylle fleſch wylle ſpere,

Syke, & ne fardher I expecte of you;   70

Be notte toe ſlacke yn love, ne overdeare;

A ſmalle fyre, yan a loude flame, proves more true.

Æ L L A.

Thie gentle wordis toe thie volunde ²⁹ kenne

To bee moe clergionde thann ys ynn meyncte of

   menne.

---

²⁷ ſtretched. ²⁸ ſervices. ²⁹ memory, underſtanding.

ÆLLA, BIRTHA, CELMONDE, MYNSTRELLES.

CELMONDE.

Alle bleſſynges ſhowre on gentle Ælla's hedde !   75
Oft maie the moone, yn ſylverr ſheenynge lyghte,
Inne varied chaunges varyed bleſſynges ſhedde,
Beſprengeynge far abrode miſchaunces nyghte ;
And thou, fayre Birtha ! thou, fayre Dame, ſo
     bryghte,
Long mayeſt thou wyth Ælla fynde muche peace, 80
Wythe felyneſſe, as wyth a roabe, be dyghte,
Wyth everych chaungynge mone new joies encreaſe !
I, as a token of mie love to ſpeake,
Have brought you jubbes of ale, at nyghte youre
     brayne to breake.

ÆLLA.

Whan ſopperes paſte we'lle drenche youre ale ſoe
     ſtronge,   85
Tyde lyfe, tyde death.

', C E L M O N.D E.

Ye Mynftrelles, chaunt your fonge.

Mynftrelles Songe, bie a Manne and Womanne.

M A N N E.

Tourne thee to thie Shepfterr ³⁰ fwayne;
Bryghte fonne has ne droncke the dewe
From the floures of yellowe hue;
Tourne thee, Alyce, backe agayne.   9●

W O M A N N E.

No, beftoikerre ³¹, I wylle go,
Softlie tryppynge o'ere the mees ³²,
Lyche the fylver-footed doe,
Seekeynge fhelterr yn grene trees.

M A N N E.

See the mofs-growne daifey'd banke,   95
Pereynge ynne the ftreme belowe;
Here we'lle fytte, yn dewie danke;
Tourne thee, Alyce, do notte goe.

---

³⁹ Shcpherd.   ³¹ deceiver.   ³² meadows.

WOMANNE.

I've hearde erfte mie grandame faie,
Yonge damoyfelles fchulde ne bee,   100
Inne the fwotie moonthe of Maie,
Wythe yonge menne bie the grene wode tree.

MANNE.

Sytte thee, Alyce, fytte, and harke,
Howe the ouzle 33 chauntes hys noate,
The chelandree 34, greie morn larke,   105
Chauntynge from theyre lyttel throate;

WOMANNE.

I heare them from eche grene wode tree,
Chauntynge owte fo blatauntlie 35,
Tellynge lecturnyes 36 to mee,
Myfcheefe ys whanne you are nygh.   110

---

33 The black-bird.   34 Gold-finch.   35 loudly.   36 lectures.

M A N N E.

See alonge the mees fo grene
Pied daifies, kynge-coppes fwote;
Alle wee fee, bie non bee feene,
Nete botte fhepe fettes here a fote.

W O M A N N E.

Shepfter fwayne, you tare mie gratche [37].   115
Oute uponne ye! lette me goe.
Leave mee fwythe, or I'lle alatche.
Robynne, thys youre dame fhall knowe.

M A N N E.

See ! the crokynge brionie
Rounde the popler twyfte hys fpraie;   120
Rounde the oake the greene ivie
Florryfchethe and lyveth aie.

Lette us feate us bie thys tree,
Laughe, and fynge to lovynge ayres;
Comme, and doe notte coyen bee;   125
Nature made all thynges bie payres.

[37] Apparel.

Droried

Drooried cattes wylle after kynde;
Gentle doves wylle kyfs and coe:

W O M A N N E.

Botte manne, hee mofte bee ywrynde,
Tylle fyr preefte make on of two.   130

Tempe mee ne to the foule thynge;
I wylle no mannes lemanne be;
Tyll fyr preefte hys fonge doethe fynge,
Thou fhalt neere fynde aught of mee.

M A N N E.

Bie oure ladie her yborne,   135
To-morrowe, foone as ytte ys daie,
I'lle make thee wyfe, ne bee forfworne,
So tyde me lyfe or dethe for aie.

W O M A N N E.

Whatt dothe lette, botte thatte nowe
Wee attenes [38], thos honde yn honde,   140
Unto diviniftre [39] goe,
And bee lyncked yn wedlocke bonde?

[38] At once.   [39] a divine.

G 3   MANNE.

Æ L L A:

M A N N E.

I agree, and thus I plyghte
Honde, and harte, and all that's myne ;
Good fyr Rogerr, do us ryghte,   145
Make us one, at Cothbertes fhryne.

B O T H E.

We wylle ynn a bordelle ⁴⁰ lyve,
Hailie, thoughe of no eftate ;
Everyche clocke moe love fhall gyve ;
Wee ynn godeneffe wylle bee greate.   150

Æ L L A.

I lyche thys fonge, I lyche ytt myckle well ;
And there ys monie for yer fyngeyne nowe ;
Butte have you noone thatt marriage-bleffynges telle ?

C E L M O N D E.

In marriage, bleffynges are botte fewe, I trowe.

⁴⁰ A cottage.

MYNSTRELLES.

Laverde⁴¹, we have; and, gyff you pleafe, wille

 fynge,   151

As well as owre choughe-voyces wylle permytte.

ÆLLA.

Comme then, and fee you fwotelie tune the ftrynge,

And ftret ⁴², and engyne all the human wytte,

Toe pleafe mie dame.

MYNSTRELLES.

 We'lle ftrayne owre wytte and fynge.

Mynftrelles Songe.

FYRSTE MYNSTRELLE.

The boddynge flourettes blofhes atte the lyghte; 160

The mees be fprenged wyth the yellowe hue;

Ynn daifeyd mantels ys the mountayne dyghte;

The nefh ⁴³ yonge coweflepe bendethe wyth the dewe;

  ⁴¹ Lord. ⁴² ftretch. ⁴³ tender.

        The

The trees enlefed, yntoe Heavenne ftraughte,'

Whenn gentle wyndes doe blowe, to wheftlyng dynne

   ys broughte.   165

The evenynge commes, and brynges the dewe alonge;

The roddie welkynne fheeneth to the eyne;

Arounde the aleftake Mynftrells fynge the fonge;

Yonge ivie rounde the doore pofte do entwyne;

I laie mee onn the graffe; yette, to mie wylle,   170

Albeytte alle ys fayre, there lackethe fomethynge ftylle.

SECONDE MYNSTRELLE.

So Adam thoughtenne, whann, ynn Paradyfe,

All Heavenn and Erthe dyd hommage to hys mynde;

Ynn Womman alleyne mannes pleafaunce lyes;

As Inftrumentes of joie were made the kynde.   175

Go, take a wyfe untoe thie armes, and fee

Wynter, and brownie hylles, wyll have a charme for thee.

THYRDE

THYRDE MYNSTRELLE.

Whanne Autumpne blake 44 and fonne-brente doe
    appere,
With hys goulde honde guylteynge the falkeynge lefe,
Bryngeynge oppe Wynterr to folfylle the yere,   180
Beerynge uponne hys backe the riped fhefe;
Whan al the hyls wythe woddie fede ys whyte;
Whanne levynne-fyres and lemes do mete from far the
    fyghte;

Whann the fayre apple, rudde as even fkie,
Do bende the tree unto the fructyle grounde;   185
When joicie peres, and berries of blacke die,
Doe daunce yn ayre, and call the eyne arounde;
Thann, bee the even foule, or even fayre,
Meethynckes mie hartys joie ys fteynced wyth fomme
    care.

44 Naked.

SECONDE

SECONDE MYNSTRELLE.

Angelles bee wrogte to bee of neidher kynde ;   190
Angelles alleyne fromme chafe 45 defyre bee free ;
Dheere ys a fomwhatte evere yn the mynde,
Yatte, wythout wommanne, cannot ftylled bee ;
Ne feynête yn celles, botte, havynge blodde and
    tere 46,
Do fynde the fpryte to joie on fyghte of womanne
    fayre :   195

Wommen bee made, notte for hemfelves, botte
    manne,
Bone of hys bone, and chyld of hys defire ;
Fromme an ynutyle membere fyrfte beganne,
Ywroghte with moche of water, lyttele fyre ;
Therefore theie feke the fyre of love, to hete   200
The milkynefs of kynde, and make hemfelfes complete.

Albeytte, wythout wommen, menne were pheeres
To falvage kynde, and wulde botte lyve to flea,
Botte wommenne efte the fpryghte of peace fo cheres,
Tochelod yn Angel joie heie Angeles bee ;   205

45 Hot.   46 health.

Go,

Go, take thee fwythyn [47] to thie bedde a wyfe,
Bee bante or bleffed hie, yn proovynge marryage lyfe.

Anodber Mynftrelles Songe, bie Syr *Thybbot Gorges*.

As Elynour bie the green leffelle was fyttynge,
   As from the fones hete fhe harried,
She faydè, as herr whytte hondes whyte hofen was
      knyttynge,   210
  Whatte pleafure ytt ys to be married !

Mie hufbande, Lorde Thomas, a forrefter boulde,
   As ever clove pynne, or the bafkette,
Does no cheryfauncys from Elynour houlde,
   I have ytte as foone as I afke ytte.   215

Whann I lyved wyth mie fadre yn merrie Clowd-dell,
   Tho' twas at my liefe to mynde fpynnynge,
I ftylle wanted fomethynge, botte whatte ne coulde telle,
   Mie lorde fadres barbde haulle han ne wynnynge.

[47] Quickly.

Eche

Eche mornynge I ryfe, doe I fette mie maydennes,   220
　　Somme to fpynn, fomme to curdell, fomme bleachynge,
Gyff any new entered doe afke for mie aidens,
　　Thann fwythynne you fynde mee a teachynge.

Lorde Walterre, mie fadre, he loved me welle,
　　And nothynge unto mee was nedeynge,   225
Botte fchulde I agen goe to merrie Cloud-dell,
　　In fothen twoulde bee wythoute redeynge.

Shee fayde, and lorde Thomas came over the lea,
　　As hee the fatte derkynnes wae chacynge,
Shee putte uppe her knyttynge, and to hym wente
　　　fhee;   230
　　So wee leave hem bothe kyndelie embracynge.

Æ L L A.

I lyche eke thys; goe ynn untoe the feafte;
Wee wylle permytte you antecedente bee;
There fwotelie fynge eche carolle, and yaped [48] jeafte;
And there ys monnie, that you merrie bee;   235

　　　· [48] Laughable.

　　　　　　　　　　　　　　　Comme,

Comme, gentle love, wee wylle toe fpoufe-feafte goe,
And there ynn ale and wyne bee dreynĉted 49 everych woe.

ÆLLA, BIRTHA, CELMONDE, MESSENGERE.

MESSENGERE.

Ælla, the Danes ar thondrynge onn our coafte ;
Lyche fcolles of locufts, cafte oppe bie the fea,
Magnus and Hurra, wythe a doughtie hoafte,   240
Are ragyng, to be quanfed 50 bie none botte thee ;
Hafte, fwyfte as Levynne to thefe royners flee :
Thie dogges alleyne can tame thys ragynge bulle.
Hafte fwythyn, fore anieghe the towne theie bee,
And Wedecefterres rolle of dome bee fulle.   245
Hafte, hafte, O Ælla, to the byker flie,
For yn a momentes fpace tenne thoufand menne maie die.

ÆLLA.

Befhrew thee for thie newes ! I mofte be gon.
Was ever locklefs dome fo hard as myne !
Thos from dyfportyfmente to warr to ron,   250
To chaunge the felke vefte for the gaberdyne !

49 Drouned.   50 Stilled, quenched.

I   BIRTHA.

BIRTHA.

O! lyche a nedere, lette me rounde thee twyne,
And hylte thie boddie from the fchaftes of warre.
Thou fhalte nott, muft not, from thie Birtha ryne,
Botte kenn the dynne of flughornes from afarre. 255

ÆLLA.

O love, was thys thie joie, to fhewe the treate,
Than groffyfhe to forbydde thie hongered gueftes
     to eate ?

O mie upfwalynge [51] harte, whatt wordes can faie
The peynes, thatte paffethe ynn mie foule ybrente ?
Thos to bee torne uponne mie fpoufalle daie, 260
O! 'tys a peyne beyond entendemente.
Yee mychtie Goddes, and is yor favoures fente
As thous fafte dented to a loade of peyne ?
Mofte wee aie holde yn chace the fhade content,
And for a bodykyn [52] a fwarthe obteyne ? 265

     [51] Swelling.   [52] Body, fubftance.

                         O! whie,

O! whie, yee feynctes, opprefs yee thos mie fowle?
How fhalle I fpeke mie woe, mie freme, mie dreerie dole?

CELMONDE.

Sometyme the wyfefte lacketh pore mans rede.
Reafonne and counynge wytte efte flees awaie.
Thanne, loverde, lett me faie, wyth hommaged drede
(Bieneth your fote ylayn) mie counfelle faie;   271
Gyff thos wee lett the matter lethlen 53 faie,
The foemenn, everych honde-poyncte, getteth fote.
Mie loverde, lett the fpeere-menne, dyghte for fraie,
And all the fabbataners goe aboute.   275
I fpeke, mie loverde, alleyne to upryfe
Youre wytte from marvelle, and the warriour to alyfe.

ÆLLA.

Ah! nowe thou potteft takells 54 yn mie harte;
Mie foulghe dothe nowe begynne to fee herfelle;
I wylle upryfe mie myghte, and doe mie parte,   280
To flea the foemenne yn mie furie felle.

53 Still, dead.   54 arrows, darts.

Botte

Botte howe canne tynge mie rampynge fourie telle,
Whyche ryfeth from mie love to Birtha fayre?
Ne coulde the queede, and alle the myghte of Helle,
Founde out impleafaunce of fyke blacke a geare. 285
Yette I wylle bee miefelfe, and rouze mie fpryte
To acte wythe rennome, and goe meet the bloddie
        fyghte.

B I R T H A.

No, thou fchalte never leave thie Birtha's fyde;
Ne fchall the wynde uponne us blowe alleyne;
I, lyche a nedre, wylle untoe thee byde;   290
Tyde lyfe, tyde deathe, ytte fhall behoulde us twayne.
I have mie parte of drierie dole and peyne;
Itte brafteth from mee atte the holtred eyne;
Ynne tydes of teares mie fwarthynge fpryte wyll
        drayne,   295
Gyff drerie dole ys thyne, tys twa tymes myne.
Goe notte, O Ælla; wythe thie Birtha ftaie;
For wyth thie femmlykeed mie fpryte wyll goe awaie.

                            Æ L L A:

Æ L L A.

O! tys for thee, for thee alleyne I fele;
Yett I mufte bee miefelfe; with valoures gear
I'lle dyghte mie hearte, and notte mie lymbes yn
   ftele,   300
And fhake the bloddie fwerde and fteyned fpere.

B I R T H A.

Can Ælla from hys breafte hys Birtha teare?
Is fhee fo rou and ugfomme 55 to hys fyghte?
Entrykeynge wyght! ys leathall warre fo deare?
Thou pryzeft mee belowe the joies of fyghte. 305
Thou fcalte notte leave mee, albeytte the erthe
Hong pendaunte bie thie fwerde, and craved for thy
   morthe.

Æ L L A.

Dyddeft thou kenne howe mie woes, as ftarres
   ybrente,
Headed bie thefe thie wordes doe onn mee falle,
Thou woulde ftryve to gyve mie harte contente, 310
Wakyng mie flepynge mynde to honnoures calle.

     55 Terrible.

     H   Of

Of felyneffe I pryze thee moe yan all
Heaven can mee fende, or counynge wytt acquyre,
Yette I wylle leave thee, onne the foe to falle,
Retournynge to thie eyne with double fyre.   315

BIRTHA.

Mofte Birtha boon requefte and bee denyd ?
Receyve attenes a darte yn felyneffe and pryde ?
   Doe ftaie, att leafte tylle morrowes fonne apperes.

ÆLLA.

Thou kennefte welle the Dacyannes myttee powere;
Wythe   them   a   mynnute   wurchethe   bane   for
      yeares ;   320
Theie undoe reaulmes wythyn a fyngle hower.
Rouze all thie honnoure, Birtha ; look attoure
Thie bledeynge countrie, whych for haftie dede
Calls, for the rodeynge of fome doughtie power,
To royn yttes royners, make yttes foemenne blede. 325

BIRTHA.

BIRTHA.

Rouze all thie love; falfe and entrykyng wyghte!
Ne leave thie Birtha thos uponne pretence of fyghte.

Thou nedeft notte goe; untyll thou hafte command
Under the fygnette of oure lorde the kynge.

ÆLLA.

And wouldeft thou make me then a recreande ?   330
Hollie Seynéte Marie, keepe mee from the thynge !
Heere, Birtha, thou haft potté a double ftynge,
One for thie love, anodher for thie mynde.

BIRTHA.

Agylted 56 Ælla, thie abredynge 57 blynge 58.
Twas love of thee thatte foule intente ywrynde.   335
Yette heare mie fupplycate, to mee attende,
Hear from mie groted 59 harte the lover and the friende.

56 Offended.   57 upbraiding.   39 ceafe.   59 fwollen.

Lett Celmonde yn thie armour-brace be dyghte;
And yn thie ftead unto the battle goe;
Thie name alleyne wylle putte the Danes to
    flyghte,   340
The ayre thatt beares ytt woulde preffe downe the foe.

Æ L L A.

Birtha, yn vayne thou wouldfte mee recreand doe;
I mofte, I wylle, fyghte for mie countries wele,
And leave thee for ytt. Celmonde, fweftlie goe,
Telle mie Bryftowans to dyghte yn ftele;   [345
Tell hem I fcorne to kenne hem from afar,
Botte leave the vyrgyn brydall bedde for bedde of
    warre.

Æ L L A, B I R T H A.

B I R T H A.

And thou wylt goe: O mie agroted harte!

Æ L L A.

Mie countrie waites mie marche; I mufte awaie;
Albeytte I fchulde goe to mete the darte   350
Of certen Dethe, yette here I woulde notte ftaie.

                               Botte

Botte thos to leave thee, Birtha, dothe affwaie

Moe torturynge peynes yanne canne be fedde bie
    tyngue,

Yette rouze thie honoure uppe, and wayte the daie,

Whan rounde aboute mee fonge of warre heie
    fynge.   355

O Birtha, ftrev mie agreeme [60] to accaie [61],

And joyous fee mie armes, dyghte oute ynn warre arraie.

B I R T H A.

Difficile [62] ys the pennaunce, yette I'lle ftrev

To keepe mie woe behyltren yn mie breafte.

Albeytte nete maye to mee pleafaunce yev,   360

Lyche thee, I'lle ftrev to fette mie mynde atte refte.

Yett oh! forgeve, yff I have thee dyftrefte;

Love, doughtie love, wylle beare no odher fwaie.

Jufte as I was wythe Ælla to blefte,

Shappe foullie thos hathe fnatched hym awaie, 365

It was a tene too doughtie to bee borne,

Wydhoute an ounde of feares and breafte wyth fyghes
    ytorne.

[60] Torture,   [61] affwage.   [62] difficult,

Æ L L A.

Thie mynde ys now thiefelfe; why wylte thou bee
All blanche, al kyngelie, all foe wyfe yn mynde,
Alleyne to lett pore wretched Ælla fee,   370
Whatte wondrous bighes [63] he nowe mufte leave
    behynde ?
O Birtha fayre, warde everyche commynge wynde,
On everych wynde I wylle a token fende ;
Onn mie longe fhielde ycorne thie name thoul't fynde.
Butte here commes Celmonde, wordhie knyghte and
    friende.   375

ÆLLA, BIRTHA, CELMONDE
fpeaking.

Thie Bryftowe knyghtes for thie forth-comynge
    lynge [64] ;
Echone athwarte hys backe hys longe warre-fhield dothe
    flynge.

Æ L L A.

Birtha, adieu ; but yette I cannotte goe.

[64] Jewels.   [63] ftay.

BIRTHA.

B,I R T H A.

Lyfe of mie fpryte, mie gentle Ælla ftaie.   380
Engyne mee notte wyth fyke a drierie woe.

Æ L L`A.

I mufte, I wylle; tys honnoure cals awaie.

B I R T H A.

O mie agroted harte, brafte, brafte ynn twaie.
Ælla, for honnoure, flyes awaie from mee.

Æ L L A.

Birtha, adieu; I maie notte here obaie.   385
I'm flyynge from miefelfe yn flying thee.

B I R T H A.

O Ælla, houfband, friend, and loverde, ftaie.
He's gon, he's gone, alafs! percafe he's gone for aie.

CELMONDE.

Hope, hallie fufter, fweepeynge thro' the fkie,
In crowne of goulde, and robe of lillie whyte,   390
Whyche farre abrode ynne gentle ayre doe flie,
Meetynge from dyftaunce the enjoyous fyghte,
Albeytte efte thou takeft thie hie flyghte
Hecket [65] ynne a myfte, and wyth thyne eyne
    yblente,
Nowe commeft thou to mee wythe ftarrie lyghte; 395
Ontoe thie vefte the rodde fonne ys adente [66];
The Sommer tyde, the month of Maïe appere,
Depyéte wythe fkylledd honde upponn thie wyde
    aumere.

I from a nete of hopelen am adawed,
Awhaped [67] atte the fetyvenefs of daie;   400
Ælla, bie nete moe thann hys myndbruche awed,
Is gone, and I mofte followe, toe the fraie.

[65] Wrapped clofely, covered.   [66] faftened.   [67] aftonifh'd.

Celmonde

Celmonde canne ne'er from anie byker ftaie.

Dothe warre begynne? there's Celmonde yn the place.

Botte whanne the warre ys donne, I'll hafte awaie.

The refte from nethe tymes mafque muft fhew yttes
    face.   405

I fee onnombered joies arounde mee ryfe;

Blake [68] ftondethe future doome, and joie dothe mee
    alyfe.

O honnoure, honnoure, whatt ys bie thee hanne?

Hailie the robber and the bordelyer,   410

Who kens ne thee, or ys to thee beftanne,

And nothynge does thie myckle gaftnefs fere.

Faygne woulde I from mie bofomme alle thee tare.

Thou there dyfperpelleft [69] thie levynne-bronde;

Whyleft mie foulgh's forwyned, thou art the
    gare;   415

Sleene ys mie comforte bie thie ferie honde;

As fomme talle hylle, whann wynds doe fhake the
    ground,

[68] Naked,   [69] Scattereft.

Itte

Itte kerveth all abroade, bie brafteynge hyltren wounde.

   Honnoure, whatt bee ytte? tys a fhadowes fhade,

   A thynge of wychencref, an idle dreme;   420

   On of the fonnis whych the clerche have made

   Menne wydhoute fprytes, and wommen for to fleme;

   Knyghtes, who efte kenne the loude dynne of the

      beme,

   Schulde be forgarde to fyke enfeeblynge waies,

   Make everych aĉte, alyche theyr foules, be breme,425

   And for theyre chyvalrie alleyne have prayfe.

      O thou, whatteer thie name,

         Or Zabalus or Queed,

      Comme, fteel mie fable fpryte,

         For fremde [70] and dolefulle dede.   430

            [76] Strange.

                                      MAGNUS,

MAGNUS, HURRA, *and* HIE PREESTE,
wyth the ARMIE, *neare* Watchette.

MAGNUS.

SWYTHE [71] lette the offrendes [72] to the Goddeſ
    begynne,
To knowe of hem the iſſue of the fyghte.
Potte the blodde-ſteyned ſword and pavyes ynne ;
Spreade ſwythyn all arounde the hallie lyghte.

HIE PREESTE *ſyngeth.*

Yee, who hie yn mokie ayre   435
Delethe feaſonnes foule or fayre,
Yee, who, whanne yee weere agguylte,
The mone yn bloddie gyttelles [73] hylte,
Mooved the ſtarres, and dyd unbynde
Everyche barriere to the wynde ;   440

[71] Quickly.   [72] offerings.   [73] mantels.

Whanne

Whanne the oundynge waves dyſtreſte,
Storven to be overeſt,
Sockeynge yn the ſpyre-gyrte towne,
Swolterynge wole natyones downe,
Sendynge dethe, on plagues aſtrodde,   445
Moovynge lyke the erthys Godde;
To mee ſend your heſte dyvyne,
Lyghte eletten 74 all myne eyne,
Thatt I maie now undevyſe
All the actyonnes of th'empprize.   450

              [*falleth downe and efte ryſethe.*

Thus ſayethe the Goddes; goe, yſſue to the playne;
Forr there ſhall meynte of mytte menne bee ſlayne.

MAGNUS.

Whie, ſoe there evere was, whanne Magnus foughte,
Efte have I treynted noyance throughe the hoaſte,
Athorowe ſwerdes, alyche the Queed dyſtraughte, 455
Have Magnus preſſynge wroghte hys foemen loaſte,

        74 Enlighten.

                                    As

As whanne a tempeſte vexethe foare the coaſte,
The dyngeynge ounde the fandeie ſtronde doe tare,
So dyd I inne the warre the javlynne tofte,
Full meynte a champyonnes breaſte received mie
    ſpear. 460
Mie ſheelde, lyche fommere morie gronfer droke,
Mie lethalle ſpeere, alyche a levyn-mylted oke.

H U R R A.

Thie wordes are greate, full hyghe of found, and
    eeke
Lyche thonderre, to the whych dothe comme no rayne.
Itte lacketh notte a doughtie honde to fpeke ; 465
The cocke faiethe drefte [75], yett armed ys he alleyne.
Certis thie wordes maie, thou moteſt have fayne
Of mee, and meynte of moe, who eke canne fyghte,
Who haveth trodden downe the adventayle,
And tore the heaulmes from heades of myckle
    myghte. 470
Sythence fyke myghte ys placed yn thie honde,
Lette blowes thie aƈtyons ſpeeke, and bie thie corrage
    ſtonde.

        [75] Leaſt.

                MAGNUS.

MAGNUS.

Thou are a warrioure, Hurra, thatte I kenne,
And myckle famed for thie handie dede.
Thou fyghteft anente [76] maydens and ne menne,   475
Nor aie thou makeft armed hartes to blede.
Efte I, caparyfon'd on bloddie ftede,
Havethe thee feene binethe mee ynn the fyghte,
Wythe corfes I inveftynge everich mede,
And thou afton, and wondrynge at mie myghte.   480
Thanne wouldeft thou comme yn for mie renome,
Albeytte thou wouldft reyne awaie from bloddie dome ?

HURRA.

How! butte bee bourne mie rage.   I kenne aryghte
Bothe thee and thyne maie ne bee wordhye peene.
Eftfoones I hope wee fcalle engage yn fyghte ;   485
Thanne to the fouldyers all thou wylte be wreene.

[76] Againft.

I   I'll

I'll prove mie courage onne the burled greene;

Tys there alleyne I'll telle thee whatte I bee.

Gyf I weelde notte the deadlie fphere adeene,

Thanne lett mie name be fulle as lowe as thee.   490

Thys mie adented fhielde, thys mie warre-fpeare,

Schalle telle the falleynge foe gyf Hurra's harte can

    feare.

MAGNUS.

Magnus woulde fpeke, butte thatte hys noble fpryte

Dothe foe enrage, he knowes notte whatte to faie.

He'dde fpeke yn blowes, yn gottes of blodde he'd

    wryte,   495

And on thie heafod peyncte hys myghte for aie.

Gyf thou anent an wolfynnes rage wouldeft ftaie,

'Tys here to meet ytt; botte gyff nott, bee goe;

Left I in furrie fhulde mie armes dyfplaie,

Whyche to thie boddie wylle wurche 77 myckle

    woe.   500

Oh! I bee madde, dyftraughte wyth brendyng rage;

Ne feas of fmethynge gore wylle mie chafed harte

    affwage.

77 W, ,

                HURRA.

H U R R A.

I kenne thee, Magnus, welle; a wyghte thou art
That doeſt aſlee alonge ynn doled dyſtreſſe,
Strynge bulle yn boddie, lyoncelle yn harte,   505
I almoſt wyſche thie prowes were made leſſe.
Whan Ælla (name dreſt uppe yn ugſomneſs [78]
To thee and recreandes [79]) thondered on the playne,
Howe dydſte thou thorowe fyrſte of fleers preſſe !
Swefter thanne federed takelle dydſte thou reyne.   510
A ronnynge pryze onn feynĉte daie to ordayne,
Magnus, and none botte hee, the ronnynge pryze
        wylle gayne.

M A G N U S.

Eternalle plagues devour thie baned tyngue !
Myrriades of neders pre upponne thie ſpryte !
Maieſt thou fele al the peynes of age whylſt
        yynge,   515
Unmanned, uneyned, exclooded aie the lyghte,

[75] Terror.   [79] cowards.

                                                        Thie

Thie fenfes, lyche thiefelfe, enwrapped yn nyghte,
A fcoff to foemen & to beaftes a pheere;
Maie furched levynne onne thie head alyghte,
Maie on thee falle the fhuyr of the unweere;   520
Fen vaipoures blafte thie everiche manlie powere,
Maie thie bante boddie quycke the wolfome peenes
    devoure.

Faygne woulde I curfe thee further, botte mie tyngue
Denies mie harte the favoure foe toe doe.

H U R R A.

Nowe bie the Dacyanne goddes, & Welkyns kynge, 525
Wythe fhurie, as thou dydfte begynne, perfue;
Calle on mie heade all tortures that bee rou,
Bane onne, tylle thie owne tongue thie curfes fele.
Sende onne mie heade the blyghteynge levynne blewe,
The thonder loude, the fwellynge azure rele [80].   539
Thie wordes be hie of dynne, botte nete befyde;
Bane on, good chieftayn, fyghte wythe wordes of myckle
    pryde.

Botte doe notte wafte thie breath, left Ælla come.

[80] Wave.

I   MAG.

M A G N U S.

Ælla & thee togyder fynke toe helle !
Bee youre names blafted from the rolle of dome ! 535
I feere noe Ælla, thatte thou kenneft welle.
Unlydgefulle traytoure, wylt thou nowe rebelle ?
'Tys knowen, thatte yie menn bee lyncked to myne,
Bothe fente, as troopes of wolves, to fletre felle ;
Botte nowe thou lackeft hem to be all yyne.   540
Nowe, bie the goddes yatte reule the Dacyanne ftate,
Speacke thou yn rage once moe, I wyll thee dyfregate,

H U R R A.

I pryze thie threattes jofte as I doe thie banes,
The fede of malyce and recendize al.
Thou arte a fteyne unto the name of Danes ;   545
Thou alleyne to thie tyngue for proofe canft calle.
Thou beeft a worme fo groffile and fo fmal,
I wythe thie bloude woulde fcorne to foul mie fworde,
Botte wythe thie weaponnes woulde upon thee falle,
Alyche thie owne feare, flea thee wythe a worde. 550
I Hurra amme miefel, & aie wylle bee,
As greate yn valourous actes, & yn commande as thee.

M A G-

MAGNUS, HURRA, ARMYE & MESSENGER,

MESSENGERE.

Blynne your contekions [81], chiefs ; for, as I ftode
Uponne mie watche, I fpiede an armie commynge,
Notte lyche ann handfulle of a fremded [82] foe,   555
Botte blacke wythe armoure, movynge ugfomlie,
Lyche a blacke fulle cloude, thatte dothe goe alonge
To droppe yn hayle, & hele the thonder ftorme,

MAGNUS.

Ar there meynte of them ?

MESSENGERR.

Thycke as the ante-flyes ynne a fommer's none,   560
Seemynge as tho' theie ftynge as perfante too.

HURRA.

Whatte matters thatte ? lettes fette oure warr-arraie.
Goe, founde the beme, lette champyons prepare ;

[81] Contentions.   [82] frighted,

I. 2   Ne

Ne doubtynge, we wylle ſtynge as faſte as heie.

Whatte ? doeſt forgard [83] thie blodde ? ys ytte for

    feare ?   565

Wouldeſt thou gayne the towne, & caſtle-ſtere,

And yette ne byker wythe the foldyer guarde ?

Go, hyde thee ynn mie tente annethe the lere ;

I of thie boddie wylle keepe watche & warde.

M A G N U S.

Oure goddes of Denmarke know mie harte ys

    goode.   570

H U R R A.

For nete uppon the erthe, botte to be choughens foode.

MAGNUS, HURRA, ARMIE, SECONDE
M E S S E N G E R R E.

SECONDE MESSENGERRE.

As from mie towre I kende the commynge foe,

I ſpied the croſſed ſhielde, & bloddie ſwerde,

[83] Loſe.

The

The furyous Ælla's banner; wythynne kenne
The armie ys.   Dysorder throughe oure hoaste   575
Is fleynge, borne onne wynges of Ælla's name;
Styr, styr, mie lordes!

MAGNUS.

What? Ælla? & soe neare?
Thenne Denmarques roiend; oh mie rysynge feare!

HURRA.

What doeste thou mene? thys Ælla's botte a manne.
Nowe bie mie sworde, thou arte a verie berne [84].   580
Of late I dyd thie creand valoure scanne,
Whanne thou dydst boaste soe moche of actyon derne.
Botte I toe warr mie doeynges moste atturne,
To cheere the Sabbataneres to deere dede.

MAGNUS.

I to the knyghtes onne everyche syde wylle burne, 585
Telleynge 'hem alle to make her foemen blede;
Sythe shame or deathe onne eidher syde wylle bee,
Mie harte I wylle upryse, & inne the battelle slea.

[84] Child.

I 3   ÆLLA,

ÆLLA, CELMONDE, & ARMIE *near* WATCHETTE.

Æ L L A.

NOW havynge done oure mattynes & oure vowes,
Lette us for the intended fyghte be boune,   590
And everyche champyone potte the joyous crowne
Of certane mafterfchyppe upon hys gleftreynge browes.

As for mie harte, I owne ytt ys, as ere
Itte has beene ynne the fommer-fheene of fate,
Unknowen to the ugfomme gratche of fere ;   595
Mie blodde embollen, wythe mafterie elate,
Boyles ynne mie veynes, & rolles ynn rapyd ftate,
Impatyente forr to mete the perfante ftele,
And telle the worlde, thatte Ælla dyed as greate
As anie knyghte who foughte for Englondes weale. 600
Friends, kynne, & foldyerres, ynne blacke armore
    drere,
Mie actyons ymytate, mie prefente redynge here.

                                        There

There ys ne houfe, athrow thys fhap-fcutged 85 ifle,
Thatte has ne lofte a kynne yn thefe fell fyghtes,
Fatte blodde has forfeeted the hongerde foyle,   605
And townes enlowed 86 lemed 87 oppe the nyghtes.
Inne gyte of fyre oure hallie churche dheie dyghtes ;
Oure fonnes lie ftorven 88 ynne theyre fmethynge
       gore ;
Oppe bie the rootes oure tree of lyfe dheie pyghtes,
Vexynge oure coafte, as byllowes doe the fhore.   610
Yee menne, gyf ye are menne, difplaie yor name,
Ybrende yer tropes, alyche the roarynge tempeft flame.

Ye Chryftyans, doe as wordhie of the name ;
Thefe roynerres of oure hallie houfes flea ;
Brafte, lyke a cloude, from whence doth come the
       flame,   615
Lyche torrentes, gufhynge downe the mountaines, bee.
And whanne alonge the grene yer champyons flee,
Swefte as the rodde for-weltrynge 89 levyn-bronde,
. Yatte hauntes the flyinge mortherer oere the lea,
Soe flie oponne thefe royners of the londe.   620

85 Fate-fcourged.   86 flamed, fired.   87 lighted.   88 dead.
89 blafting.

I 4   Lette·

Lette thofe yatte are unto yer battayles fledde,
Take flepe eterne uponne a feerie lowynge bedde.

Let cowarde Londonne fee herre towne onn fyre,
And ftrev wythe goulde to ftaie the royners honde,
Ælla & Bryftowe havethe thoughtes thattes
 hygher,   625
Wee fyghte notte forr ourfelves, botte all the londe.
As Severnes hyger lyghethe banckes of fonde,
Preffynge ytte downe binethe the reynynge ftreme,
Wythe dreerie dynn enfwolters 90 the hyghe ftronde,
Beerynge the rockes alonge ynn fhurye breme,   830
Soe wylle wee beere the Dacyanne armie downe,
And throughe a ftorme of blodde wyll reache the cham-
 pyon crowne.

Gyff ynn thys battelle locke ne wayte oure gare,
To Bryftowe dheie wylle tourne yeyre fhuyrie dyre;
Bryftowe, & alle her joies, wylle fynke toe ayre,   635
Brendeynge perforce wythe unenhantende 91 fyre:
Thenne lette oure fafetie doublie moove oure ire,
Lyche wolfyns, rovynge for the evnynge pre,

   90 fwallows, fucks in.   91 unaccuftomed.

    2   See

See[ing] the lambe & ſhepſterr nere the brire,
Doth th'one forr ſafetie, th'one for hongre flea ; 640
Thanne, whanne the ravenne crokes uponne the
    playne,
Oh! lette ytte bee the knelle to myghtie Dacyanns
    ſlayne.

Lyche a rodde gronſer, ſhalle mie anlace ſheene,
Lyche a ſtrynge lyoncelle I'lle bee ynne fyghte,
Lyche fallynge leaves the Dacyannes ſhalle bee
    fleene,   645
Lyche[a]loud dynnynge ſtreeme ſcalle be mie myghte.
Ye menne, who woulde deſerve the name of knyghte,
Lette bloddie teares bie all your paves be wepte ;
To commynge tymes no poyntelle ſhalle ywrite,
Whanne Englonde han her foemenn, Bryſtow
    ſlepte.   650
Yourſelfes, youre chyldren, & youre fellowes crie,
Go, fyghte ynne rennomes gare, be brave, & wynne or
    die.

I ſaie ne moe ; youre ſpryte the reſte wylle ſaie ;
Youre ſpryte wylle wrynne, thatte Bryſtow ys yer
    place ;
                                            To

To honoures houſe I nede notte marcke the waie; 655
Inne youre owne hartes you maie the foote-pathe
  trace.
'Twexte ſhappe & us there ys botte lyttelle ſpace;
The tyme ys nowe to proove yourſelves bee menne;
Drawe forthe the bornyſhed bylle wythe fetyve grace,
Rouze, lyche a wolfynne rouzing from hys denne. 660
Thus I enrone mie anlace; go thou ſhethe;
I'lle potte ytt ne ynn place, tyll ytte ys fycke wythe
  deathe.

SOLDYERS.

Onn, Ælla, onn; we longe for bloddie fraie;
Wee longe to here the raven ſynge yn vayne;
Onn, Ælla, onn; we eertys gayne the daie,   665
Whanne thou doſte leade us to the leathal playne.

CELMONDE.

Thie ſpeche, O Loverde, fyrethe the whole trayne;
Theie pancte for war, as honted wolves for breathe;
Go, & fytte crowned on corſes of the ſlayne;
Go, & ywielde the maſſie ſwerde of deathe,   670

SOL-

SOLDYERRES.

From thee, O Ælla, alle oure courage reygnes ;
Echone yn phantafie do lede the Danes ynne chaynes.

Æ L L A.

Mie countrymenne, mie friendes, your noble fprytes
Speke yn youre eyne, & doe yer mafter telle.
Swefte as the rayne-ftorme toe the erthe alyghtes, 675
Soe wylle we fall upon thefe royners felle.
Oure mowynge fwerdes fhalle plonge hem downe to
    helle ;
Theyre throngynge corfes fhall onlyghte the ftarres ;
The barrowes braftynge wythe the fleene fchall fwelle,
Brynnynge 92 to commynge tymes our famous
    warres ;   680
Inne everie eyne I kenne the lowe of myghte,
Sheenynge abrode, alyche a hylle-fyre ynne the nyghte.

. Whanne poyntelles of oure famous fyghte fhall faie,
Echone wylle marvelle atte the dernie dede,

92 Declaring.

Echone

Echone wylle wyffen hee hanne feene the daie,   685

And bravelie holped to make the foemenn blede ;

Botte for yer holpe oure battelle wylle notte nede ;

Oure force ys force enowe to ftaie theyre honde ;

Wee wylle retourne unto thys grened mede,

Oer corfes of the foemen of the londe.   690

Nowe to the warre lette all the flughornes founde,

The Dacyanne troopes appere on yinder ryfynge
    grounde.

Chiefes, heade youre bandes, and leade.

DANES *flyinge, neare* WATCHETTE.

FYRSTE DANE.

FLY, fly, ye Danes; Magnus, the chiefe, ys fleene;
The Saxonnes comme wythe Ælla atte theyre
    heade;   695
Lette's ftrev to gette awaie to yinder greene;
Flie, flie; thys ys the kyngdomme of the deadde.

SECONDE DANE.

O goddes! have thoufandes bie mie anlace bledde,
And mufte I nowe for fafetie flie awaie?
See! farre befprenged alle oure troopes are
    fpreade,   700
Yette I wylle fynglie dare the bloddie fraie.
Botte ne; I'lle flie, & morther yn retrete;
Deathe, blodde, & fyre, fcalle [93] marke the goeynge of
    my feete.

[93] Shall.

THYRDE

T H Y R D E   D A N E.

Enthoghteynge forr to fcape the brondeynge foe,
As nere unto the byllowd beche I came,   705
Farr offe I fpied a fyghte of myckle woe,
Oure fpyrynge battayles wrapte ynn fayles of flame.
The burled Dacyannes, who were ynne the fame,
Fro fyde to fyde fledde the purfuyte of deathe;
The fwelleynge fyre yer corrage doe enflame,   710
Theie lepe ynto the fea, & bobblynge yield yer
       breathe;
Whyleft thofe thatt bee uponne the bloddie playne,
Bee deathe-doomed captyves taene, or yn the battle
       flayne.

H U R R A.

Nowe bie the goddes, Magnus, dyfcourteous knyghte,
Bie cravente 94 havyoure havethe don oure woe,   715
Dyfpendynge all the talle menne yn the fyghte,
And placeyng valourous menne where draffs mote
       goe.
Sythence oure fourtunie havethe tourned foe,
Gader the fouldyers lefte to future fhappe,

94 Coward.

To

To fomme newe place for fafetie wee wylle goe, 720
Inne future daie wee wylle have better happe.
Sounde the loude flughorne for a quicke forloyne 95 ;
Lette alle the Dacyannes fwythe untoe oure banner joyne.

Throw hamlettes wee wylle fprenge fadde dethe &
    dole,
Bathe yn hotte gore, & wafch ourefelves there-
    ynne ;   725
Goddes ! here the Saxonnes lyche a byllowe rolle.
I heere the anlacis detefted dynne.
Awaie, awaie, ye Danes, to yonder penne ;
Wee now wylle make forloyne yn tyme to fyghte
    agenne.

95 Retreat.

CELMONDE,

CÉLMONDE, *near* WATCHETTE,

O forr a fpryte al feere ! to telle the daie,   730
The daie whyche fcal aftounde the herers rede,
Makeynge oure foemennes envyynge hartes to blede,
Ybereynge thro the worlde oure rennomde name for
    aie.

Bryghte fonne han ynn hys roddie robes byn dyghte,
From the rodde Eafte he flytted wythe hys trayne,735
The howers drewe awaie the geete of nyghte,
Her fable tapiftrie was rente yn twayne.
The dauncynge ftreakes bedecked heavennes playne,
And on the dewe dyd fmyle wythe fhemrynge eie,
Lyche gottes of blodde whyche doe blacke armoure
    fteyne,   740
Sheenynge upon the borne 96 whyche ftondeth bie ;
The fouldyers ftoode uponne the hillis fyde,
Lyche yonge enlefed trees whyche yn a forrefte byde.

96 Burnifh.

AElla

Ælla rofe lyche the tree befette wyth brieres;
Hys talle fpeere fheenynge as the ftarres at nyghte, 745
Hys eyne enfemeynge as a lowe of fyre;
Whanne he encheered everie manne to fyghte,
Hys gentle wordes dyd moove eche valourous knyghte;
Itte moovethe 'hem, as honterres lyoncelle;
In trebled armoure ys theyre courage dyghte;   750
Eche warrynge harte forr prayfe & rennome fwelles;
Lyche flowelie dynnynge of the croucheynge ftreme,
Syche dyd the mormrynge founde of the whol armie
     feme.

Hee ledes 'hem onne to fyghte; oh! thenne to faie
How Ælla loked, and lokyng dyd encheere,   755
Moovynge alyche a mountayne yn affraie,
Whanne a lowde whyrlevynde doe yttes boefomme
     tare,
To telle howe everie loke wuld banyfhe feere,
Woulde afke an angelles poyntelle or hys tyngue.
Lyche a talle rocke yatte ryfeth heaven-were,   760
Lyche a yonge wolfynne brondeous & ftrynge,

K   Soe

Soe dydde he goe, & myghtie warriours hedde ;
Wythe gore-depyćted wynges mafterie arounde hym
   fledde.

The battelle jyned ; fwerdes uponne fwerdes dyd
   rynge ;
Ælla was chafed, as lyonns madded bee ;   765
Lyche fallynge ftarres, he dydde the javlynn flynge ;
Hys mightie anlace mightie menne dyd flea ;
Where he dydde comme, the flemed 97 foe dydde flee,
Or felle benethe hys honde, as fallynge rayne,
Wythe fythe a fhuyrie he dydde onn 'hemm dree, 770
Hylles of yer bowkes dyd ryfe opponne the playne ;
Ælla, thou arte—botte ftaie, mie tynge ; faie nee ;
Howe greate I hymme maye make, ftylle greater hee
   wylle bee.

Nor dydde hys fouldyerres fee hys aćtes yn vayne.
Heere a ftoute Dane uponne hys compheere felle ; 775
Heere lorde & hyndlette fonke uponne the playne ;
Heere fonne & fadre trembled ynto helle.
Chief Magnus fought hys waie, &, fhame to telle !
Hee foughte hys waie for flyghte ; botte Ælla's fpeere

97 Frighted.

Uponne

Uponne the flyynge Dacyannes fchoulder felle,   780
Quyte throwe hys boddie, & hys harte ytte tare,
He groned, & fonke uponne the gorie greene,
And wythe hys corfe encreafed the pyles of Dacyannes
    fleene.

Spente wythe the fyghte, the Danyfhe champyons
    ftonde,
Lyche bulles, whofe ftrengthe & wondrous myghte ys
    fledde;   785
Ælla, a javelynne grypped yn eyther honde,
Flyes to the thronge, & doomes two Dacyannes
    deadde.
After hys acte, the armie all yfpedde;
Fromm everich on unmyffynge javlynnes flewe;
Theie ftraughte yer doughtie fwerdes; the foemenn
    bledde;   790
Fulle three of foure of myghtie Danes dheie flewe;
The Danes, wythe terroure rulynge att their head,
Threwe downe theyr bannere talle, & lyche a ravenne
    fledde.

        K 2   The

The foldyerres followed wythe a myghtie crie,

Cryes, yatte welle myghte the ftoutefte hartes affraie.   795

Swefte, as yer fhyppes, the vanquyfhed Dacyannes
flie;

Swefte, as the rayne uponne an Aprylle daie,

Preffynge behynde, the Englyfche foldyerres flaie.

Botte halfe the tythes of Danyfhe menne remayne;

Ælla commaundes 'heie fhoulde the fleetre ftaie,   800

Botte bynde 'hem pryfonners on the bloddie playne.

The fyghtynge beynge done, I came awaie,

In odher fieldes to fyghte a moe unequalle fraie.

Mie fervant fquyre!

CELMONDE, SERVITOURE.

CELMONDE.

Prepare a fleing horfe,

Whofe feete are wynges, whofe pace ys lycke the
wynde,   805

Who

Whoe wylle outeftreppe the morneynge lyghte yn
 courfe,

Leaveynge the gyttelles of the merke behynde.

Somme hyltren matters doe mie prefence fynde.

Gyv oute to alle yatte I was fleene ynne fyghte.

Gyff ynne thys gare thou doeft mie order mynde, 810

Whanne I returne, thou fhalte be made a knyghte ;

Flie, flie, be gon ; an howerre ys a daie ;

Quycke dyghte mie befte of ftedes, & brynge hymm
 heere—awaie !

C E L M O N D E.

Ælla ys woundedd fore, & ynne the toune

He waytethe, tylle hys woundes bee broghte to ethe. 815

And fhalle I from hys browes plocke off the croune,

Makynge the vyctore yn hys vyctorie blethe ?

O no ! fulle fooner fchulde mie hartes blodde fmethe,

Fulle foonere woulde I tortured bee toe deathe ;

Botte—Birtha ys the pryze ; ahe ! ytte were ethe 820

To gayne fo gayne a pryze wythe loffe of breathe ;

Botte thanne rennome æterne 98—ytte ys botte ayre ;

Bredde ynne the phantafie, & alleyn lyvynge there.

98 Eternal.

K 3   Albeytte

Albeytte everyche thynge yn lyfe confpyre

To telle me of the faulte I nowe fchulde doe,   825

Yette woulde I battentlie affuage mie fyre,

And the fame menes, as I fcall nowe, purfue.

The qualytyes I fro mie parentes drewe,

Were blodde, & morther, mafterie, and warre';

Thie I wylle holde to now, & hede ne moe   830

A wounde yn rennome, yanne a boddie fcarre.

Nowe, Ælla, nowe Ime plantynge of a thorne,

Bie whyche thie peace, thie love, & glorie fhalle be
    torne.

BRYSTOWE.

BRYSTOWE.

BIRTHA, EGWINA.

BIRTHA,

GENTLE Egwina, do notte preche me joie;
I cannotte joie ynne anie thynge botte weere 99.   835
Oh! yatte aughte fchulde oure fellyneffe deftroie,
Floddynge the face wythe woe, & brynie teare!

EGWINA.

You mufte, you mufte endeavour for to cheere
Youre harte unto fomme cherifaunied refte.
Youre loverde from the battelle wylle appere,   840
Ynne honnoure, & a greater love, be drefte;
Botte I wylle call the mynftrelles roundelaie;
Perchaunce the fwotie founde maie chafe your wiere 99
     awaie.

     99 Grief.

     K 4   BIRTHA,

BIRTHA, EGWINA, MYNSTRELLES.

MYNSTRELLES SONGE.

O! fynge untoe mie roundelaie,
O! droppe the brynie teare wythe mee,   845
Daunce ne moe atte hallie daie,
Lycke a reynynge [100] ryver bee;
  Mie love ys dedde,
  Gon to hys death-bedde,
  Al under the wyllowe tree.   850

Blacke hys cryne [101] as the wyntere nyghte,
Whyte hys rode [102] as the fommer fnowe,
Rodde hys face as the mornynge lyghte,
Cale he lyes ynne the grave belowe;
  Mie love ys dedde,   855
  Gon to hys deathe-bedde,
  Al under the wyllowe tree.

Swote hys tyngue as the throftles note,
Quycke ynn daunce as thoughte canne bee,

[100] Running.   [101] hair.   [102] complexion.

Defte

Defte hys taboure, codgelle ftote,   860
O! hee lyes bie the wyllowe tree:
    Mie love ys dedde,
      Gonne to hys deathe-bedde,
      Alle underre the wyllowe tree.

Harke! the ravenne flappes hys wynge,   865
In the briered delle belowe;
Harke! the dethe-owle loude dothe fynge,
To the nyghte-mares as heie goe;
    Mie love ys dedde,
      Gonne to hys deathe-bedde,   870
      Al under the wyllowe tree.

See! the whyte moone fheenes onne hie;
Whyterre ys mie true loves fhroude;
Whyterre yanne the mornynge fkie,
Whyterre yanne the evenynge cloude;   875
    Mie love ys dedde,
      Gon to hys deathe-bedde,
      Al under the wyllowe tree.

Heere, uponne mie true loves grave,
Schalle the baren fleurs be layde,   880
  3   Nee

Nee one hallie Seyncte to fave
Al the celnefs of a mayde.
   Mie love ys dedde,
   Gonne to hys death-bedde,
   Alle under the wyllowe tree.   885

Wythe mie hondes I'lle dente the brieres
Rounde his hallie corfe to gre,
Ouphante fairie, lyghte youre fyres,
Heere mie boddie ftylle fchalle bee,
   Mie love ys dedde,   890
   Gon to hys death-bedde,
   Al under the wyllowe tree.

Comme, wythe acorne-coppe & thorne,
Drayne mie hartys blodde awaie;
Lyfe & all yttes goode I fcorne,   895
Daunce bie nete, or feafte by daie.
   Mie love ys dedde,
   Gon to hys death-bedde,
   Al under the wyllowe tree.

Waterre wytches, crownede wythe reytes [103],   900
Bere mee to yer leathalle tyde.
    [103] Water-flags

        I die;

I die ; I comme ; mie true love waytes,
Thos the damselle spake, and dyed.

B I R T H A,

Thys syngeyng haveth whatte coulde make ytte
pleafe ;
Butte mie uncourtlie shappe benymmes mee of all
case.   905

ÆLLA,

CURSE onne mie tardie woundes! brynge mee a
   ſtede!
I wylle awaie to Birtha bie thys nyghte;
Albeytte fro mie woundes mie ſoul doe blede,
I wylle awaie, & die wythynne her ſyghte.
Brynge   mee   a   ſtede,   wythe   eagle-wynges   for
   flyghte;   910
Swefte as mie wyſhe, &, as mie love ys, ſtronge.
The   Danes   have   wroughte   mee   myckle   woe   ynne
   fyghte,
Inne kepeynge mee from Birtha's armes ſo longe.
O! whatte a dome was myne, ſythe maſterie
Canne yeve ne pleaſaunce, nor mie londes goode leme
   myne eie!   915

Yee goddes, howe ys a loverres temper formed!
Sometymes the ſamme thynge wylle bothe bane, &
   bleſſe;

                                                    On

On tyme encalede ¹⁰⁴, yanne bie the fame thynge
    warmed,

Eftroughted foorthe, and yanne ybrogten lefs.

*Tys Birtha's lofs whyche doe mie thoughtes pof-
    feffe;   920

I wylle, I mufte awaie: whie ftaies mie ftede?

Mie hufcarles, hyther hafte; prepare a dreffe,

Whyche couracyers ¹⁰⁵ yn haftie journies nede.

O heavens! I mofte awaie to Byrtha eyne,

For yn her lookes I fynde mie beynge doe entwyne. 925

---

104 Frozen, cold.   105 horfe courfers, couriers.

CELMONDE,

CELMONDE, att BRYSTOWE.

THE worlde ys darke wythe nyghte; the wyndes
    are ftylle;
Fayntelie the mone her palyde lyghte makes gleme;
The upryfte [106] fprytes the fylente letten [107] fylle,
Wythe ouphant faeryes joynyng ynne the dreme;
The forrefte fheenethe wythe the fylver leme;   930
Nowe maie mie love be fated ynn yttes treate;
Uponne the lynche of fomme fwefte reynyng ftreme,
Att the fwote banquette I wylle fwotelie eate.
Thys ys the howfe; yee hyndes, fwythyn appere.

CELMONDE, SERVYTOURE.

CELMONDE.

Go telle to Birtha ftrayte, a ftraungerr waytethe
    here.   935

[106] Rifen.   [107] church-yard.

CELMONDE, BIRTHA.

BIRTHA.

Celmonde! yee feynétes! I hope thou hafte goode
newes.

CELMONDE.

Ths hope ys lofte; for heavie newes prepare.

BIRTHA.

Is Ælla welle?

CELMONDE.

. Hee lyves; & ftylle maie ufe
The behylte [108] bleffynges of a future yeare.

BIRTHA.

Whatte heavie tydynge thenne have I to feare? 940
Of whatte mifchaunce dydfte thou fo latelie faie?

[108] Promifed.

CEL-

CELMONDE.

For heavie tydynges fwythyn nowe prepare.
Ælla fore wounded ys, yn bykerous fraie;
In Wedecefter's wallid toune he lyes.

BIRTHA,

O mie agroted breaft!

CELMONDE.

Wythoute your fyghte, he dyes.   945

BIRTHA.

Wylle Birtha's prefence ethe herr Ælla's payne?
I flie; newe wynges doe from mie fchoulderrs fprynge.

CELMONDE.

Mie ftede wydhoute wylle deftelie beere us twayne.

BIRTHA.

Oh! I wyll flie as wynde, & no waie lynge;

Sweftlie

Sweftlie caparifons for rydynge brynge; 950
I have a mynde wynged wythe the levyn ploome.
O Ælla, Ælla! dydfte thou kenne the ftynge,
The whyche doeth canker ynne mie hartys roome,
Thou wouldfte fee playne thiefelfe the gare to bee;
Aryfe, uponne thie love, & flie to meeten mee. 955

CELMONDE.

The ftede, on whyche I came, ys fwefte as ayre;
Mie fervytoures doe wayte mee nere the wode;
Swythynne wythe mee unto the place repayre;
To Ælla I wylle gev you conducte goode.
Youre eyne, alyche a baulme, wylle ftaunche hys
 bloode, 960
Holpe oppe hys woundes, & yev hys harte alle
 cheere;
Uponne your eyne he holdes hys lyvelyhode [109];
You doe hys fpryte, & alle hys pleafaunce bere.
Comme, lette's awaie, albeytte ytte ys moke,
Yette love wille bee a tore to tourne to feere nyghtes
 fmoke. 965

[109] Life.

L   BIR-

B I R T H A.

Albeytte unwears dyd the welkynn rende,

Reyne, alyche fallynge ryvers, dyd ferſe bee,

Erthe wythe the ayre enchafed dyd contende,

Everychone breathe of wynde wythe plagues dyd

flee,

Yette I to Ælla's eyne eftſoones woulde flee;   970

Albeytte hawethornes dyd mie fleſhe enſeme,

Owlettes, wythe ſcrychynge, ſhakeynge everyche tree,

And water-neders wrygglynge yn eche ſtreme,

Yette woulde I flie, ne under coverte ſtaie,

Botte ſeke mie Ælla owte ; brave Celmonde, leade the

waie.   975

A WODE.

A WODE.

HURRA, DANES.

HURRA.

HEERE ynn yis forreſte lette us watche for pree,
Bewreckeynge on oure foemenne oure ylle warre;
Whatteverre ſchalle be Englyſch wee wylle ſlea,
Spreddynge our ugſomme rennome to afarre.
Ye Dacyanne menne, gyff Dacyanne menne yee
    are,   980
Lette nete botte blodde ſuffycyle for yee bee;
On everich breaſte yn gorie letteres ſcarre,
Whatt ſprytes you have, & howe thoſe ſprytes maie
    dree.
And gyf yee gette awaie to Denmarkes ſhore,
Efteſoones we will retourne, & wanquiſhed bee ne
    moere,   985

              The

The battelle lofte, a battelle was yndede ;

Note queedes hemfelfes culde ftonde fo harde a fraie ;

Oure verie armoure, & oure heaulmes dyd blede,

The Dacyannes fprytes, lyche dewe drops, fledde
    awaie.

Ytte was an Ælla dyd commaunde the daie ;   990

Ynn fpyte of foemanne, I mofte faie hys myghte ;

Botte wee ynn hyndlettes blodde the lofs wylle paie,

Brynnynge, thatte we knowe howe to wynne yn
    fyghte ;

Wee wylie, lyke wylfes enloofed from chaynes,
    deftroie ;—

Oure armoures—wynter nyghte fhotte oute the daie of
    joie.   995

Whene fwefte-fote tyme doe rolle the daie alonge,

Somme hamlette fcalle onto oure fhuyrie brende ;

Braftynge alyche a rocke, or mountayne ftronge,

The talle chyrche-fpyre upon the grene fhalle bende ;

Wee wylle the walles, & auntyante tourrettes
    rende,   1000

Pete everych tree whych goldyn fruyte doe beere,

Downe

Downe to the goddes the ownerrs dhereof fende,

Befprengynge alle abrode fadde warre & bloddie weere.

Botte fyrfte to yynder oke-tree wee wylle flie;

And thence wylle yffue owte onne all yatte commeth
    bie.   1005

ANODHER PARTE OF THE WOODE.

CELMONDE, BIRTHA.

BIRTHA.

Thys merknefs doe affraie mie wommanns breafte.

Howe fable ys the fpreddynge fkie arrayde!

Hallie the bordeleire, who lyves to refte,

Ne ys att nyghtys flemynge hue dyfmayde;

The ftarres doe fcantillie [110] the fable brayde;   1010

Wyde ys the fylver lemes of comforte wove;

Speke, Celmonde, does ytte make thee notte afrayde?

CELMONDE.

Merker the nyghte, the fitter tyde for love.

[110] Scarcely, fparingly.

B I R T H A.

Saieſt thou for love? ah! love is far awaie.
Faygne would I ſee once moe the roddie lemes of
  daie.   1015

C E L M O N D E.

Love maie bee nie, woulde Birtha calle ytte here.

B I R T H A.

How, Celmonde, dothe thou mene?

C E L M O N D E.

     Thys Celmonde menes.
No leme, no eyne, ne mortalle manne appere,
Ne lyghte, an acte of love for to bewreene;
Nete in thys forreſte, botte thys tore [111], dothe
  ſheene,   1020
The whych, potte oute, do leave the whole yn nyghte;
See! howe the brauncynge trees doe here entwyne,
Makeynge thys bower ſo pleaſynge to the ſyghte;

   [111] Torch.

          Thys

Thys was for love fyrſte made, & heere ytt ſtondes,
Thatte hereynne lovers maie enlyncke yn true loves
    bondes.   1025

BIRTHA.

Celmonde, ſpeake whatte thou meneſt, or alſe mie
    thoughtes
Perchaunce maie robbe thie honeſtie ſo fayre.

CELMONDE.

Then here, & knowe, hereto I have you broughte,
Mie longe hydde love unto you to make clere.

BIRTHA.

Oh heaven & earthe! whatte ys ytt I doe heare? 1030
Am I betraſte [112]? where ys mie Ælla, ſaie!

CELMONDE.

O! do nete nowe to Ælla ſyke love bere,
Botte geven ſome onne Celmondes hedde.

[112] Betrayed.

L 4   BIRj

B I R T H A.

Awaie!
1 wylle be gone, & groape mie paſſage oute,
Albeytte neders ſtynges mie legs du twyne aboute.   1035

C E L M O N D E.

Nowe bie the ſeynctes I wylle notte lette thee goe,
Ontylle thou doeſte mie brendynge love amate.
Thoſe eyne have cauſed Celmonde myckle woe,
Yenne lette yer ſmyle fyrſt take hymm yn regrate.
O ! didſt thou ſee mie breaſtis troblous ſtate,   1040
Theere love doth harrie up mie joie, and ethe !
Iwretched bee, beyonde the hele of fate,
Gyff Birtha ſtylle wylle make mie harte-veynes blethe.
Softe as the ſommer flowreets, Birtha, looke,
Fulle ylle I canne thie frownes & harde dyſpleaſaunce
        brooke.   1045

B I R T H A.

Thie love ys foule ; I woulde bee deafe for aie,
Radher thanne heere ſyche deſlavatie [113] ſedde.

[113] Letchery.

Swythynne

Swythynne flie from mee, and ne further faie;

Radher thanne heare thie love, I woulde bee dead.

Yee feynctes ! & fhal I wronge mie Ælla's bedde, 1050

And wouldft thou, Celmonde, tempte me to the
thynge ?

Lett mee be gone—alle curfes onne thie hedde !

Was ytte for thys thou dydfte a meffage brynge !

Lette me be gone, thou manne of fable harte !

Or welkyn ¹¹⁴ & her ftarres wyll take a maydens
parte.   1055

CELMONDE.

Sythence you wylle notte lette mie fuyte avele,

Mie love wylle have yttes joie, altho wythe guylte ;

Youre lymbes fhall bende, albeytte ftrynge as ftele ;

The merkye feefonne wylle your blofhes hylte ¹¹⁵.

BIRTHA.

Holpe, holpe, yee feynctes ! oh thatte mie blodde was
fpylte !   1060

---

¹¹⁴ heaven.   ¹¹⁵ hide.

2   C E L-

CELMONDE.

The feynctes att diftaunce ftonde ynn tyme of nede.
Strev notte to goe; thou canfte notte, gyff thou wylte.
Unto mie wyfche bee kinde, & nete alfe hede.

BIRTHA.

No, foule beftoykerre, I wylle rende the ayre,
Tylle dethe do ftaie mie dynne, or fomme kynde roder
    heare.   1065
    Holpe! holpe! oh godde!

CELMONDE, BIRTHA, HURRA, DANES.

HURRA.

        Ah! thatts a wommanne cries.
I kenn hem; faie, who are you, yatte bee theere?

CELMONDE.

Yee hyndes, awaie! orre bie thys fwerde yee dies.

             HURRA.

HURRA.

Thie wordes wylle ne mie hartis fete affere.

BIRTHA.

Save mee, oh! fave mee from thys royner heere! 1070

HURRA.

Stonde thou bie mee; nowe faie thie name & londe;
Or fwythyne fchall mie fwerde thie boddie tare.

CELMONDE.

Bothe I wylle fhewe thee bie mie brondeous [116] honde;

HURRA.

Befette hym rounde, yee Danes.

CELMONDE.

Comme onne, and fee
Gyff mie ftrynge anlace maie bewryen whatte I bee. 1075
[*Fygbte al anenfte* Celmonde, *meynte Danes he fleath,
and faleth to* Hurra.

[116] Furious.

.CEL-

CELMONDE.

Oh! I forflagen [117] be! ye Danes, now kenne,
I amme yatte Celmonde, feconde yn the fyghte,
Who dydd, atte Watchette, fo forflege youre menne;
I fele myne eyne to fwymme yn æterne nyghte;—
To her be kynde.   [*Dieth.*

HURRA.

      Thenne felle a wordhie knyghte.   1080
Saie, who bee you?

BIRTHA.

      I am greate Ælla's wyfe.

HURRA.

Ah!

BIRTHA.

Gyff anenfte hym you harboure foule defpyte,
Nowe wythe the lethal anlace take mie lyfe,

    [117] flain.

                      Bie

Bie thankes I ever onne you wylle beſtowe,

From ewbryce [118] you mee pyghte, the worſte of mortal
woe.   1085

H U R R A.

I wylle; ytte ſcalle bee ſoe: yee Dacyans, heere.

Thys Ælla havethe been oure foe for aie.

Thorrowe the battelle he dyd brondeous teare,

Beyng the lyfe and head of everych fraie;

From everych Dacyanne power he won the daie, 1090

Forſlagen Magnus, all oure ſchippes ybrente;

Bie hys felle arme wee now are made to ſtraie;

The ſpeere of Dacya he ynne pieces ſhente;

Whanne hantoned barckes unto our londe dyd comme,

Ælla the gare dheie ſed, & wyſched hym bytter
dome.   1095

B I R T H A.

Mercie!

H U R R A.

Bee ſtylle.

[118] Adultery.

Botte

Botte yette he ys a foemanne goode and fayre;
Whanne wee are fpente, he foundethe the forloyne;
The captyves chayne he toffeth ynne the ayre,
Cheered the wounded bothe wythe bredde & wyne;
Has hee notte untoe fomme of you bynn dygne? 1100
You would have fmethd onne Wedeceftrian fielde,
Botte hee behylte the flughorne for to cleyne,
Throwynge onne hys wyde backe, hys wyder fpred-
        dynge fhielde.
Whanne you, as caytyfned, yn fielde dyd bee,
Hee oathed you to bee ftylle, & ftrayte dydd fette you
        free,   1105

Scalle wee forflege [119] hys wyfe, becaufe he's brave?
Bicaus hee fyghteth for hys countryes gare?
Wylle hee, who havith bynne yis Ælla's flave,
Robbe hym of whatte percafe he holdith deere?
Or fcalle we menne of mennys fprytes appere, 1110
Doeynge hym favoure for hys favoure donne,
Swefte to hys pallace thys damoifelle bere,
Bewrynne oure cafe, and to oure waie be gonne?

        [119] Slay.

                                        The

The laſt you do approve ;. ſo lette ytte bee ;
Damoyſelle, comme awaie ; you ſafe ſcalle bee wythe
   mee. 1115

BIRTHA.

Al bleſſynges maie the ſeynctes unto yee gyve !
Al pleaſaunce maie youre longe-ſtraughte livynges
   bee !
Ælla, whanne knowynge thatte bie you I lyve,
Wylle thyncke too ſmalle a guyfte the londe & ſea.
O Celmonde ! I maie deftlie rede bie thee, 1120
Whatte ille betydethe the enfouled kynde ;
Maie ne thie croſs-ſtone [120] of thie cryme bewree !
Maie alle menne ken thie valoure, fewe thie mynde !
Soldyer ! for ſyke thou arte ynn noble fraie,
I wylle thie goinges 'tende, & doe thou lede the waie. 1125

HURRA.

The mornynge 'gyns' alonge the Eaſte to ſheene ;
Darklinge the lyghte doe onne the waters plaie ;
   The feynte rodde leme ſlowe creepeth oere the greene,
   Toe chaſe the merkyneſs of nyghte awaie ;

[120] Monument.

                        Swifte

Swifte flies the howers thatte wylle brynge oute the
.   daie ;   1130
The fofte dewe falleth onne the greeynge graffe ;
The fhepfter mayden, dyghtynge her arraie,
Scante [121] fees her vyfage yn the wavie glaffe ;
Bie the fulle daylieghte wee fcalle Ælla fee,
Or Bryftowes   wallyd   towne ;   damoyfelle,   followe
     mee.   1135

[121] Scarce.

AT BRYSTOWE.

ÆLLA AND SERVITOURES.

ÆLLA.

TYS nowe fulle morne; I thoughten, bie lafte
   nyghte
To have been heere; mie ftede han notte mie love;
Thys ys mie pallace; lette mie hyndes alyghte,
Whylfte I goe oppe, & wake mie flepeynge dove.
Staie here, mie hyndlettes; I fhal goe above.   1140
Nowe, Birtha, wyll thie loke enhele mie fpryte,
Thie fmyles unto mie woundes a baulme wylle prove;
Mie ledanne boddie wylle bee fette aryghte.
Egwina, hafte, & ope the portalle doore,
Yatte I on Birtha's brefte maie thynke of warre ne
   more.   1145

      M   ÆLLA.

Æ L L A, E G W I N A.

E G W I N A.

Oh Ælla!

Æ L L A.

Ah! that femmlykeene to me
Speeketh a legendary tale of woe.

E G W I N A.

Birtha is —

Æ L L A.

Whatt? where? how? faie, whatte of fhee?

E G W I N A.

Gone —

Æ L L A.

Gone! ye goddes!

E G W I N *A*

E G W I N A.

Alas! ytte ys toe true.
Yee feynctes, hee dies awaie wythe myckle woe! 1150
Ælla! what? Ælla! oh! hee lyves agen.

Æ L L A.

Çal mee notte Ælla; I am hymme ne moe.
Where ys fhee gon awaie? ah! fpeake! how? when?

E G W I N A.

I will.

Æ L L A.

Caparyfon a fcore of ftedes; flie, flie,
Where ys fhee? fwythynne fpeeke, or inftante thou
fhalte die. 1155

E G W I N A.

Stylle thie loud rage, & here thou whatte I knowe.

Æ L L A.

Oh! fpeek.

M 2   E G W I N A.

E G W I N A.

Lyche prymrofe, droopynge wythe the heavie rayne,
Lafte nyghte I lefte her, droopynge wythe her wiere,
Her love the gare, thatte gave her hearte fyke peyne—

Æ L L A.

Her love! to whomme?

E G W I N A.

To thee, her fpoufe alleyne [121].　1160
As ys mie hentylle everyche morne to goe,
I wente, and oped her chamber doore ynn twayne,
Botte found her notte, as I was wont to doe;
Thanne alle arounde the pallace I dyd feere [123],
Botte culde (to mie hartes woe) ne fynde her anie
　　wheere.　　　　　　　　　　　1165

Æ L L A.

Thou lyeft, foul hagge! thou lyeft; thou art her
　　ayde
To chere her loufte;—botte noe; ytte cannotte bee.

[121] Only, alone.　　[123] Search.

I　　　　　　　　　　　E G W I N A,

EGWINA.

Gyff trouthe appear notte inne whatte I have fayde,
Drawe forthe thie anlace fwythyn, thanne mee flea.

ÆLLA.

Botte yette ytte mufte, ytte mufte bee foe; I fee, 1170
Shee wythe fomme louftie paramoure ys gone;
Itte mofte bee foe—oh! how ytt wracketh mee!
Mie race of love, mie race of lyfe ys ronne;
Nowe rage, & brondeous ftorm, & tempefte comme;
Nete lyvynge upon erthe can now enfwote mie
  domme.   1175

ÆLLA, EGWINA, SERVYTOURE.

SERVYTOURE.

Loverde! I am aboute the trouthe to faie.
Lafte nyghte, fulle late I dydde retourne to refte.
As to mie chamber I dydde bende mie waie,
To Birtha onne hys name & place addrefte;

Downe

Downe to hym camme ſhee ; butte thereof the

reſte 1180

I ken ne matter ; ſo, mie hommage made—

Æ L L A.

O ! ſpeake ne moe ; mie harte flames yn yttes heſte ;

I once was Ælla ; nowe bee notte yttes ſhade.

Hanne alle the fuirie of mysfortunes wylle

Fallen onne mie benned [124] headde I hanne been Ælla

ſtylle. 1185

Thys alleyn was unburled [125] of alle mie ſpryte ;

Mie honnoure, honnoure, frownd on the dolce [126]

wynde,

Thatte ſteeked on ytte ; nowe wyth rage Im pyghte ;

A brondeous unweere ys mie engyned mynde.

Mie hommeur yette ſomme drybblet joie maie

fynde, 1190

To the Danes woundes I wylle another yeve ;

Whanne thos mie rennome [127] & mie peace ys rynde,

Itte were a recrandize to thyncke toe lyve ;

[124] Curſed, tormented. [125] unarmed. [126] ſoft, gentle.
[127] renown.

Mie

Mie hufcarles, untoe everie afker telle,
Gyffe noblie Ælla lyved, as noblie Ælla felle.   1195

[Stabbeth hys brefte.

SERVYTOURE.

Ælla ys fleene; the flower of Englonde's marrde!

Æ L L A.

Be ftylle: ftythe lette the chyrches rynge mie knelle.
Call hyther brave Coernyke; he, as warde
Of thys mie Bryftowe caftle, wyll doe welle.

[Knelle ryngeth.

ÆLLA, EGWINA, SERVYTOURE, COERNYKE.

Æ L L A.

Thee I ordeyne the warde; fo alle maie telle.   1200
I have botte lyttel tym to dragge thys lyfe;
Mie lethal tale, alyche a lethalle belle,
Dynne yn the eares of her I wyfchd mie wyfe!

Botte

Botte, ah ! fhee maie be fayre.

E G W I N A.

Yatte fhee mofte bee

Æ L L A.

Ah ! faie notte foe ; yatte worde woulde Ælla dobblie
flee.   1205

ÆLLA, EGWINA, SERVYTOURE, COERNYKE,
BIRTHA, HURRA.

Æ L L A.

Ah ! Birtha here !

B I R T H A.

Whatte dynne ys thys? whatte menes yis leathalle
knelle ?
Where ys mie Ælla? fpeeke ; where ? howe ys hee ?
Oh Ælla ! art thou yanne alyve and welle !

Æ L L A.

Æ L L A.

I lyve yndeed; botte doe notte lyve for thee.

B I R T H A.

Whatte menes mie Ælla?

Æ L L A.

Here mie meneynge fee.   1210
Thie foulnefs urged mie honde to gyve thys wounde,
Ytte mee unfprytes [118].

B I R T H A.

Ytte hathe unfpryted mee.

Æ L L A.

Ah heavens! mie Birtha fallethe to the grounde!
Botte yette I am a manne, and fo wylle bee.

[118] Un-fouls.

H U R R A.

H U R R A.

Ælla! I amme a Dane; botte yette a friende to
    thee.   1215

Thys damoyfelle I founde wythynne a woode,
Strevynge fulle harde anenfte a burled fwayne;
I fente hym myrynge ynne mie compheeres blodde,
Celmonde hys name, chief of thie warrynge trayne.
Yis damoifelle foughte to be here agayne;   1220
The whyche, albeytte foemen, wee dydd wylle;
So here wee broughte her wythe you to remayne.

C O E R N I K E.

Yee nobylle Danes! wythe goulde I wyll you fylle.

Æ L L A.

Birtha, mie lyfe! mie love! oh! fhe ys fayre.
Whatte faultes coulde Birtha have, whatte faultes could
    Ælla feare?   1225

B I R T H A.

. BIRTHA.

Amm I yenne thyne? I cannotte blame thie feere.
Botte doe refte mĕe uponne mie Ælla's breafte;
I wylle to thee bewryen the woefulle gare.
Celmonde dyd comme to mee at tyme of refte,
Wordeynge for mee to flie, att your requefte,   1230
To Watchette towne, where you deceafynge laie;
I wyth hym fledde; thro' a murke wode we prefte,
Where hee foule love unto mie eares dyd faie;
The Danes —

Æ L L A.

Oh! I die contente.—   [*dieth.*

BIRTHA.

                    Oh! ys mie Ælla dedde?
O! I will make hys grave mie vyrgyn fpoufal
        bedde.   1235
                    [Birtha *feynEteth.*

COERNYKE.

Whatt? Ælla deadde! & Birtha dyynge toe!
Soe falles the fayreft flourettes of the playne.

                                Who

Who canne unplyte the wurchys heaven can doe,

Or who untwefte the role of fhappe yn twayne ?

Ælla, thie rennome was thie onlie gayne ;   1240

For yatte, thie pleafaunce, & thie joie was lofte.

Thie countrymen fhall rere thee, on the playne,

A pyle of carnes, as anie grave can boafte ;

Further, a juft amede to thee to bee,

Inne heaven thou fynge of Godde, on erthe we'lle fynge

    of thee.   1245

THE ENDE.

GODDWYN;

GODDWYN;

A TRAGEDIE.

By THOMAS ROWLEIE.

PERSONS REPRESENTED.

HAROLDE,   bie *T. Rowleie*, the Aucthoure.

GODDWYN,   bie *Johan de Iscamme*.

ELWARDE,   bie Syrr *Thybbot Gorges*.

ALSTAN,   bie Syrr *Alan de Vere*.

KYNGE EDWARDE, bie Maftre *Willyam Canynge*.

Odhers bie *Knyghtes Mynnftrells*.

PROLOGUE,

Made bie Maiftre WILLIAM CANYNGE.

WHYLOMME¹ bie penfmenne² moke³ ungentle⁴
    name
Have upon Goddwynne Erle of Kente bin layde,
Dherebie benymmynge⁵ hymme of faie⁶ and fame;
Unliart⁷ diviniftres⁸ haveth faide,
Thatte he was knowen toe noe hallie⁹ wurche¹⁰;   5
Botte thys was all hys faulte, he gyfted ne¹¹ the churche.

The aucthoure¹¹ of the piece whiche we enacte,
Albeytte¹³ a clergyon¹⁴, trouthe wyll wrytte.
Inne drawynge of hys menne no wytte ys lackte;
Entyn¹⁵ a kynge mote¹⁶ bee full pleafed to nyghte. 10
Attende, and marcke the partes nowe to be done;
Wee better for toe doe do champyon¹⁷ anie onne.

---

¹ Of old, formerly. ² writers, hiftorians. ³ much. ⁴ inglorious.
⁵ bereaving. ⁶ faith. ⁷ unforgiving. ⁸ divines, clergymen, monks.
⁹ holy. ¹⁰ work. ¹¹ not. ¹² author. ¹³ though, notwithftanding.
¹⁴ clerk, or clergyman. ¹⁵ entyn, even. ¹⁶ might. ¹⁷ challenge.

GODDWYN;

GODDWYN; A TRAGEDIE.

GODDWYN and HAROLDE.

GODDWYN.

HAROLDE!

HAROLDE.

Mie loverde [18]!

GODDWYN.

O! I weepe to thyncke,
What foemen [19] rifeth to ifrete [20] the londe.
Theie batten [21] onne her flefhe, her hartes bloude
dryncke,
And all ys graunted from the roieal honde.

[18] Lord. [19] foes, enemies. [20] devour, deftroy. [21] fatten.

HAROLDE.

HAROLDE.

Lette notte thie agreme [22] blyn [23], ne aledge [24] ftonde; 5
Bee I toe wepe, I wepe in teres of gore:
Am I betraffed [25], fyke [26] fhulde mie burlie [27] bronde
Depeyncte [28] the wronges on hym from whom I bore.

GODDWYN.

I ken thie fpryte [29] ful welle ; gentle thou art,
Stringe [30], ugfomme [31], rou [32], as fmethynge [33] armyes
    feeme ;   10
Yett efte [34], I feare, thie chefes [35] toe grete a parte,
And that thie rede [36] bee efte borne downe bie breme [37].
What tydynges from the kynge ?

HAROLDE.

          His Normans know.
I make noe compheeres of the fhemrynge [38] trayne.

[22] Grievance; a fenfe of it.   [23] ceafe, be ftill,   [24] idly.
[25] deceived, impofed on.   [26] fo.   [27] fury, anger, rage.
[28] paint, difplay.   [29] foul.   [30] ftrong.   [31] terrible;
[32] horrid, grim.   [33] fmoking, bleeding.   [34] oft.   [35] heat, rafhnefs.
[36] counfel, wifdom.   [37] ftrength, alfo ftrong.   [38] taudry, glimmering.

     N   GODD-

G O D D W Y N.

Ah Harolde ! tis a fyghte of myckle woe,   15
To kenne thefe Normannes everich rennome gayne.
What tydynge withe the foulke [39] ?

H A R O L D E.

Stylle mormorynge atte yer fhap [40], ftylle toe the
    kynge
Theie rolle theire trobbles, lyche a forgie fea.
Hane Englonde thenne a tongue, butte notte a
    ftynge ?   20
Dothe alle compleyne, yette none wylle ryghted bee ?

G O D D W Y N.

Awayte the tyme, whanne Godde wylle fende us ayde.

H A R O L D E.

No, we mufte ftreve to ayde ourefelves wyth powre.
Whan Godde wylle fende us ayde ! tis fetelie [41] prayde.

[39] People.   [40] fate, deftiny.   [41] nobly.

Mofte

Mofte we thofe calke 4² awaie the lyve-longe howre? 25
Thos croche 43 oure armes, and ne toe lyve dareygne44,
Unburled 45, undelievre 46, unefpryte 47 ?
Far fro mie harte be fled thyk 48 thoughte of peyne,
Ile free mie countrie, or Ille die yn fyghte.

G O D D W Y N.

Botte lette us wayte untylle fomme feafon fytte.   30
Mie Kentyfhmen, thie Summertons fhall ryfe;
Adented 49 prowefs 50 to the gite 51 of witte,
Agayne the argent 5² horfe fhall daunce yn fkies.
Oh Harolde, heere forftraughteynge 53 wanhope 54
  lies.
Englonde, oh Englonde, tys for thee I blethe 55.   35
Whylfte Edwarde to thie fonnes wylle nete alyfe 56,
Shulde anie of thie fonnes fele aughte of ethe 57 ?
Upponne the trone 58 I fette thee, helde thie crowne;
Botte oh! twere hommage nowe to pyghte 59 thee downe.

---

42 Caft. 43 crofs, from crouche, a crofs. 44 attempt, or endeavour.
45 unarmed. 46 unactive. 47 unfpirited. 48 fuch. 49 faftened, annexed.   50 might, power.   51 mantle, or robe.   52 white, alluding to the arms of Kent, a horfe faliant, argent.   53 diftracting.
54 defpair. 55 bleed. 56 allow. 57 eafe. 58 throne. 59 pluck.

Thou

Thou arte all preefte, & notheynge of the kynge. 40
Thou arte all Norman, nothynge of mie blodde.
Know, ytte befeies [60] thee notte a maffe to fynge; ·
· Servynge thie leegefolcke [61] thou arte fervynge Godde.

H A R O L D E.

Thenne Ille doe heaven a fervyce.   To the fkyes
The dailie contekes [62] of the londe afcende.   45
The wyddowe, fahdreleffe, & bondemennes cries
Acheke [63] the mokie [64] aire & heaven aftende [65].
On us the rulers doe the folcke depende;
Hancelled [66] from erthe thefe Normanne [67] hyndes
     fhalle bee ;
Lyche a battently [68] low [69], mie fwerde fhalle
     brende [70] ;   50
Lyche fallynge fofte rayne droppes, I wyll hem [71] flea [72];
Wee wayte too longe ; our purpofe wylle defayte [73];
Aboune [74] the hyghe empryze [75], & rouze the cham-
     pyones ftrayte.

---

[60] Becomes.   [61] fubjects.   [61] contentions, complaints.   [63] choke.
[64] dark, cloudy.   [65] aftonifh.   [66] cut off, deftroyed.   [67] flaves.
[68] loud roaring.   [69] flame of fire.   [70] burn, confume.   [71] them.
[72] flay.   [73] decay.   [74] make ready.   [75] enterprize.

GODDWYN.

Thie fufter —

HAROLDE.

Aye, I knowe, fhe is his queene.
Albeytte 76, dyd fhee fpeeke her foemen 77 fayre,   55
I wulde dequace 78 her comlie femlykeene 79,
And foulde mie bloddie anlace 80 yn her hayre.

GODDWYN.

Thye fhuir 81 blyn 82.

HAROLDE.

No, bydde the leathal 83 mere 84,
Uprifte 85 withe hiltrene 86 wyndes & caufe unkend 87,
Behefte 88 it to be lete 89; fo twylle appeare,   60
Eere Harolde hyde hys name, his contries frende.

---

76 Notwithftanding.   77 foes.   78 mangle, deftroy.
79 beauty, countenance.   80 an ancient fword.   81 fury.   82 ceafe.
83 deadly.   84 lake.   85 fwollen.   86 hidden.   87 unknown.
88 command.   89 ftill.

The

The gule-fteynct [90] brygandyne [91], the adventayle [92],
The feerie anlace [92] brede [93] fhal make mie gare [94] pre-
vayle.

G O D D W Y N.

Harolde, what wuldeft doe?

H A R O L D E.

Bethyncke thee whatt.
Here liethe Englonde, all her drites [95] unfree,   65
Here liethe Normans coupynge [96] her bie lotte,
Caltyfnyng [97] everich native plante to gre [98],
Whatte woulde I doe? I brondeous [99] wulde hem
    flee [1];
Tare owte theyre fable harte bie ryghtefulle breme [2];
Theyre deathe a meanes untoe mie lyfe fhulde bee, 70
Mie fpryte fhulde revelle yn theyr harte-blodde ftreme.
Eftfoones I wylle bewryne [3] mie ragefulle ire,
And Goddis anlace [4] wielde yn furie dyre.

---

[90] Red-ftained.   [91] [92] parts of armour.   [93] broad.   [94] caufe.
[95] rights, liberties.   [96] cutting, mangling.   [97] forbidding.   [98] grow.
[99] furious.   [1] flay.   [2] ftrength.   [3] declare.   [4] fword.

GODDWYN.

Whatte wouldeft thou wythe the kynge?

HAROLDE.

Take offe hys crowne;
The ruler of fomme mynfter 5 hym ordeyne;   75
Sette uppe fom dygner 6 than I han pyghte 7 downe;
And peace in Englonde fhulde be bray'd 8 agayne.

GODDWYN.

No, lette the fuper-hallie 9 feyncte kynge reygne,
Ande fomme moe reded 10 rule the untentyff 11
  reaulme;
Kynge Edwarde, yn hys cortefie, wylle deygne   80
To yielde the fpoiles, and alleyne were the heaulme:
Botte from mee harte bee everych thoughte of gayne,
Not anie of mie kin I wyfche him to ordeyne.

---

5 Monaftery.   6 more worthy.   7 pulled, plucked.   8 difplayed.
9 over-righteous.   10 counfelled, more wife.   11 uncareful, neglected.

HAROLDE.

H A R O L D E.

Tell me the meenes, and I wylle boute ytte ſtrayte;
Bete [12] mee to ſlea [13] mieſelf, ytte ſhalle be done.   85

G O D D W Y N.

To thee I wylle ſwythynne [14] the menes unplayte [15],
Bie whyche thou, Harolde, ſhalte be proved mie ſonne.
I have longe ſeen whatte peynes were undergon,
Whatte agrames [16] braunce [17] out from the general tree;
The tyme ys commynge, whan the mollock [18] gron [19]   90
Drented [20] of alle yts ſwolynge [21] owndes [22] ſhalle bee;
Mie remedie is goode; our menne ſhall ryſe:
Eftſoons the Normans and owre agrame [23] flies.

H A R O L D E.

I will to the Weſt, and gemote [24] alle mie knyghtes,
Wythe bylles that pancte for blodde, and ſheeldes as brede [25]   95

[12] Bid, command.   [13] flay.   [14] preſently.   [15] explain.
[16] grievances.   [17] branch.   [18] wet, moiſt.   [19] fen, moor.
[20] drained.   [21] ſwelling.   [22] waves.   [23] grievance.   [24] aſſemble.
[25] broad.

As

As the ybroched [26] moon, when blaunch [27] fhe dyghtes [28]
The wodeland grounde or water-mantled mede;
Wythe hondes whofe myghte canne make the dough-
tieft [29] blede,
Who efte have knelte upon forflagen [30] foes,
Whoe wythe yer fote orrefts [31] a caftle-ftede [32],   100
Who dare on kynges for to bewrecke [33] yiere woes;
Nowe wylle the menne of Englonde haile the daie,
Whan Goddwyn leades them to the ryghtfulle fraie.

G O D D W Y N.

Botte firfte we'll call the loverdes of the Weft,
The erles of Mercia, Conventrie and all;   105
The moe wee gayne, the gare [34] wylle profper befte,
Wythe fyke a nomber wee can never fall.

H A R O L D E.

True, fo wee fal doe beft to lyncke the chayne,
And alle attenes [35] the fpreddynge kyngedomme
bynde.

[26] Horned.   [27] white.   [28] decks.   [29] mightieft, moft valiant.
[30] flain.   [31] overfets.   [32] a caftle.   [33] revenge.   [34] caufe.
[35] at once.

No crouched [36] champyone wythe an harte moe
feygne   100
Dyd yffue owte the hallie [37] fwerde to fynde,
Than I nowe ftrev to ryd mie londe of peyne.
Goddwyn, what thanckes owre laboures wylle enhepe !
I'lle ryfe mie friendes unto the bloddie pleyne ;
I'lle wake the honnoure thatte ys now aflepe.   115
When wylle the chiefes mete atte thie feaftive halle,
That I wythe voice alowde maie there upon 'em calle ?

G O D D W Y N.

Next eve, mie fonne.

H A R O L D E.

Nowe, Englonde, ys the tyme,
Whan thee or thie felle foemens caufe mofte die.
Thie geafon [38] wronges bee reyne [39] ynto theyre
pryme ;   120
Nowe wylle thie fonnes unto thie fuccoure flie.
Alyche a ftorm egederinge [40] yn the fkie,
Tys fulle ande brafteth [41] on the chaper [42] grounde ;

---

[36] One who takes up the crofs in order to fight againft the Saracens.
[37] holy.   [38] rare, extraordinary, ftrange.   [39] run; fhot up.
[40] affembling, gathering, [41] burfteth. [42] dry, barren.

I   Sycke

Sycke fhalle mie fhuirye on the Normans flie,

And alle theyre mittee 43 menne be fleene 44
   arounde. 125

Nowe, nowe, wylle Harolde or oppreffionne falle,

Ne moe the Englyfhmenne yn vayne for hele 45 fhal
   calle.

43 Mighty.   44 flain.   45 help.

KYNGE

KYNGE EDWARDE AND HYS QUEENE.

QUEENE.

BOTTE, loverde [46], whie fo manie Normannes here?
Mee thynckethe wee bee notte yn Englyfhe londe.
Thefe browded [47] ftraungers alwaie doe appere,   130
Theie parte yor trone [48], and fete at your ryghte
      honde.

KYNGE.

Go to, goe. to, you doe ne underftonde :
Theie yeave mee lyffe, and dyd mie bowkie [49] kepe ;
Theie dyd mee feefte, and did embowre [50] me gronde;
To trete hem ylle wulde lette mie kyndneffe flepe. 135

---

[46] Lord.   [47] embroidered ; 'tis conjectured, embroidery was not
ufed in England till Hen. II.   [48] throne.   [49] perfon, body.
[50] lodge.

QUEÉNE.

QUEENE.

Mancas [51] you have yn ftore, and to them parte;
Youre leege-folcke [52] make moke [53] dole [54], you have
theyr worthe afterte [55].

KYNGE.

I hefte [56] no rede of you. I ken mie friendes.
Hallie [57] dheie are, fulle ready mee to hele [58].
Theyre volundes [59] are yftorven [60] to felf endes; 140
No denwere [61] yn mie brefte I of them fele:
I mufte to prayers; goe yn, and you do wele;
I mufte ne lofe the dutie of the daie;
Go inne, go ynne, ande viewe the azure rele [62],
Fulle welle I wote you have noe mynde toe praie. 145

QUEENE.

I leeve youe to doe hommage heaven-were [63];
To ferve yor leege-folcke toe is doeynge hommage there.

---

[51] Marks. [52] fubjects. [53] much. [54] lamentation.
[55] neglected, or paffed by. [56] require, afk. [57] holy. [58] help.
[59] will. [60] dead. [61] doubt. [62] waves.
[63] heaven-ward, or God-ward.

KYNGE and Syr HUGHE.

K Y N G E.

Mie friende, Syr Hughe, whatte tydynges brynges
. thee here ?

H U G H E.

There is no mancas yn mie loverdes ente [64] ;
The hus dyfpenfe [65] unpaied doe appere ; 150
The lafte receivure [66] ys eftefoones [67] difpente [68].

K Y N G E.

Thenne guylde the Wefte.

H U G H E.

    Mie loverde, I dyd fpeke
Untoe the mitte [69] Erle Harolde of the thynge ;
He rayfed hys honde, and fmoke me onne the cheke,
Saieynge, go beare thatte meffage to the kynge. 155

---

[64] Purfe, ufed here probably as a treafury. [65] expence.
[66] receipt. [67] foon. [68] expended. [69] a contradiction of mighty.

K Y N G E.

K Y N G E.

Arace [70] hym of hys powere; bie Goddis worde,
Ne moe thatte Harolde fhall ywield the erlies fwerde.

H U G H E.

Atte feefon fytte, mie loverde, lette itt bee;
Botte nowe the folcke doe foe enalfe [71] hys name,
Inne ftrevvynge to flea hymme, ourfelves wee flea; 160
Syke ys the doughtynefs [72] of hys grete fame.

K Y N G E.

Hughe, l beethyncke, thie rede [73] ys notte to blame.
Botte thou maieft fynde fulle ftore of marckes yn
Kente.

H U G H E.

Mie noble loverde, Godwynn ys the fame;
He fweeres he wylle notte fwelle the Normans ent. 165

[70] Diveft.   [71] embrace.   [72] mightinefs.   [73] counfel.

K Y N G E.

K Y N G E.

Ah traytoure ! botte mie rage I wylle commaunde.
Thou arte a Normanne, Hughe, a ſtraunger to the
    launde.

Thou kenneſte howe theſe Englyſche erle doe bere
Such ſtedneſs 74 in the yll and evylle thynge;
Botte atte the goode theie hover yn denwere 75,   170
Onknowlachynge 76 gif thereunto to clynge.

H U G H E.

Onwordie ſyke a marvelle 77 of a kynge !
O Edwarde, thou deſerveſt purer leege 78 ;
To thee heie 79 ſhulden al theire mancas brynge ;
Thie nodde ſhould ſave menne, and thie glomb 80
    forſlege 81.   175
I amme no curriedowe 82, I lacke no wite 83,
I ſpeke whatte bee the trouthe, and whatte all ſee is
    ryghte.

---

74 Firmneſs, ſtedfaſtneſs.   75 doubt, ſuſpenſe.   76 not knowing.
77 wonder.   78 homage, obeyſance.   79 they.   80 frown.   81 kill.
82 curriedowe, flatterer.   83 reward.

                                            K Y N G E.

KYNGE.

Thou arte a hallie [84] manne, I doe thee pryze.

Comme, comme, and here and hele [85] mee ynn mie

    praires.

Fulle twentie mancas I wylle thee alife [86],   180

And twayne of hamlettes [87] to thee and thie heyres.

Soe fhalle all Normannes from mie londe be fed,

Theie alleyn [88] have fyke love as to acquyre yet

    bredde.

[84] holy.   [85] help.   [86] allow.   [87] manors.   [88] alone.

O   CHORUS.

C H O R U S.

WHAÑ Freedom, dreſte yn blodde-ſteyned veſte,
 To everie knyghte her warre-ſonge ſunge, 185
Uponne her hedde wylde wedes were ſpredde ;
 A gorie anlaee bye her honge.
  She daunced onne the heathe ;
  She hearde the voice of deathe ;
Pale-eyned affryghte, hys harte of ſylver hue, 190
In vayne aſſayled ¹ her boſomme to acale ² ;
She hearde onflemed ³ the ſhriekynge voice of woe,
And ſadneſſe ynne the owlette ſhake the dale.
  She ſhooke the burled ⁴ ſpeere,
  On hie ſhe jeſte ⁵ her ſheelde, 195
  Her foemen ⁶ all appére,
  And flizze ⁷ alonge the feelde.
Power, wythe his heafod ⁸ ſtraught ⁹ ynto the ſkyes,
Hys ſpeere a ſonne-beame, and his ſheelde a ſtarre,

---

¹ Endeavoured. ² freeze. ³ undiſmayed. ⁴ armed, pointed.
⁵ hoiſted on high, raiſed. ⁶ foes, enemies. ⁷ fly. ⁸ head.
⁹ ſtretched.

           Alyche

Alyche [10] twaie [11] brendeynge [12] gronfyres [13] rolls hys
   eyes,   200
Chaftes [14] with hys yronne feete and foundes to war.
       She fyttes upon a rocke,
       She bendes before hys fpeere,
       She ryfes from the fhocke,
       Wieldynge her owne yn ayre.   205
Harde as the thonder dothe fhe drive ytte on,
Wytte fcillye [15] wympled [16] gies [17] ytte to hys crowne,
Hys longe fharpe fpeere, hys fpreddynge fheelde ys
   gon,
He falles, and fallynge rolleth thoufandes down.
   War, goare-faced war, bie envie burld [18],
    arift [19],   210
Hys feerie heaulme [20] noddynge to the ayre,
Tenne bloddie arrowes ynne hys ftreynynge fyfte—

   *   *   *   *   *   *   *   *

[10] Like [11] two. [12] flaming. [13] meteors. [14] beats, ftamps. clofely. [16] mantled, covered. [17] guides. [18] armed. [19] arofe. helmet.

ENGLYSH METAMORPHOSIS:

Bie T. ROWLEIE.

BOOKE Ift[1].

WHANNE Scythyannes, falvage as the wolves
     theie chacde,
Peynĉed in horrowe[2] formes bie nature dyghte,
Heckled[3] yn beaftſkyns, flepte uponne the wafte,
And wyth the morneynge rouzed the wolfe to fyghte,
Swefte as defcendeynge lemes[4] of roddie lyghte   5
Plonged to the hulftred[5] bedde of faveynge feas,
Gerd[6] the blacke mountayn okes yn drybbfets[7]
    twighte[8],
And ranne yn thoughte alonge the azure mees,
Whofe eyne dyd feerie fheene, like blue-hayred
    defs[9],
That dreerie hange upon Dover's emblaunched[10] clefs. 10

[1] I will endeavour to get the remainder of thefe poems.
[2] unfeemly, difagreeable. [3] wrapped. [4] rays. [5] hidden, fecret.
[6] broke, rent. [7] fmall pieces. [8] pulled, rent. [9] vapours, meteors.
[10] emblaunched.

Soft

Soft boundeynge over fwelleynge azure reles [11]
The falvage natyves fawe a fhyppe appere ;
An uncouthe [12] denwere [13] to theire bofomme fteles ;
Theyre myghte ys knopped [14] ynne the frofte of fere.
The headed javlyn liffeth [15] here and there ;   15
Theie ftonde, theie ronne, theie loke wyth eger eyne ;
The fhyppes fayle, boleynge [16] wythe the kyndelie
          ayre,
Ronneth to harbour from the beateynge bryne ;
Theie dryve awaie aghafte, whanne to the ftronde
A burled [17] Trojan lepes, wythe Morglaien fweerde yn
          honde.   20

Hymme followede eftfoones hys compheeres [18], whofe
          fwerdes
Gleftred lyke gledeynge [19] ftarres ynne froftic nete,
Hayleynge theyre capytayne in chirckynge [20] wordes
Kynge of the lande, whereon theie fet theyre fete.
The greete kynge Brutus thanne theie dyd hym
          greete,   25
Prepared for battle, marefchalled the fyghte ;

---

[11] Ridges, rifing waves.   [12], [13] unknown tremour.
[14] faftened, chained, congealed.   [15] boundeth.   [16] fwelling.
[17] armed.   [18] companions.   [19] livid.   [20] a confufed noife.

Theie

Theie urg'd the warre, the natyves fledde, as flete

As fleaynge cloudes that fwymme before the fyghte;

Tyll tyred with battles, for to ceefe the fraie,

Theie unſted [21] Brutus kynge, and gave the Trojanns
    fwaie.   30

Twayne of twelve years han lemed [22] up the myndes,

Leggende [23] the falvage unthewes [24] of theire brefte,

Improved in myfterk [25] warre, and lymmed [26] theyre
    kyndes,

Whenne Brute from Brutons fonke to æterne refte.

Eftfoons the gentle Locryne was poffeft   35

Of fwaie, and vefted yn the paramente [27];

Halceld [28] the bykrous [29] Huns, who dyd infefte

Hys wakeynge kyngdom wyth a foule intente;

As hys broade fwerde oer Homberres heade was
    honge,

He tourned toe ryver wyde, and roarynge rolled
    alonge.   40

He wedded Gendolyne of roieal fede,

Upon whofe countenance rodde healthe was fpreade;

[21] Anointed.   [22] enlightened.   [23] alloyed.   [24] favage barbarity.
[25] myftic.   [26] polifhed.   [27] a princely robe.   [28] defeated.   [29] warring.

                                   Bloufhing,

Bloufhing, alyche [30] the fcarlette of herr wede,

She fonke to pleafaunce on the marryage bedde.

Eftfoons her peacefull joie of mynde was fledde; 45

Elftrid ametten with the kynge Locryne;

Unhombered beauties were upon her fhedde,

Moche fyne, moche fayrer thanne was Gendolyne;

The mornynge tynge, the rofe, the lillie floure,

In ever ronneynge race on her dyd peyncte theyre

powere. 50

The gentle fuyte of Locryne gayned her love;

Theie lyved foft momentes to a fwotie [31] age;

Eft [32] wandringe yn the coppyce, delle, and grove,

Where ne one eyne mote theyre difporte engage;

There dydde theie tell the merrie lovynge fage [33], 55

Croppe the prymrofen floure to decke theyre headde;

The feerie Gendolyne yn woman rage

Gemoted [34] warriours to bewrecke [35] her bedde;

Theie rofe; ynne battle was greete Locryne fleene;

The faire Elftrida fledde from the enchafed [36] queene. 60

[30] Like.   [31] fweet.   [32] oft.   [33] a tale.   [34] affembled.
[35] revenge.   [36] heated, enraged.

O 4   A tye

A tye of love, a dawter fayre fhe hanne,
Whofe boddeynge morneyng fhewed a fayre daie,
Her fadre Locrynne, once an hailie manne.
Wyth the fayre dawterre dydde fhe hafte awaie,
To where the Weftern mittee ³⁷ pyles of claie   65
Arife ynto the cloudes, and doe them beere;
There dyd Elftrida and Sabryna ftaie;
The fyrfte tryckde out a whyle yn warryours gratch ³⁸
      and gear;
Vyncente was fhe ycleped, butte fulle foone fate
Sente deathe, to telle the dame, fhe was notte yn re-
      grate ³⁹.   70

The queene Gendolyne fente a gyaunte knyghte,
Whofe doughtie heade fwepte the emmertleynge ⁴⁰
      fkies,
To flea her wherefoever fhe fhulde be pyghte ⁴¹,
Eke everychone who fhulde her ele ⁴² emprize ⁴³.
Swefte as the roareynge wyndes the gyaunte flies,   75
Stayde the loude wyndes, and fhaded reaulmes yn
      nyghte,

³⁷ Mighty.   ³⁸ apparel.   ³⁹ efteem, favour.   ⁴⁰ glittering.
⁴¹ fettled.   ⁴² help.   ⁴³ adventure.

                                                    Stept

Stepte over cytties, on meint 44 acres lies,

Meeteynge the herehaughtes of morneynge lighte;

Tyll mooveynge to the Wefte, myfchaunce hys gye 45,

He thorowe warriours gratch fayre Elftrid did efpie.   80

He tore a ragged mountayne from the grounde,

Harried 46 uppe noddynge forrefts to the fkie,

Thanne wythe a fuirie, mote the erthe aftounde 47,

To meddle ayre he lette the mountayne fle.

The flying wolfynnes fente a yelleynge crie;   85

Onne Vyncente and Sabryna felle the mount;

To lyve æternalle dyd theie eftfoones die;

Thorowe the fandie grave boiled up the pourple founte,

On a broade graffic playne was layde the hylle,

Staieynge the rounynge courfe of meint a limmed 43 rylle.   90

The goddes, who kenned the actyons of the wyghte,

To leggen 49 the fadde happe of twayne fo fayre,

Houton 50 dyd make the mountaine bie theire mighte,

Forth from Sabryna ran a ryverre cleere,

44 Many.   45 guide.   46 toft.   47 aftonifh.   48 glaffy, reflecting.
49 leffen, alloy.   50 hollow.

Roarynge

Roarynge and rolleynge on yn courfe byfmare 51 ;   95
From female Vyncente fhotte a ridge of ftones,
Eche fyde the ryver ryfynge heavenwere ;
Sabrynas floode was helde ynne Elftryds bones.
So are theie cleped ; gentle and the hynde
Can telle, that Severnes ftreeme bie Vyncentes rocke's
    ywrynde 52.   100

The bawfyn 53 gyaunt, hee who dyd them flee,
To telle Gendolyne quycklie was yfped 54 ;
Whanne, as he ftrod alonge the fhakeynge lee,
The roddie levynne 55 glefterrd on hys headde :
Into hys hearte the azure vapoures fpreade ;   105
He wrythde arounde yn drearie dernie 56 payne ;
Whanne from his lyfe-bloode the rodde lemes 57 were
    fed,
He felle an hepe of afhes on the playne :
Stylle does hys afhes fhoote ynto the lyghte,
A wondrous mountayne hie, and Snowdon ys ytte
    hyghte.   110

---

51 Bewildered, curious.   52 hid, covered,   53 huge, bulky.
54 difpatched.   55 red lightning.   56 cruel.   57 flames, rays.

F I N I S.

AN

AN EXCELENTE BALADE

OF CHARITIE:

As wroten bie the gode Priefte Thomas Rowley[1],
1464.

IN Virgyne the fweltrie fun gan fheene,
 And hotte upon the mees[2] did cafte his raie;
The apple rodded[3] from its palie greene,
And the mole[4] peare did bende the leafy fpraie;
The peede chelandri[5] funge the livelong daie;   5
'Twas nowe the pride, the manhode of the yeare,
And eke the grounde was dighte[6] in its mofe defte[7]
   aumere[8].

The fun was glemeing in the midde of daie,
Deadde ftill the aire, and eke the welken[9] blue,

---

[1] Thomas Rowley, the author, was born at Norton Mal-reward in Somerfetfhire, educated at the Convent of St. Kenna at Keynefham, and died at Weftbury in Gloucefterfhire.   [2] meads.   [3] reddened, ripened.   [4] foft.   [5] pied goldfinch.   [6] dreft, arayed.   [7] neat, ornamental.   [8] a loofe robe or mantle.   [9] the fky, the atmofphere.

When

When from the fea arift [10] in drear arraie   10

A hepe of cloudes of fable fullen hue,

The which full faft unto the woodlande drewe,

Hiltring [11] attenes [12] the funnis fetive [13] face,

And the blacke tempefte fwolne and gatherd up apace.

Beneathe an holme, fafte by a pathwaie fide,   15

Which dide unto Seynĉte Godwine's covent [14] lede,

A haplefs pilgrim moneynge did abide,

Pore in his viewe, ungentle [15] in his weede,

Longe bretful [16] of the miferies of neede,

Where from the hail-ftone coulde the almer [17] flie? 20

He had no houfen theere, ne anie covent nie.

Look in his glommed [18] face, his fprighte there fcanne;

Howe woe-be-gone, how withered, forwynd [19], deade!

[10] Arofe.   [11] hiding, fhrouding.   [12] at once.   [13] beauteous.
[14] It would have been *charitable*, if the author had not pointed at per-
fonal charaĉters in this Ballad of Charity. The Abbot of St. Godwin's
at the time of the writing of this was Ralph de Bellomont, a great ftickler
for the Lancaftrian family. Rowley was a Yorkift.   [15] beggarly.
[16] filled with.   [17] beggar.   [18] clouded, dejeĉted. A perfon of fome
note in the literary world is of opinion, that *glum* and *glom* are modern
cant words; and from this circumftance doubts the authenticity of
Rowley's Manufcripts. Glum-mong in the Saxon fignifies twilight, a
dark or dubious light; and the modern word *gloomy* is derived from the
Saxon *glum*.   [19] dry, faplefs.

Hafte

Hafte to thie church-glebe-houfe [20], afshrewed [21]
    manne!
Hafte to thie kifte [22], thie onlie dortoure [23] bedde. 25
Cale, as the claie whiche will gre on thie hedde,
Is Charitie and Love aminge highe elves;
Knightis and Barons live for pleafure and themfelves.

The gatherd ftorme is rype; the bigge drops falle;
The forfwat [24] meadowes fmethe [25], and drenche [26] the
    raine; 30
The comyng ghaftnefs do the cattle pall [27],
And the full flockes are drivynge ore the plaine;
Dafhde from the cloudes the waters flott [28] againe;
The welkin opes; the yellow levynne [29] flies; 35
And the hot fierie fmothe [30] in the wide lowings [31]
    dies.

Lifte! now the thunder's rattling clymmynge [32] found
Cheves [33] flowlie on, and then embollen [34] clangs,

[20] The grave.   [21] accurfed, unfortunate.   [22] coffin.
[23] a fleeping room.   [24] fun-burnt.   [25] fmoke.   [26] drink.
[27] *pall*, a contraction from *appall*, to fright.   [28] fly.   [29] lightning.
[30] fteam, or vapours.   [31] flames.   [32] noify.   [33] moves.
[34] fwelled, ftrengthened.

Shakes

Shakes the hie fpyre, and lofft, difpended, drown'd,

Still on the gallard 35 eare of terroure hanges ;

The windes are up ; the lofty elmen fwanges ;   40

Again the levynne and the thunder poures,

And the full cloudes are brafte 36 attenes in ftonen
   fhowers.

Spurreynge his palfrie oere the watrie plaine,

The Abbote of Seyncte Godwynes convente came ;

His chapournette 37 was drented with the reine,   45

And his pencte 38 gyrdle met with mickle fhame ;

He aynewarde tolde his bederoll 39 at the fame ;

The ftorme encreafen, and he drew afide,

With the mift 40 almes craver neere to the holme to
   bide.

His cope 41 was all of Lyncolne clothe fo fyne,   50

With a gold button faften'd neere his chynne ;

His autremete 42 was edged with golden twynne,

---

35 Frighted.   36 burft.   37 a fmall round hat, not unlike the
fhapournette in heraldry, formerly worn by Ecclefiaftics and Lawyers.
38 painted.   39 He told his beads backwards ; a figurative expreffion
to fignify curfing.   40 poor, needy.   41 a cloke.   42 a loofe white
robe, worn by Priefts.

And

And his fhoone pyke a loverds [43] mighte have binne ;
Full well it fhewn he thoughten cofte no finne :
The trammels of the palfrye pleafde his fighte,   55
For the horfe-millanare [44] his head with rofes dighte.

An almes, fir priefte ! the droppynge pilgrim faide,
O ! let me waite within your covente dore,
Till the funne fheneth hie above our heade,
And the loude tempefte of the aire is oer ;   60
Helplefs and ould am I alas ! and poor ;
No houfe, ne friend, ne moneie in my pouche ;
All yatte I call my owne is this my filver crouche.

Varlet, replyd the Abbatte, ceafe your dinne ;
This is no feafon almes and prayers to give ;   65
Mie porter never lets a faitour [45] in ;
None touch mie rynge who not in honour live.
And now the fonne with the blacke cloudes did
     ftryve,
And fhettynge on the grounde his glairie raie,
The Abbatte fpurrde his fteede, and eftfoones roadde
     awaie.   70

[43] A lord.   [44] I believe this trade is ftill in being, though but el dom employed.   [45] a beggar, or vagabond.

7   Once

Once moe the fkie was blacke, the thounder rolde ;
Fafte reyneynge oer the plaine a priefte was feen ;
Ne dighte full proude, ne buttoned up in golde ;
His cope and jape [46] were graie, and eke were clene ;
A Limitoure he was of order feene ;   75
And from the pathwaie fide then turned hee,
Where the pore almer laie binethe the holmen tree.

An almes, fir prieft ! the droppynge pilgrim fayde,
For fweete Seyncte Marie and your order fake.
The Limitoure then loofen'd his pouche threade, 80
And did thereoute a groate of filver take ;
The mifter pilgrim dyd for halline [47] fhake.
Here take this filver, it maie eathe [48] thie care ;
We are Goddes ftewards all, nete [49] of oure owne we
    bare.

But ah ! unhailie [50] pilgrim, lerne of me,   85
Scathe anie give a rentrolle to their Lorde.
Here take my femecope [51], thou arte bare I fee ;

---

[46] A fhort furplice, worn by Friars of an inferior clafs, and fecular priefts.   [47] joy.   [48] eafe.   [49] nought.   [50] unhappy.
[51] a fhort under-cloke.

Tis

Tis thyne; the Seynctes will give me mie rewarde.

He left the pilgrim, and his waie aborde.

Virgynne and hallie Seyncte, who sitte yn gloure [52],

Or give the mittee [53] will, or give the gode man power.

[52] Glory.   [53] mighty, rich.

P   BATTLE

BATTLE OF HASTINGS.

[Nº 1.]

O CHRYSTE, it is a grief for me to telle,
   How manie a nobil erle and valrous knyghte
In fyghtynge for Kynge Harrold noblie fell,
Al fleyne in Haftyngs feeld in bloudie fyghte.
O fea! our teeming donore han thy floude,   5
Han anie fructuous entendement,
Thou wouldft have rofe and fank wyth tydes of bloude,
Before Duke Wyllyam's knyghts han hither went;
   Whofe cowart arrows manie erles fleyne,
   And brued the feeld wyth bloude as feafon rayne.   10

And of his knyghtes did eke full manie die,
All paffyng hie, of mickle myghte echone,
Whofe poygnant arrowes, typp'd with deftynie,
Caus'd manie wydowes to make myckle mone.
                         Lordynges,

Lordynges, avaunt, that chycken-harted are,   15
From out of hearynge quicklie now departe;
Full well I wote, to fynge of bloudie warre
Will greeve your tenderlie and mayden harte.
   Go, do the weaklie womman inn mann's geare,
   And fcond your manfion if grymm war come there. 20

Soone as the erlie maten belle was tolde,
And fonne was come to byd us all good daie,
Bothe armies on the feeld, both brave and bolde,
Prepar'd for fyghte in champyon arraie.
As when two bulles, deftynde for Hocktide fyghte, 25
Are yoked bie the necke within a fparre,
Theie rend the erthe, and travellyrs affryghte,
Lackynge to gage the fportive bloudie warre;
   Soe lacked Harroldes menne to come to blowes,
   The Normans lacked for to wielde their bowes. 30

Kynge Harrolde turnynge to hys leegemen fpake;
My merrie men, be not cafte downe in mynde;
Your onlie lode for aye to mar or make,
Before yon funne has donde his welke, you'll fynde.
Your lovyng wife, who erft dyd rid the londe 35
Of Lurdanes, and the treafure that you han,

Wyll

Wyll falle into the Normanne robber's honde,
Unleffe with honde and harte you plaie the manne.
 Cheer up youre hartes, chafe forrowe farre awaie,
 Godde and Seyncte Cuthbert be the worde to daie. 40

And thenne Duke Wyllyam to his knyghtes did faie;
My merrie menne, be bravelie everiche;
Gif I do gayn the honore of the daie,
Ech one of you I will make myckle riche.
Beer you in mynde, we for a kyngdomm fyghte;   45
Lordfhippes and honores echone fhall poffeffe;
Be this the worde to daie, God and my Ryghte;
Ne doubte but God will oure true caufe bleffe.
 The clarions then founded fharpe and fhrille;
 Deathdoeynge blades were out intent to kille.   50

And brave Kyng Harrolde had nowe donde hys faie;
He threwe wythe myghte amayne hys fhorte horfe-fpear,
The noife it made the duke to turn awaie,
And hytt his knyghte, de Beque, upon the ear.
His criftede beaver dyd him fmalle abounde;   55
The cruel fpear went thorough all his hede;
The purpel bloude came goufhynge to the grounde,
And at Duke Wyllyam's feet he tumbled deade:

So fell the myghtie tower of Standrip, whenne
It felte the furie of the Danifh menne.   60

O Afflem, fon of Cuthbert, holie Saynĉte,
Come ayde thy freend, and fhewe Duke Wyllyams payne;
Take up thy pencyl, all hys features painĉte;
Thy coloryng excells a fynger ftrayne.
Duke Wyllyam fawe hys freende fleyne piteouflie,   65
His lovynge freende whome he muche honored,
For he han lovd hym from puerilitie,
And theie together bothe han bin ybred :
  O! in Duke Wyllyam's harte it rayfde a flame,
  To whiche the rage of emptie wolves is tame.   70

He tooke a brafen croffe-bowe in his honde,
And drewe it harde with all hys myghte amein,
Ne doubtyng but the braveft in the londe
Han by his foundynge arrowe-lede bene fleyne.
Alured's ftede, the fyneft ftede alive,   75
Bye comelie forme knowlached from the reft ;
But nowe his deftind howre dyd aryve,
The arrowe hyt upon his milkwhite brefte ;
  So have I feen a ladie-fmock foe white,
  Blown in the mornynge, and mowd downe at night. 80

P 3   With

With thilk a force it dyd his bodie gore,
That in his tender guttes it entered,
In veritee a fulle clothe yarde or more,
And downe with flaiten noyfe he funken dede.
Brave Alured, benethe his faithfull horfe,   85
Was fmeerd all over withe the gorie dufte,
And on hym laie the recer's lukewarme corfe,
That Alured coulde not hymfelf alufte.
 The ftandyng Normans drew theyr bowe echone,
 And broght full manie Englyfh champyons downe. 90

The Normans kept aloofe, at diftaunce ftylle,
The Englyfh nete but fhort horfe-fpears could welde;
The Englyfh manie dethe-fure dartes did kille,
And manie arrowes twang'd upon the fheelde.
Kynge Haroldes knyghts defir'de for hendie ftroke,   95
And marched furious o'er the bloudie pleyne,
In bodie clofe, and made the pleyne to fmoke;
Theire fheelds rebounded arrowes back agayne.
 The Normans ftode aloofe, nor hede the fame,
 Their arrowes woulde do dethe, tho' from far of they
  came.   100

         Duke

Duke Wyllyam drewe agen hys arrowe ftrynge,
An arrowe withe a fylver-hede drewe he ;
The arrowe dauncynge in the ayre dyd fynge,
And hytt the horfe Toffelyn on the knee.
At this brave Tofslyn threwe his fhort horfe-fpeare ; 105
Duke Wyllyam ftooped to avoyde the blowe ;
The yrone weapon hummed in his eare,
And hitte Sir Doullie Naibor on the prowe :
   Upon his helme foe furious was the ftroke,
   It fplete his bever, and the ryvets broke.   110

Downe fell the beaver by Tofslyn fplete in tweine,
And onn his hede expos'd a punie wounde,
But on Deftoutvilles fholder came ameine,
And fell'd the champyon to the bloudie grounde.
Then Doullie myghte his boweftrynge drewe,   115
Enthoughte to gyve brave Tofslyn bloudie wounde,
But Harolde's afenglave ftopp'd it as it flewe,
And it fell bootlefs on the bloudie grounde.
   Siere Doullie, when he fawe hys venge thus broke,
   Death-doynge blade from out the fcabard toke. 120

And now the battail clofde on everych fyde,
And face to face appeard the knyghts full brave;
P 4

They

They lifted up theire bylles with myckle pryde,.
And manie woundes unto the Normans gave.
So have I fene two weirs at once give grounde,   125
White fomyng hygh to rorynge combat runne ;
In roaryng dyn and heaven-breaking founde,
Burfte waves on waves, and fpangle in the funne ;
   And when their myghte in burftynge waves is fled,
   Like cowards, ftele alonge their ozy bede.   130

Yonge Egelrede, a knyghte of comelie mien,
Affynd unto the kynge of Dynefarre,
At echone tylte and tourney he was feene,
And lov'd to be amonge the bloudie warre ;
He couch'd hys launce, and ran wyth mickle myghte 135
Ageinfte the breft of Sieur de Bonoboe;
He grond and funken on the place of fyghte,
O Chryfte ! to fele his wounde, his harte was woe.
   Ten thoufand thoughtes pufh'd in upon his mynde,
   Not for hymfelfe, but thofe he left behynde.   140

He dy'd and leffed wyfe and chyldren tweine,
Whom he wyth cheryfhment did dearlie love;
In England's court, in goode Kynge Edwarde's regne,
He wonne the tylte, and ware her crymfon glove ;
                                  And

And thence unto the place where he was borne,   145
Together with hys welthe & better wyfe,
To Normandie he dyd perdie returne,
In peace and quietneffe to lead his lyfe;
    And now with fovrayn Wyllyam he came,
      To die in battel, or get welthe and fame.   150

Then, fwefte as lyghtnynge, Egelredus fet
Agaynft du Barlie of the mounten head;
In his dere hartes bloude his longe launce was wett,
And from his courfer down he tumbled dede.
So have I fene a mountayne oak, that longe   155
Has cafte his fhadowe to the mountayne fyde,
Brave all the wyndes, tho' ever they fo ftronge,
And view the briers belowe with felf-taught pride;
    But, whan throwne downe by mightie thunder ftroke,
      He'de rather bee a bryer than an oke.   160

Then Egelred dyd in a declynie
Hys launce uprere with all hys myghte ameine,
And ftrok Fitzport upon the dexter eye,
And at his pole the fpear came out agayne.
Butt as he drewe it forthe, an arrowe fledde   165
Wyth mickle myght fent from de Tracy's bowe,

                        And

And at hys fyde the arrowe entered,
And oute the crymfon ftreme of bloude gan flowe;
   In purple ftrekes it dyd his armer ftaine,
   And fmok'd in puddles on the duftie plaine.   170

But Egelred, before he funken downe,
With all his myghte amein his fpear befped,
It hytte Bertrammil Manne upon the crowne,
And bothe together quicklie funken dede.
So have I feen a rocke o'er others hange,   175
Who ftronglie plac'd laughde at his flippry ftate,
But when he falls with heaven-peercynge bange
That he the fleeve unravels all theire fate,
   And broken onn the beech thys leffon fpeak,
   The ftronge and firme fhould not defame the weake.180

Howel ap Jevah came from Matraval,
Where he by chaunce han flayne a noble's fon,
And now was come to fyghte at Harold's call,
And in the battel he much goode han done;
Unto Kyng Harold he foughte mickle near,   185
For he was yeoman of the bodie guard;
And with a targyt and a fyghtyng fpear,
He of his boddie han kepte watch and ward:

                          True

True as a fhadow to a fubftant thynge,
So true he guarded Harold hys good kynge.   190

But when Egelred tumbled to the grounde,
He from Kynge Harolde quicklie dyd advaunce,
And ftrooke de Tracie thilk a crewel wounde,
Hys harte and lever came out on the launce.
And then retreted for to guarde his kynge,   195
On dented launce he bore the harte awaie;
An arrowe came from Auffroie Griel's ftrynge,
Into hys heele betwyxt hys yron ftaie;
    The grey-goofe pynion, that thereon was fett,
    Eftfoons wyth fmokyng crymfon bloud was wett. 200

His bloude at this was waxen flaminge hotte,
Without adoe he turned once agayne,
And hytt de Griel thilk a blowe, God wote,
Maugre hys helme, he fplete his hede in twayne.
This Auffroie was a manne of mickle pryde,   205
Whofe featlieft bewty ladden in his face;
His chaunce in warr he ne before han tryde,
But lyv'd in love and Rofaline's embrace;
    And like a ufeleis weede amonge the haie
    Amonge the fleine warriours Griel laie.   210

Kynge

Kynge Harolde then he putt his yeomen bie,
And ferſlie ryd into the bloudie fyghte ;
Erle Ethelwolf, and Goodrick, and Alfie,
Cuthbert, and Goddard, mical menne of myghte,
Ethelwin, Ethelbert, and Edwin too,   215
Effred the famous, and Erle Ethelwarde,
Kynge Harolde's leegemenn, erlies hie and true,
Rode after hym, his bodie for to guarde ;
    The reſte of erlies, fyghtynge other wheres,
    Stained with Norman bloude theire fyghtynge
       ſperes.   220

As when ſome ryver with the ſeaſon raynes
White fomynge hie doth breke the bridges oft,
Oerturns the hamelet and all conteins,
And layeth oer the hylls a muddie ſoft ;
So Harold ranne upon his Normanne foes,   225
And layde the greate and ſmall upon the grounde,
And delte among them thilke a ſtore of blowes,
Full manie a Normanne fell by him dede wounde ;
    So who he be that ouphant faieries ſtrike,
    Their ſoules will wander to Kynge Offa's dyke. 230

                                  Fitz

Fitz Salnarville, Duke William's favourite knyghte,
'To noble Edelwarde his life dyd yielde;
Withe hys tylte launcé hee ftroke with thilk a myghte,
The Norman's bowels fteemde upon the feeld.
Old Salnarville beheld hys fon lie ded,   235
Againft Erle Edelward his bowe-ftrynge drewe;
But Harold at one blowe made tweine his head;
He dy'd before the poignant arrowe flew.
    So was the hope of all the iffue gone,
    And in one battle fell the fire and fon.   240

De Aubignee rod fercely thro' the fyghte,
'To where the boddie of Salnarville laie;
Quod he; And art thou ded, thou manne of myghte?
I'll be revengd, or die for thee this daie.
Die then thou fhalt, Erle Ethelwarde he faid;   245
I am a cunnynge erle, and that can tell;
Then drewe hys fwerde, and ghaftlie cut hys hede,
And on his freend eftfoons he lifelefs fell,
    Stretch'd on the bloudie pleyne; great God forefend,
    It be the fate of no fuch truftie freende!   250

Then Egwin Sieur Pikeny did attaque;
He turned aboute and vilely fouten flie;

                                        But

But Egwyn cutt fo deepe into his backe,
He rolled on the grounde and foon dyd die.
His diftant fonne, Sire Romara de Biere,   255
Soughte to revenge his fallen kynfman's lote,
But foone Erle Cuthbert's dented fyghtyng fpear
Stucke in his harte, and ftayd his fpeed, God wote.
 He tumbled downe clofe by hys kynfman's fyde,
 Myngle their ftremes of pourple bloude, and dy'd. 260

And now an arrowe from a bowe unwote
Into Erle Cuthbert's harte eftfoons dyd flee;
Who dying fayd; ah me! how hard my lote!
Now flayne, mayhap, of one of lowe degree.
So have I feen a leafie elm of yore   265
Have been the pride and glorie of the pleine;
But, when the fpendyng landlord is growne poore,
It falls benethe the axe of fome rude fweine;
 And like the oke, the fovran of the woode,
 It's fallen boddie tells you how it ftoode.   270

When Edelward perceevd Erle Cuthbert die,
On Hubert ftrongeft of the Normanne crewe,
As wolfs when hungred on the cattel flie,
So Edelward amaine upon him flewe.
   I   With

With thilk a force he hyt hym to the grounde;   275
And was demafing howe to take his life,
When he behynde received a ghaftlie wounde
Gyven by de Torcie, with a ftabbyng knyfe;
   Bafe trecherous Normannes, if fuch actes you doe,
   The conquer'd maie clame victorie of you.   280

The erlie felt de Torcie's trecherous knyfe
Han made his crymfon bloude and fpirits floe;
And knowlachyng he foon muft quyt this lyfe,
Refolved Hubert fhould too with hym goe.
He held hys truftie fwerd againft his brefte,   285
And down he fell, and peerc'd him to the harte;
And both together then did take their refte,
Their foules from corpfes unaknell'd depart;
   And both together foughte the unknown fhore,
   Where we fhall goe, where manie's gon before.   290

Kynge Harolde Torcie's trechery dyd fpie,
And hie alofe his temper'd fwerde dyd welde,
Cut offe his arme, and made the bloude to flie,
His proofe fteel armoure did him littel fheelde;
And not contente, he fplete his hede in twaine,   295
And down he tumbled on the bloudie grounde;
                            Mean

Mean while the other erlies on the playne
Gave and received manie a bloudie wounde,
   Such as the arts in warre han learnt with care,
   But manie knyghtes were men in women's geer. 300

Herrewald, borne on Sarim's fpreddyng plaine,
Where Thor's fam'd temple manie ages ftoode ;
Where Druids, auncient preefts, did ryghtes ordaine,
And in the middle fhed the victyms bloude ;
Where auncient Bardi dyd their verfes fynge   305
Of Cæfar conquer'd, and his mighty hofte,
And how old Tynyan, necromancing kynge,
Wreck'd all hys fhyppyng on the Brittifh coafte,
   And made hym in his tatter'd barks to flie,
   'Till Tynyan's dethe and opportunity.   310

To make it more renomed than before,
(I, tho a Saxon, yet the truthe will telle)
The Saxonnes fteynd the place wyth Brittifh gore,
Where nete but bloud of facrifices felle.
Tho' Chryftians, ftylle they thoghte mouche of the
    pile,   315
And here theie mett when caufes dyd it neede ;

                           'Twas

'Twas here the auncient Elders of the Iſle
Dyd by the trecherie of Hengiſt bleede;
  O Hengiſt! han thy-cauſe bin good and true,
  Thou wouldſt ſuch murdrous acts as theſe eſchew. 320

The erlie was a manne of hie degree,
And han that daie full manie Normannes ſleine;
Three Norman Champyons of hie degree
He lefte to ſmoke upon the bloudie pleine:
The Sier Fitzbotevilleine did then advaunce,   325
And with his bowe he ſmote the erlies hede;
Who eftſoons gored hym with his tylting launce,
And at his horſes feet he tumbled dede:
  His partyng ſpirit hovered o'er the floude
  Of ſoddayne rouſhynge mouche lov'd pourple
    bloude.   330

De Viponte then, a ſquier of low degree,
An arrowe drewe with all his myghte ameine;
The arrowe graz'd upon the erlies knee,
A punie wounde, that cauſd but littel peine.
So have I ſeene a Dolthead place a ſtone,   335
Enthoghte to ſtaie a driving rivers courſe;

But better han it bin to lett alone,
It onlie drives it on with mickle force;
    The erlie, wounded by fo bafe a hynde,
    Rays'd furyous doyngs in his noble mynde.   340

The Siere Chatillion, yonger of that name,
Advaunced next before the erlie's fyghte;
His fader was a manne of mickle fame,
And he renomde and valorous in fyghte.
Chatillion his truftie fwerd forth drewe,   345
The erle drawes his, menne both of mickle myghte;
And at eche other vengouflie they flewe,
As maftie dogs at Hocktide fet to fyghte;
    Bothe fcornd to yeelde, and bothe abhor'de to flie,
    Refolv'd to vanquifhe, or refolv'd to die.   350

Chatillion hyt the erlie on the hede,
Thatt fplytte eftfoons his crifted helm in twayne;
Whiche he perforce withe target covered,
And to the battel went with myghte ameine.
The erlie hytte Chatillion thilke a blowe   355
Upon his brefte, his harte was plein to fee;
He tumbled at the horfes feet alfoe,
And in dethe panges he feez'd the recer's knee:

                          Fafte

Fafte as the ivy rounde the oke doth clymbe,
So fafte he dying gryp'd the recer's lymbe.   360

The recer then beganne to flynge and kicke,
And tofte the erlie farr off to the grounde;
The erlie's fquier then a fwerde did fticke
Into his harte, a dedlie ghaftlie wounde;
And downe he felle upon the crymfon pleine,   365
Upon Chatillion's foullefs corfe of claie;
A puddlie ftreme of bloude flow'd oute ameine;
Stretch'd out at length befmer'd with gore he laie;
  As fome tall oke fell'd from the greenie plaine,
  To live a fecond time upon the main.   370

The erlie nowe an horfe and beaver han,
And nowe agayne appered on the feeld;
And manie a mickle knyghte and mightie manne
To his dethe-doyng fwerd his life did yeeld;
When Siere de Broque an arrowe longe lett flie,   375
Intending Herewaldus to have fleyne;
It mifs'd; butt hytte Edardus on the eye,
And at his pole came out with horrid payne.
  Edardus felle upon the bloudie grounde,
  His noble foule came roufhyng from the wounde. 380

Q 2

Thys Herewald perceevd, and full of ire
He on the Siere de Broque with furie came;
Quod he; thou'ſt ſlaughtred my beloved ſquier,
But I will be revenged for the ſame.
Into his bowels then his launce he thruſte,   385
And drew thereout a ſteemie drerie lode;
Quod he; theſe offals are for ever curſt,
Shall ſerve the coughs, and rooks, and dawes, for foode.
  Then on the pleine the ſteemie lode hee throwde,
    Smokynge wyth lyfe, and dy'd with crẏmſon
      bloude.   390

Fitz Broque, who ſaw his father killen lie,
Ah me! ſayde he; what woeful ſyghte I ſee!
But now I muſt do ſomethyng more than ſighe;
And then an arrowe from the bowe drew he.
Beneth the erlie's navil came the darte;   495
Fitz Broque on foote han drawne it from the bowe;
And upwards went into the erlie's harte,
And out the crymſon ſtreme of bloude 'gan flowe.
  As fromm a hatch, drawne with a vehement geir,
    White ruſhe the burſtynge waves, and roar along the
      weir.   400
        Z   The

The erle with one honde grafp'd the recer's mayne,
And with the other he his launce befped;
And then felle bleedyng on the bloudie plaine.
His launce it hytte Fitz Broque upon the hede;
Upon his hede it made a wounde full flyghte, 405
But peerc'd his fhoulder, ghaftlie wounde inferne,
Before his optics daunced a fhade of nyghte,
Whyche foone were clofed ynn a fleepe eterne.
    The noble erlie than, withote a grone,
    Took flyghte, to fynde the regyons unknowne. 410

Brave Alured from binethe his noble horfe
Was gotten on his leggs, with bloude all fmore;
And now eletten on another horfe,
Eftfoons he withe his launce did manie gore.
The cowart Norman knyghtes before hym fledde, 415
And from a diftaunce fent their arrowes keene;
But noe fuch deftinie awaits his hedde,
As to be fleyen by a wighte fo meene.
    Tho oft the oke falls by the villen's fhock,
    'Tys moe than hyndes can do, to move the rock. 420

Q 3   Upon

Upon du Chatelet he ferſelie ſett,
And peerc'd his bodie with a force full grete;
The aſenglave of his tylt-launce was wett,
The rollynge bloude alonge the launce did fleet.
Advauncynge, as a maſtie at a bull,   425
He rann his launce into Fitz Warren's harte;
From Partaies bowe, a wight unmercifull,
Within his owne he felt a cruel darte;
    Cloſe by the Norman champyons he han ſleine,
    He fell; and mixd his bloude with theirs upon the
        pleine.   430

Erle Ethelbert then hove, with clinie juſt,
A launce, that ſtroke Partaie upon the thighe,
And pinn'd him downe unto the gorie duſte;
Cruel, quod he, thou cruellie ſhalt die.
With that his launce he enterd at his throte;   435
He ſcritch'd and ſcreem'd in melancholie mood;
And at his backe eftſoons came out, God wote,
And after it a crymſon ſtreme of bloude:
    In agonie and peine he there dyd lie,
    While life and dethe ſtrove for the maſterrie,   440

                          He

He gryped hard the bloudie murdring launce,
And in a grone he left this mortel lyfe.
Behynde the erlie Fifcampe did advaunce,
Bethoghte to kill him with a ftabbynge knife;
But Egward, who perceevd his fowle intent,   445
Eftfoons his truftie fwerde he forthwyth drewe,
And thilke a cruel blowe to Fifcampe fent,
That foule and bodie's bloude at one gate flewe.
 Thilk deeds do all deferve, whofe deeds fo fowle
 Will black theire earthlie name, if not their foule. 450

When lo! an arrowe from Walleris honde,
Winged with fate and dethe daunced alonge;
And flewe the noble flower of Powyflonde,
Howel ap Jevah, who yclepd the ftronge.
Whan he the firft mifchaunce received han,   455
With horfemans hafte he from the armie rodde;
And did repaire unto the cunnynge manne,
Who fange a charme, that dyd it mickle goode;
 Then praid Seynéte Cuthbert, and our holie Dame,
 To bleffe his labour, and to heal the fame.   460

Then

Then drewe the arrowe, and the wounde did feck,
And putt the teint of holie herbies on;
And putt a rowe of bloude-ftones' round his neck;
And then did fay; go, champyon, get agone.
And now was comynge Harrolde to defend,   465
And metten with Walleris cruel darte;
His fheelde of wolf-fkinn did him not attend,
The arrow peerced into his noble harte;
   As fome tall oke, hewn from the mountayne hed,
   Falls to the pleine; fo fell the warriour dede.   470

His countryman, brave Mervyn ap Teudor,
Who love of hym han from his country gone,
When he perceevd his friend lie in his gore,
As furious as a mountayn wolf he ranne.
As ouphant faieries, whan the moone fheenes bryghte, 475
In littel circles daunce upon the greene,
All living creatures flie far from their fyghte,
Ne by the race of deftinie be feen;
   For what he be that ouphant faieries ftryke,
   Their foules will wander to Kyng Offa's dyke.   480

So from the face of Mervyn Tewdor brave
The Normans eftfoons fled awaie aghafte;

                            And

And left behynde their bowe and afenglave,
For fear of hym, in thilk a cowart hafte.
His garb fufficient were to meve affryghte;   485
A wolf fkin girded round his myddle was;
A bear fkyn, from Norwegians wan in fyghte,
Was tytend round his fhoulders by the claws:
    So Hercules, 'tis funge, much like to him,
        Upon his fhoulder wore a lyon's fkin.   490

Upon his thyghes and harte-fwefte legges he wore
A hugie goat fkyn, all of one grete peice;
A boar fkyn fheelde on his bare armes he bore;
His gauntletts were the fkynn of harte of greece.
They fledde; he followed clofe upon their heels,   495
Vowynge vengeance for his deare countrymanne;
And Siere de Sancelotte his vengeance feels;
He peerc'd hys backe, and out the bloude ytt ranne.
    His bloude went downe the fwerde unto his arme,
        In fpringing rivulet, alive and warme.   500

His fwerde was fhorte, and broade, and myckle keene,
And no mann's bone could ftonde to ftoppe itts waie;
The Normann's harte in partes two cutt cleane,
He clos'd his eyne, and clos'd hys eyne for aie.
                                            Then

Then with his·fwerde he fett on Fitz du Valle,   505

A knyghte mouch famous for to runne at tylte;

With thilk a furie on hym he dyd falle,

Into his neck he ranne the fwerde and hylte;

   As myghtie lyghtenynge often has been founde,

   To drive an oke into unfallow'd grounde.   510

And with the fwerde, that in his neck yet ftoke,

The Norman fell unto the bloudie grounde;

And with the fall ap Tewdore's fwerde he broke,

And bloude afrefhe came trickling from the wounde.

As whan the hyndes, before a mountayne wolfe,   515

Flie from his paws, and angrie vyfage grym;

But when he falls into the pittie golphe,

They dare hym to his bearde, and battone hym;

   And caufe he fryghted them fo muche before,

   Lyke cowart hyndes, they battone hym the more.   520

So, whan they fawe ap Tewdore was bereft

Of his keen fwerde, thatt wroghte thilke great difmaie,

They turned about, eftfoons upom hym lept,

And full a fcore engaged in the fraie.

Mervyn ap Tewdore, ragyng as a bear,   525

Seiz'd on the beaver of the Sier de Laque;

                      And

And wring'd his hedde with fuch a vehement gier,
His vifage was turned round unto his backe.
   Backe to his harte retyr'd the ufelefs gore,
   And felle upon the pleine to rife no more.   530

Then on the mightie Siere Fitz Pierce he flew,
And broke his helm and feiz'd hym bie the throte:
Then manie Normann knyghtes their arrowes drew,
That enter'd into Mervyn's harte, God wote.
In dying panges he gryp'd his throte more ftronge, 535
And from their fockets ftarted out his eyes;
And from his mouthe came out his blamelefs tonge;
And bothe in peyne and anguifhe eftfoon dies.
   As fome rude rocke torne from his bed of claie,
   Stretch'd onn the pleyne the brave ap Tewdore
     laie.   540

And now Erle Ethelbert and Egward came
Brave Mervyn from the Normannes to affift;
A myghtie fiere, Fitz Chatulet bie name,
An arrowe drew, that dyd them littel lift.
Erle Egward points his launce at Chatulet,   545
And Ethelbert at Walleris fet his;

                        And

And Egwald dyd the fiere a hard blowe hytt,
But Ethelbert by a myfchaunce dyd mifs :‐
   Fear laide Walleris flat upon the ftrande,
   He ne deferved a death from erlies hande.   550

Betwyxt the ribbes of Sire Fitz Chatelet
The poynted launce of Egward did ypafs ;
The diftaunt fyde thereof was ruddie wet,
And he fell breathlefs on the bloudie grafs.
As cowart Walleris laie on the grounde,   555
The dreaded weapon hummed oer his heade,
And hytt the fquier thylke a lethal wounde,
Upon his fallen lorde he tumbled dead :
   Oh fhame to Norman armes ! a lord a flave,
   A captyve villeyn than a lorde more brave !   560

From Chatelet hys launce Erle Egward drew,
And hit Wallerie on the dexter cheek ;
Peerc'd to his braine, and cut his tongue in two :
There, knyght, quod he, let that thy actions fpeak—

      *   *   *   *   *   *   *

BATTLE OF HASTINGS.

OH Truth! immortal daughter of the fkies,
   Too lyttle known to wryters of thefe daies,
Teach me, fayre Sainête! thy paffynge worthe to
   pryze,
To blame a friend and give a foeman prayfe.
The fickle moone, bedeckt wythe fylver rays,   5
Leadynge a traine of ftarres of feeble lyghte,
With look adigne the worlde belowe furveies,
The world, that wotted not it coud be nyghte;
Wyth armour dyd, with human gore ydeyd,
She fees Kynge Harolde ftande, fayre Englands curfe and
   pryde.   10

With ale and vernage drunk his fouldiers lay;
Here was an hynde, anie an erlie fpredde;

                    Sad

Sad keepynge of their leaders natal daie !

This even in drinke, toomorrow with the dead !

Thro' everie troope diforder reer'd her hedde ;   15

Dancynge and heideignes was the onlie theme ;

Sad dome was theires, who lefte this eafie bedde,

And wak'd in torments from fo fweet a dream.

Duke Williams menne, of comeing dethe afraide,

All nyghte to the great Godde for fuccour afkd and

  praied.   20

Thus Harolde to his wites that ftoode arounde ;

Goe, Gyrthe and Eilward, take bills halfe a fcore,

And fearch how farre our foeman's campe doth

  bound ;

Yourfelf have rede ; I nede to faie ne more.

My brother beft belov'd of anie ore,   25

My Leofwinus, goe to everich wite,

Tell them to raunge the battel to the grore,

And waiten tyll I fende the heft for fyghte.

He faide ; the loieaul broders lefte the place,

Succefs and cheerfulnefs depicted on ech face.   30

Slowelie brave Gyrthe and Eilwarde dyd advaunce,

And markd wyth care the armies dyftant fyde,

        When

When the dyre clatterynge of the shielde and launce
Made them to be by Hugh Fitzhugh espyd.
He lyfted up his voice, and lowdlie cryd ;   35
Like wolfs in wintere did the Normanne yell ;
Girthe drew hys swerde, and cutte hys burled hyde ;
The proto-slene manne of the fielde he felle ;
Out streemd the bloude, and ran in smokynge curles,
Reflected bie the moone seemd rubies mixt wyth
    pearles.   40

A troope of Normannes from the mafs-songe came,
Roufd from their praiers by the slotting crie ;
Thoughe Girthe and Ailwardus perceevd the same,
Not once theie stoode abashd, or thoghte to flie.
He seizd a bill, to conquer or to die ;   45
Fierce as a clevis from a rocke ytorne,
That makes a vallie wherefoe're it lie ;
* Fierce as a ryver burstynge from the borne ;
So fiercelie Gyrthe hitte Fitz du Gore a blowe,
And on the verdaunt playne he layde the champyone
    lowe.   50

* In Turgott's tyme Holenwell braste of erthe so fierce that it threw
a stone-mell carrying the same awaie.   J. Lydgate ne knowynge this
lefte out o line.

                                    Tancarville

Tancarville thus; alle peace in Williams name;
Let none édraw his arcublafter bowe.
Girthe cas'd his weppone, as he hearde the fame,
And vengynge Normannes ftaid the flyinge floe.
The fire wente onne; ye menne, what mean ye fo 55
Thus unprovokd to courte a bloudie fyghte?
Quod Gyrthe; oure meanynge we ne care to fhowe,
Nor dread thy duke wyth all his men of myghte;
Here fingle onlie thefe to all thie crewe
Shall fhewe what Englyfh handes and heartes can doe. 60

Seek not for bloude, Tancarville calme replyd,
Nor joie in dethe, lyke madmen moft diftraught;
In peace and mercy is a Chryftians pryde;
He that dothe conteftes pryze is in a faulte.
And now the news was to Duke William brought, 65
That men of Haroldes armie taken were;
For theyre good cheere all caties were enthoughte,
And Gyrthe and Eilwardus enjoi'd goode cheere.
Quod Willyam; thus fhall Willyam be founde
A friend to everie manne that treades on Englifh
ground.   70

Erle

Erle Leofwinus throwghe the campe ypafs'd,
And fawe bothe men and erlies on the grounde;
They flepte, as thoughe they woulde have flepte theyr
   laft,
And hadd alreadie felte theyr fatale wounde.
He ftarted backe, and was wyth fhame aftownd; 75
Loked wanne wyth anger, and he fhooke wyth rage;
When throughe the hollow tentes thefe wordes dyd
   found,
Rowfe from your fleepe, detratours of the age!
Was it for thys the ftoute Norwegian bledde?
Awake, ye hufcarles, now, or waken wyth the dead. 80

As when the fhepfter in the fhadie bowre
In jintle flumbers chafe the heat of daie,
Hears doublyng echoe wind the wolfins rore,
That neare hys flocke is watchynge for a praie,
He tremblynge for his fheep drives dreeme awaie, 85
Gripes fafte hys burled croke, and fore adradde
Wyth fleeting ftrides he haftens to the fraie,
And rage and prowefs fyres the coiftrell lad;
With truftie talbots to the battel flies,
And yell of men and dogs and wolfins tear the fkies. 90

            R   Such

Such was the dire confufion of eche witt,

That rofe from fleep and walfome power of wine ;

Theie thoughte the foe by trechit yn the nyghte

Had broke theyr camp and gotten pafte the line ;

Now here now there the burnyfht fheeldes and byll-
    fpear fhine ;   95

Throwote the campe a wild confufionne fpredde ;

Eche bracd hys armlace fiker ne defygne,

The crefted helmet nodded on the hedde;

Some caught a flughorne, and an onfett wounde;

Kynge Harolde hearde the charge, and wondred at the
    founde.   100

Thus Leofwine ; O women cas'd in ftele !

Was itte for thys Norwegia's ftubborn fede

Throughe the black armoure dyd the anlace fele,

And rybbes of folid braffe were made to bleede ?

Whylft yet the worlde was wondrynge at the
    deede.   105

You fouldiers, that fhoulde ftand with byll in hand,

Get full of wine, devoid of any rede.

Oh fhame ! oh dyre difhonoure to the lande !

He

He fayde; and fhame on everie vifage fpredde,
Ne fawe the erlies face, but addawd hung their head. 110

Thus he; rowze yee, and forme the boddie tyghte.
The Kentyfh menne in fronte, for ftrenght renownd,
Next the Bryftowans dare the bloudie fyghte,
And laft the numerous crewe fhall preffe the grounde.
I and my king be wyth the Kenters founde;   115
Bythric and Alfwold hedde the Bryftowe bande;
And Bertrams fonne, the man of glorious wounde,
Lead in the rear the menged of the lande;
And let the Londoners and Suffers plie
Bie Herewardes memuine and the lighte fkyrts anie.   120

He faide; and as a packe of hounds belent,
When that the trackyng of the hare is gone,
If one perchaunce fhall hit upon the fcent,
With twa redubbled fhuir the alans run;
So ftyrrd the valiante Saxons everych one;   125
Soone linked man to man the champyones ftoode;
To 'tone for their bewrate fo foone 'twas done,
And lyfted bylls enfeem'd an yron woode;

Here glorious Alfwold towr'd above the wites,
And feem'd to brave the fuir of twa ten thoufand
    fights.   130

Thus Leofwine; today will Englandes dome
Be fyxt for aie, for gode or evill ftate;
This funnes aunture be felt for years to come;
Then bravelie fyghte, and live till deathe of date.
Thinke of brave Ælfridus, yclept the grete,   135
From porte to porte the red-haird Dane he chafd,
The Danes, with whomme not lyoncels coud mate,
Who made of peopled reaulms a barren wafte;
Thinke how at once by you Norwegia bled
Whilfte dethe and victorie for magyftrie befted.   140

Meanwhile did Gyrthe unto Kynge Harolde ride,
And tolde howe he dyd with Duke Willyam fare.
Brave Harolde lookd afkaunte, and thus replyd;
And can thie fay be bowght wyth drunken cheer?
Gyrthe waxen hotte; fhuir in his eyne did glare; 145
And thus he faide; oh brother, friend, and kynge,
Have I deferved this fremed fpeche to heare?
Bie Goddes hie hallidome ne thoughte the thynge.
                                  When

When Toſtus ſent me golde and ſylver ſtore,
I ſcornd hys preſent vile, and ſcorn'd hys treaſon
   more.   150

Forgive me, Gyrthe, the brave Kynge Harolde cryd ;
Who can I truſt, if brothers are not true ?
Ithink of Toſtus, once my joie and pryde.
Girthe ſaide, with looke adigne ; my lord, I doe.
But what oure foemen are, quod Girth, I'll ſhewe ; 155
By Gods hie hallidome they preeſtes are.
Do not, quod Harolde, Girthe, myſtell them ſo,
For theie are everich one brave men at warre.
Quod Girthe ; why will ye then provoke theyr hate ?
Quod Harolde ; great the foe, ſo is the glorie grete. 160

And nowe Duke Willyam marefchalled his band,
And ſtretchd his armie owte a goodlie rowe.
Firſt did a ranke of arcublaſtries ſtande,
Next thoſe on horſebacke drewe the aſcendyng flo,
Brave champyones, eche well lerned in the bowe, 165
Theyr aſenglave acroſſe theyr horſes ty'd,
Or with the loverds ſquier behinde dyd goe,
Or waited ſquier lyke at the horſes ſyde.

When thus Duke Willyam to a Monke dyd faie,
Prepare thyfelfe wyth fpede, to Harolde hafte awaie. 170

Telle hym from me one of thefe three to take;
That hee to mee do homage for thys lande,
Or mee hys heyre, when he deceafyth, make,
Or to the judgment of Chryfts vicar ftande.
He faide; the Monke departyd out of hande, 175
And to Kyng Harolde dyd this meffage bear;
Who faid; tell thou the duke, at his likand
If he can gette the crown hee may itte wear.
He faid, and drove the Monke out of his fyghte,
And with his brothers rouz'd each manne to bloudie
fyghte. 180

A ftandarde made of fylke and jewells rare,
Wherein alle coloures wroughte aboute in bighes,
An armyd knyghte was feen deth doynge there,
Under this motte, He conquers or he dies.
This ftandard rych, endazzlynge mortal eyes, 185
Was borne neare Harolde at the Kenters heade,
Who chargd hys broders for the grete empryze
That ftraite the heft for battle fhould be fpredde.

To evry erle and knyghte the worde is gyven,
And cries *a guerre* and flughornes fhake the vaulted
heaven.   190

As when the erthe, torne by convulfyons dyre,
In reaulmes of darknefs hid from human fyghte,
The warring force of water, air, and fyre,
Braft from the regions of eternal nyghte,
Thro the darke caverns feeke the reaulmes of
lyght;   195
Some loftie mountaine, by its fury torne,
Dreadfully moves, and caufes grete affryght;
Now here, now there, majeftic nods the bourne,
And awfulle fhakes, mov'd by the almighty force,
Whole woods and forefts nod, and ryvers change theyr
courfe.   200

So did the men of war at once advaunce,
Liakd man to man, enfeemed one boddie light;
Above a wood, yform'd of bill and launce,
That noddyd in the ayre moft ftraunge to fyght.
Harde as the iron were the menne of mighte,   205
Ne neede of flughornes to enrowfe theyr minde;

Eche

Eche fhootynge fpere yreaden for the fyghte,
More feerce than fallynge rocks, more fwefte than
    wynd;
With folemne ftep, by ecchoe made more dyre,
One fingle boddie all theie marchd, theyr eyen on
    fyre.   210

And now the greie-eyd morne with vi'lets dreft,
Shakyng the dewdrops on the flourie meedes,
Fied with her rofie radiance to the Weft :
Forth from the Eafterne gatte the fyerie fteedes
Of the bright funne awaytynge fpirits leedes :   215
The funne, in fierie pompe enthrond on hie,
Swyfter than thoughte alonge hys jernie gledes,
And fcatters nyghtes remaynes from oute the fkie :
He fawe the armies make for bloudie fraie,
And kept his driving fteeds, and hid his lyghtfome
    raye.   220

Kynge Harolde hie in ayre majeftic rayfd
His mightie arme, deckt with a manchyn rare ;
With even hande a mighty javlyn paizde,
Then furyoufe fent it whyftlynge thro the ayre.

It ſtruck the helmet of the Sieur de Beer;   225
In vayne did braſſe or yron ſtop its waie;
Above his eyne it came, the bones dyd tare,
Peercynge quite thro, before it dyd allaie;
He tumbled, ſcritchyng wyth hys horrid payne;
His hollow cuiſhes rang upon the bloudie pleyne.   230

This Willyam ſaw, and ſoundynge Rowlandes ſonge
He bent his yron interwoven bowe,
Makynge bothe endes to meet with myghte full
      ſtronge,
From out of mortals ſyght ſhot up the floe;
Then ſwyfte as fallynge ſtarres to earthe belowe   235
It flaunted down on Alfwoldes paynćted ſheelde;
Quite thro the ſilver-bordurd croſſe did goe,
Nor loſte its force, but ſtuck into the feelde;
The Normannes, like theyr ſovrin, dyd prepare,
And ſhotte ten thouſande floes upryſynge in the aire. 240

As when a flyghte of cranes, that takes their waie
In houſeholde armies thro the flanched ſkie,
Alike the cauſe, or companie or prey,
If that perchaunce ſome boggie fenne is nie,
                                    Soon

                                    I

Soon as the muddie natyon theie efpie,   245
Inne one blacke cloude theie to the erth defcende ;
Feirce as the fallynge thunderbolte they flie ;
In vayne do reedes the fpeckled folk defend :
So prone to heavie blowe the arrowes felle,
And peercd thro braffe, and fente manie to heaven or
    helle.   250

Ælan Adelfred, of the ftowe of Leigh,
Felte a dire arrowe burnynge in his brefte ;
Before he dyd, he fente hys fpear awaie,
Thenne funke to glorie and eternal refte.
Nevylle, a Normanne of alle Normannes befte,   255
Throw the joint cuifhe dyd the javlyn feel,
As hee on horfebacke for the fyghte addrefs'd,
And fawe hys bloude come fmokynge oer the fteele ;
He fente the avengynge floe into the ayre,
And turnd hys horfes hedde, and did to leeche re-
    payre.   260

And now the javelyns, barbd with deathhis wynges,
Hurld from the Englyfh handes by force aderne,
Whyzz dreare alonge, and fonges of terror fynges,
Such fonges as alwaies clos'd in lyfe eterne.
                                   Hurld

Hurld by fuch ftrength along the ayre theie burne, 265
Not to be quenched butte ynn Normannes bloude;
Wherere theie came they were of lyfe forlorn,
And alwaies followed by a purple floude;
Like cloudes the Normanne arrowes did defcend,
Like cloudes of carnage full in purple drops dyd
    end. 270

Nor, Leöfwynus, dydft thou ftill eftande;
Full foon thie pheon glytted in the aire;
The force of none but thyne and Harolds hande
Could hurle a javlyn with fuch lethal geer;
Itte whyzzd a ghaftlie dynne in Normannes ear, 275
Then thundryng dyd upon hys greave alyghte,
Peirce to his hearte, and dyd hys bowels tear,
He closd hys eyne in everlaftynge nyghte;
Ah! what avayld the lyons on his crefte!
His hatchments rare with him upon the grounde was
    preft. 280

Willyam agayne ymade his bowe-ends meet,
And hie in ayre the arrowe wynged his waie,
Defcendyng like a fhafte of thunder fleete,
Lyke thunder rattling at the noon of daie,
                        Önne

Onne Algars fheelde the arrowe dyd affaie,   285
There throghe dyd peerfe, and ftycke into his groine;
In grypynge torments on the feelde he laie,
Tille welcome dethe came in and clos'd his eyne;
Diftort with peyne he laie upon the borne,
Lyke fturdie elms by ftormes in uncothe wrythynges
    torne.   290

Alrick his brother, when hee this perceevd,
He drewe his fwerde, his lefte hande helde a fpeere,
Towards the duke he turnd his prauncyng fteede,
And to the Godde of heaven he fent a prayre;
Then fent his lethale javlyn in the ayre,   295
On Hue de Beaumontes backe the javelyn came,
Thro his redde armour to hys harte it tare,
He felle and thondred on the place of fame;
Next with his fwerde he 'fayld the Seiur de Roe,
And brafte his fylver helme, fo furyous was the
    blowe.   300

But Willyam, who had feen hys proweffe great,
And fcered muche how farre his bronde might goe,
Tooke a ftrong arblafter, and bigge with fate
From twangynge iron fente the fleetynge floe.

          As

As Alric hoiftes hys arme for dedlie blowe,   305
Which, han it came, had been Du Roees lafte,
The fwyfte-wyngd meffenger from Willyams bowe
Quite throwe his arme into his fyde ypafte;
His eyne fhotte fyre, lyke blazyng ftarre at nyghte,
He grypd his fwerde, and felle upon the place of
    fyghte.   310

O Alfwolde, faie, how fhalle I fynge of thee
Or telle how manie dyd benethe thee falle;
Not Haroldes felf more Normanne knyghtes did flee,
Not Haroldes felf did for more praifes call;
How fhall a penne like myne then fhew it all?   315
Lyke thee their leader, eche Briftowyanne foughte;
Lyke thee, their blaze muft be canonical,
Fore theie, like thee, that daie bewrecke yroughte:
Did thirtie Normannes fall upon the grounde,
Full half a fcore from thee and theie receive their fatale
    wounde.   320

Firft Fytz Chivelloys felt thie direful force;
Nete did hys helde out brazen fheelde availe;
Eftfoones throwe that thie drivynge fpeare did peerce,
Nor was ytte ftopped by his coate of mayle;

                                            Into

Into his breafte it quicklie did affayle;   325
Out ran the bloude, like hygra of the tyde;
With purple ftayned all hys adventayle;
In fcarlet was his cuifhe of fylver dyde:
Upon the bloudie carnage houfe he laie,
Whylft hys longe fheelde dyd gleem with the fun's ryfing
    ray.   330

Next Fefcampe felle; O Chriefte, howe harde his fate
To die the leckedft knyghte of all the thronge!
His fprite was made of malice deflavate,
Ne fhoulden find a place in anie fonge.
The broch'd keene javlyn hurld from honde fo
    ftronge   335
As thine came thundrynge on his cryfted beave;
Ah! neete avayld the brafs or iron thonge,
With mightie force his fkulle in twoe dyd cleave;
Fallyng he fhooken out his fmokyng braine,
As witherd oakes or elmes are hewne from off the
    playne.   340

Nor, Norcie, could thie myghte and fkilfulle lore
Preferve thee from the doom of Alfwold's fpeere;
    Couldft

Couldfte thou not kenne, moft fkyll'd After la goure,
How in the battle it would wythe thee fare?
When Alfwolds javelyn, rattlynge in the ayre, 345
From hande dyvine on thie habergeon came,
Oute at thy backe it dyd thie hartes bloude bear,
It gave thee death and everlaftynge fame;
Thy deathe could onlie come from Alfwolde arme,
As diamondes onlie can its fellow diamonds harme. 350

Next Sire du Mouline fell upon the grounde,
Quite throughe his throte the lethal javlyn prefte,
His foule and bloude came roufhynge from the
    wounde;
He closd his eyen, and opd them with the bleft.
It can ne be I fhould behight the reft, 355
That by the myghtie arme of Alfwolde felle,
Pafte bie a penne to be counte or exprefte,
How manie Alfwolde fent to heaven or helle;
As leaves from trees fhook by derne Autumns hand,
So laie the Normannes flain by Alfwold on the ftrand. 360

As when a drove of wolves withe dreary yelles
Affayle fome flocke, ne care if fhepfter ken't,
                                Befprenge

Befprenge deftructione oer the woodes and delles ;
The fhepfter fwaynes in vayne theyr lees lement ;
So foughte the Bryftowe menne ; ne one crevent, 365
Ne onne abafhd enthoughten for to flee ;
With fallen Normans all the playne befprent,
And like theyr leaders every man did flee ;
In vayne on every fyde the arrowes fled ;
The Bryftowe menne ftyll ragd, for Alfwold was not
    dead.   370

Manie meanwhile by Haroldes arm did falle,
And Leofwyne and Gyrthe encreasd the flayne ;
'Twould take a Neftor's age to fynge them all,
Or telle how manie Normannes prefte the playne ;
But of the erles, whom recorde nete hath flayne, 375
O Truthe ! for good of after-tymes relate,
That, thowe they're deade, theyr names may lyve
    agayne,
And be in deathe, as they in life were, greate ;
So after-ages maie theyr actions fee,
And like to them æternal alwaie ftryve to be.   380

Adhelm, a knyghte, whofe holie deathlefs fire
For ever bended to S^t. Cuthbert's fhryne,

                              Whofe

Whofe breaft for ever burnd with facred fyre,
And een on erthe he myghte be calld dyvine;
To Cuthbert's church he dyd his goodes refygne, 385
And lefte hys fon his God's and fortunes knyghte;
His fon the Sainɛte behelde with looke adigne,
Made him in gemot wyfe, and greate in fyghte;
Sainɛte Cuthberte dyd him ayde in all hys deedes,
His friends he lets to live, and all his fomen bleedes. 390

He married was to Kenewalchae faire,
The fyneft dame the fun or moone adave;
She was the myghtie Aderedus heyre,
Who was alreadie haftynge to the grave;
As the blue Bruton, ryfinge from the wave, 395
Like fea-gods feeme in moft majeftic guife,
And rounde aboute the rifynge waters lave,
And their longe hayre arounde their bodie flies,
Such majeftie was in her porte difplaid,
To be excelld bie none but Homer's martial maid. 400

White as the chaulkie clyffes of Brittaines ifle,
Red as the higheft colour'd Gallic wine,
Gaie as all nature at the mornynge fmile,
Thofe hues with pleafaunce on her lippes combine,

S   Her

Her lippes more redde than fummer evenynge
    fkyne,   405
Or Phœbus ryfinge in a froftie morne,
Her brefte more white than fnow in feeldes that lyene,
Or lillie lambes that never have been fhorne,
Swellynge like bubbles in a boillynge welle,
Or new-brafte brooklettes gently whyfpringe in the
    delle.   410

Browne as the fylberte droppyng from the fhelle,
Browne as the nappy ale at Hocktyde game,
So browne the crokyde rynges, that featlie fell
Over the neck of the all-beauteous dame.
Greie as the morne before the ruddie flame   415
Of Phebus charyotte rollynge thro the fkie,
Greie as the fteel-horn'd goats Conyan made tame,
So greie appeard her featly fparklyng eye;
Thofe eyne, that did oft mickle pleafed look
On Adhelm valyaunt man, the virtues doomfday
    book.   420

Majeftic as the grove of okes that ftoode
Before the abbie buylt by Ofwald kynge;

                                       Majeftic

Majeſtic as Hybernies holie woode,
Where ſainctes and ſoules departed maſſes ſynge;
Such awe from her ſweete looke forth iſſuynge   425
At once for reveraunce and love did calle;
Sweet as the voice of thraſlarkes in the Spring,
So ſweet the wordes that from her lippes did falle;
None fell in vayne; all ſhewed ſome entent;
Her wordies did diſplaie her great entendement.   430

Tapre as candles layde at Cuthberts ſhryne,
Tapre as elmes that Goodrickes abbie ſhrove,
Tapre as ſilver chalices for wine,
So tapre was her armes and ſhape ygrove.
As ſkyllful mynemenne by the ſtones above   435
Can ken what metalle is ylach'd belowe,
So Kennewalcha's face, ymade for love,
The lovelie ymage of her ſoule did ſhewe;
Thus was ſhe outward form'd; the ſun her mind
Did guilde her mortal ſhape and all her charms re-
     fin'd.   440

What blazours then, what glorie ſhall he clayme,
What doughtie Homere ſhall hys praiſes ſynge,

           That

That lefte the bofome of fo fayre a dame .

Uncall'd, unafkt, to ferve his lorde the kynge?

To his fayre fhrine goode fubjects oughte to bringe445

The armes, the helmets, all the fpoyles of warre,

Throwe everie reaulm the poets blaze the thynge,

And travelling merchants fpredde hys name to farre;

The ftoute Norwegians had his anlace felte, .

And nowe amonge his foes dethe-doynge blowes he

   delte.   450

As when a wolfyn gettynge in the meedes

He rageth fore, and doth about hym flee,

Nowe here a talbot, there a lambkin bleeds,

And alle the graffe with clotted gore doth ftree;

As when a rivlette rolles impetuouflie,   455

And breaks the bankes that would its force reftrayne,

Alonge the playne in fomynge rynges doth flee,

Gaynfte walles and hedges doth its courfe maintayne;

As when a manne doth in a corn-fielde mowe,

With eafe at one felle ftroke full manie is laide

   lowe.   460

So manie, with fuch force, and with fuch eafe,

Did Adhelm flaughtre on the bloudie playne;

                                Before

Before hym manie dyd theyr hearts bloude leafe,
Ofttymes he foughte on towres of fmokynge flayne.
Angillian felte his force, nor felte in vayne;   465
He cutte hym with his fwerde athur the breafte;
Out ran the bloude, and did hys armoure ftayne,
He clos'd his eyen in æternal refte;
Lyke a tall oke by tempefte borne awaie,
Stretched in the armes of dethe upon the plaine he
          laie.   470

Next thro the ayre he fent his javlyn feerce,
That on De Clearmoundes buckler did alyghte,
Throwe the vafte orbe the fharpe pheone did peerce,
Rang on his coate of mayle and fpente its mighte.
But foon another wingd its aiery flyghte,   475
The keen broad pheon to his lungs did goe;
He felle, and groand upon the place of fighte,
Whilft lyfe and bloude came iffuynge from the blowe.
Like a tall pyne upon his native playne,
So fell the mightie fire and mingled with the flaine. 480

Hue de Longeville, a force doughtre mere,
Advauncyd forwarde to provoke the darte,

          S 3   When

When foone he founde that Adhelmes poynted fpeere
Had founde an eafie paffage to his hearte.
He drewe his bowe, nor was of dethe aftarte,   485
Then fell down brethleffe to encreafe the corfe ;
But as he drewe hys bowe devoid of arte,
So it came down upon Troyvillains horfe ;
Deep thro hys hatchments wente the pointed floe ;
Now here, now there, with rage bleedyng he rounde
    doth goe.   490

Nor does he hede his maftres known commands,
Tyll, growen furioufe by his bloudie wounde,
Erect upon his hynder feete he ftaundes,
And throwes hys maftre far off to the grounde.
Near Adhelms feete the Normanne laie aftounde, 495
Befprengd his arrowes, loofend was his fheelde,
Thro his redde armoure, as he laie enfoond,
He peercd his fwerde, and out upon the feelde
The Normannes bowels fteemd, a dedlie fyghte !
He opd and closd hys eyen in everlaftynge nyghte. 500

Caverd, a Scot, who for the Normannes foughte,
A man well fkilld in fwerde and foundynge ftrynge,

    3   Who

Who fled his country for a crime enftrote,
For darynge with bolde worde hys loiaule kynge,
He at Erle Aldhelme with grete force did flynge 505
An heavie javlyn, made for bloudie wounde,
Alonge his fheelde afkaunte the fame did ringe,
Peercd thro the corner, then ftuck in the grounde;
So when the thonder rauttles in the fkie,
Thro fome tall fpyre the fhaftes in a torn clevis flie. 510

Then Addhelm hurld a croched javlyn ftronge,
With mighte that none but fuch grete championes
    know;
Swifter than thoughte the javlyn paft alonge,
Ande hytte the Scot moft feirclie on the prowe;
His helmet brafted at the thondring blowe,   515
Into his brain the tremblyn javlyn fteck;
From eyther fyde the bloude began to flow,
And run in circling ringlets rounde his neck;
Down fell the warriour on the lethal ftrande,
Lyke fome tall veffel wreckt upon the tragick fande. 520

CONTINUED.

Where fruytlefs heathes and meadowes cladde in greie;
Save where derne hawthornes reare theyr humble
    heade,
The hungrie traveller upon his waie
Sees a huge defarte alle arounde hym fpredde,
The diftaunte citie fcantlie to be fpedde,   525
The curlynge force of fmoke he fees in vayne,
Tis too far diftaunte, and hys onlie bedde
Iwimpled in hys cloke ys on the playne,
Whylfte rattlynge thonder forrey oer his hedde,
And raines come down to wette hys harde uncouthlie
    bedde.   530

A wondrous pyle of rugged mountaynes ftandes,
Placd on eche other in a dreare arraie,
It ne could be the worke of human handes,
It ne was reard up bie menne of claie.
Here did the Brutons adoration paye   535
To the falfe god whom they did Tauran name,

2   Dightynge

Dightynge hys altarre with greete fyres in Maie,
Roaftynge theyr vyctualle round aboute the flame,
'Twas here that Hengyft did the Brytons flee,
As they were mette in council for to bee.   540

Neere on a loftie hylle a citie ftandes,
That lyftes yts fcheafted heade ynto the fkies,
And kynglie lookes arounde on lower landes,
And the longe browne playne that before itte lies.
Herewarde, borne of parentes brave and wyfe,   545
Within this vylle fyrfte adrewe the ayre,
A bleffynge to the erthe fente from the fkies,
In anie kyngdom nee coulde fynde his pheer;
Now rybbd in fteele he rages yn the fyghte,
And fweeps whole armies to the reaulmes of nyghte. 550

So when derne Autumne wyth hys fallowe hande
Tares the green mantle from the lymed trees,
The leaves befprenged on the yellow ftrande
Flie in whole armies from the blataunte breeze ;
Alle the whole fielde a carnage-howfe he fees,   555
And fowles unknelled hover'd oer the bloude ;
From place to place on either hand he flees,
And fweepes alle neere hym lyke a bronded floude ;
                                        Dethe

Dethe honge upon his arme ; he fleed fo maynt,
'Tis pafte the pointel of a man to paynte.   560

Bryghte fonne in hafte han drove hys fierie wayne
A three howres courfe alonge the whited fkyen,
Vewynge the fwarthlefs bodies on the playne,
And longed greetlie to plonce in the bryne.
For as hys beemes and far-ftretchynge eyne   565
Did view the pooles of gore yn purple fheene,
The wolfomme vapours rounde hys lockes dyd twyne,
And dyd disfygure all hys femmlikeen ;
Then to harde actyon he hys wayne dyd rowfe,
In hyffynge ocean to make glair hys browes.   570

Duke Wyllyam gave commaunde, eche Norman
        knyghte,
That beer war-token in a fhielde fo fyne,
Shoulde onward goe, and dare to clofer fyghte
The Saxonne warryor, that dyd fo entwyne,
Lyke the nefhe bryon and the eglantine,   575
Orre Cornyfh wraftlers at a Hocktyde game.
The Normannes, all emarchialld in a lyue,
To the ourt arraie of the thight Saxonnes came ;
                                        There

There 'twas the whaped Normannes on a parre
Dyd know that Saxonnes were the fonnes of warre. 580

Oh Turgotte, wherefoeer thie fpryte dothe haunte,
Whither wyth thie lovd Adhelme by thie fyde,
Where thou mayfte heare the fwotie nyghte larke
  chaunte,
Orre wyth fome mokynge brooklette fwetelie glide,
Or rowle in ferfelie wythe ferfe Severnes tyde, 585
Whereer thou art, come and my mynde enleme
Wyth fuch greete thoughtes as dyd with thee abyde,
Thou fonne, of whom I ofte have caught a beeme,
Send mee agayne a drybblette of thie lyghte,
That I the deeds of Englyfhmenne maie wryte. 590

Harold, who faw the Normannes to advaunce,
Seiz'd a huge byll, and layd hym down hys fpere;
Soe dyd ech wite laie downe the broched launce,
And groves of bylles did glitter in the ayre.
Wyth fhowtes the Normannes did to battel fteere; 595
Campynon famous for his ftature highe,
Fyrey wythe braffe, benethe a fhyrte of lere,
In cloudie daie he reechd into the fkie;

         Neere

Neere to Kyng Harolde dyd he come alonge,
And drewe hys fteele Morglaien fworde fo ftronge. 600

Thryce rounde hys heade hee fwung hys anlace wyde,
On whyche the funne his vifage did agleeme,
Then ftraynynge, as hys membres would dyvyde,
Hee ftroke on Haroldes fheelde yn manner breme;
Alonge the fielde it made an horrid cleembe,   605
Coupeynge Kyng Harolds payncted fheeld in twayne,
Then yn the bloude the fierie fwerde dyd fteeme,
And then dyd drive ynto the bloudie playne;
So when in ayre the vapours do abounde,
Some thunderbolte tares trees and dryves ynto the
          grounde.   6.0

Harolde upreer'd hys bylle, and furious fente
A ftroke, lyke thondre, at the Normannes fyde;
Upon the playne the broken braffe befprente
Dyd ne hys bodie from dethe-doeynge hyde;
He tournyd backe, and dyd not there abyde;   615
With ftraught oute fheelde hee ayenwarde did goe,
Threwe downe the Normannes, did their rankes
          divide,
To fave himfelfe lefte them unto the foe;
                                                So

So olyphauntes, in kingdomme of the funne,
When once provok'd doth throwe theyr owne troopes
    runne.   620

Harolde, who ken'd hee was his armies ftaie,
Nedeynge the rede of generaul fo wyfe,
Byd Alfwoulde to Campynon hafte awaie,
As thro the armie ayenwarde he hies,
Swyfte as a feether'd takel Alfwoulde flies,   625
The fteele bylle blufhynge oer wyth lukewarm
    bloude;
Ten Kenters, ten Briftowans for th' emprize
Hafted wyth Alfwoulde where Campynon ftood,
Who aynewarde went, whylfte everie Normanne
    knyghte
Dyd blufh to fee their champyon put to flyghte. 630

As painctyd Bruton, when a wolfyn wylde,
When yt is cale and bluftrynge wyndes do blowe,
Enters hys bordeile, taketh hys yonge chylde,
And wyth his bloude beftreynts the lillie fnowe,
He thoroughe mountayne hie and dale doth goe, 635
Throwe the quyck torrent of the bollen ave,
                 Throwe

Throwe Severne rollynge oer the fandes belowe
He fkyms alofe, and blents the beatynge wave,
Ne ftynts, ne lagges the chace, tylle for hys eyne
In peecies hee the morthering theef doth chyne.   640

So Alfwoulde he dyd to Campynon hafte;
Hys bloudie bylle awhap'd the Normannes eyne;
Hee fled, as wolfes when bie the talbots chac'd,
To bloudie byker he dyd ne enclyne.
Duke Wyllyam ftroke hym on hys brigandyne,   645
And fayd ; Campynon, is it thee I fee?
Thee? who dydft aétes of glorie fo bewryen,
Now poorlie come to hyde thiefelfe bie mee?
Awaie! thou dogge, and aéte a warriors parte,
Or with mie fwerde I'll perce thee to the harte.   650

Betweene Erle Alfwoulde and Duke Wyllyam's bronde
Campynon thoughte that nete but deathe coulde bee,
Seezed a huge fwerde Morglaien yn his honde,
Mottrynge a praier to the Vyrgyne:
So hunted deere the dryvynge hounds will flee,   655
When theie dyfcover they cannot efcape;

                         And

And feerful lambkyns, when theie hunted bee,
Theyre ynfante hunters doe theie oft awhape;
Thus ftoode Campynon, greete but hertleffe knyghte,
When feere of dethe made hym for deathe to fyghte. 660

Alfwoulde began to dyghte hymfelfe for fyghte,
Meanewhyle hys menne on everie fyde dyd flee,
Whan on hys lyfted fheelde withe alle hys myghte
Campynon's fwerde in burlie-brande dyd dree;
Bewopen Alfwoulde fellen on his knee;   665
Hys Bryftowe menne came in hym for to fave;
Eftfoons upgotten from the grounde was hee,
And dyd agayne the touring Norman brave;
Hee grafpd hys bylle in fyke a drear arraie,
Hee feem'd a lyon catchynge at hys preie.   670

Upon the Normannes brazen adventayle
The thondrynge bill of myghtie Alfwould came;
It made a dentful brufe, and then dyd fayle;
Fromme rattlynge weepons fhotte a fparklynge flame;
Eftfoons agayne the thondrynge bill ycame,   675
Peers'd thro hys adventayle ànd fkyrts of lare;

                                        A tyde

A tyde of purple gore came wyth the fame,
As out hys bowells on the feelde it tare;
Campynon felle, as when fome cittie-walle
Inne dolefulle terrours on its mynours falle, 680

He felle, and dyd the Norman rankes dyvide;
So when an oke, that fhotte ynto the fkie,
Feeles the broad axes peerfynge his broade fyde,
Slowlie hee falls and on the grounde doth lie,
Preffynge all downe that is wyth hym anighe, 685
And ftoppynge wearie travellers on the waie;
So ftraught upon the playne the Norman hie

* * * * * * *

Bled, gron'd, and dyed: the Normanne knyghtes
aftound
To fee the bawfin champyon prefte upon the grounde.699

As when the hygra of the Severne roars,
And thunders ugfom on the fandes below,
The cleembe reboundes to Wedecefters fhore,
And fweeps the black fande rounde its horie prowe;
So bremie Alfwoulde thro the warre dyd goe; 695
Hys Kenters and Bryftowans flew ech fyde,

Betreinted

Betreinted all alonge with bloudlefs foe,

And feemd to fwymm alonge with bloudie tyde;

Fromme place.to place befmeard with bloud they went,

And rounde aboute them fwarthlefs corfe befprente. 700

A famous Normanne who yclepd Aubene,

Of fkyll in bow, in tylte, and handefworde fyghte,

That daie yn feelde han manie Saxons fleene,

Forre hee in fothen was a manne of myghte.

Fyrfte dyd his fwerde on Adelgar alyghte, 705

As hee on horfeback was, and peersd hys gryne,

Then upwarde wente: in everlaftynge nyghte

Hee closd hys rollyng and dymfyghted eyne.

Next Eadlyn, Tatwyn, and fam'd Adelred,

Bie various caufes funken to the dead. 710

But now to Alfwoulde he oppofynge went,

To whom compar'd hee was a man of ftre,

And wyth bothe hondes a myghtie blowe he fente

At Alfwouldes head, as hard as hee could dree;

But on hys paynĉted fheelde fo bifmarlie 715

Aflaunte his fwerde did go ynto the grounde;

T

Then

Then Alfwould him attack'd moſt furyouſlie,
Athrowe hys gaberdyne hee dyd him wounde,
Then ſoone agayne hys ſwerde hee dyd upryne,
And clove his creſte and ſplit hym to the eyne.   720

*   *   *   *   *   *   *

ONN OURE LADIES CHYRCHE.

A S onn a hylle one eve fittynge,
   At oure Ladie's Chyrche mouche wonderynge,
The counynge handieworke fo fyne,
Han well nighe dazeled mine eyne;
Quod I; fome counynge fairie hande   5
Yreer'd this chapelle in this lande;
Full well I wote fo fine a fyghte
Was ne yreer'd of mortall wighte.
Quod Trouthe; thou lackeft knowlachynge;
Thou forfoth ne wotteth of the thynge.   10
A Rev'rend Fadre, William Canynge hight,
Yreered uppe this chapelle brighte;
And eke another in the Towne,
Where glaffie bubblynge Trymme doth roun.
Quod I; ne doubte for all he's given   15
His fowle will certes goe to heaven.
Yea, quod Trouthe; than goe thou home,
And fee thou doe as hee hath donne.

Quod

Quod I; I doubte, that can ne bee;

I have ne gotten markes three.   20

Quod Trouthe; as thou haft got, give almes-dedes foe;

Canynges and Gaunts culde doe ne moe.

T. R.

ON THE SAME.

STAY, curyous traveller, and pafs not bye,
   Until this fetive piie aftounde thine eye.
Whole rocks on rocks with yron joynd furveie,
And okes with okes entremed difponed lie.
This mightie pile, that keeps the wyndes at baie,   5
Fyre-levyn and the mokie ftorme defie,
That fhootes aloofe into the reaulmes of daie,
Shall be the record of the Buylders fame for aie.

Thou feeft this mayftrie of a human hand,
The pride of Bryftowe and the Wefterne lande,   10
Yet is the Buylders vertues much moe greete,
Greeter than can bie Rowlies pen be fcande.
Thou feeft the faynctes and kynges in ftonen ftate,
That feemd with breath and human foule difpande,

As

As payrde to us enſeem theſe men of ſtate,   15
Such is greete Canynge's mynde when payrd to God
    elate.

Well maieſt thou be aſtound, but view it well ;
Go not from hence before thou ſee thy'fill,
And learn the Builder's vertues and his name ;
Of this tall ſpyre in every countye telle,   20
And with thy tale the lazing rych men ſhame ;
Showe howe the glorious Canynge did excelle ;
How hee good man a friend for kynges became,
And gloryous paved at once the way to heaven and
    fame.

EPITAPH ON ROBERT CANYNGE.

THYS mornynge ſtarre of Radcleves ryſynge
        raie,
A true manne good of mynde and Canynge hyghte,
Benethe thys ſtone lies moltrynge ynto claie,
Untylle the darke tombe ſheene an eterne lyghte.
Thyrde fromme hys loynes the preſent Canynge came ;
Houton are wordes for to telle hys doe ;

For

For aye fhall lyve hys heaven-recorded name,
Ne fhall yt dye whanne tyme fhalle bee no moe;
Whanne Mychael's trumpe fhall founde to rife the
    folle,
He'll wynge to heavn wyth kynne, and happie bee hys
    dolle. ⸫

THE STORIE OF WILLIAM CANYNGE.

ANENT a brooklette as I laie reclynd,
  Lifteynge to heare the water glyde alonge,
Myndeynge how thorowe the grene mees yt twynd,
Awhilft the cavys refpons'd yts mottring fonge,
At dyftaunt ryfyng Avonne to he fped,   5
Amenged wyth ryfyng hylles dyd fhewe yts head;

Engarlanded wyth crownes of ofyer weedes
And wraytes of alders of a bercie fcent,
And ftickeynge out wyth clowde agefted reedes,
The hoarie Avonne fhow'd dyre femblamente,   10
Whyleft blataunt Severne, from Sabryna clepde,
Rores flemie o'er the fandes that fhe hepde.

Thefe

Thefe eynegears fwythyn bringethe to mie thowghte
Of hardie champyons knowen to the floude,
How onne the bankes thereof brave Ælle foughte, 15
Ælle defcended from Merce kynglie bloude,
Warden of Bryftowe towne and caftel ftede,
Who ever and anon made Danes to blede.

Methoughte fuch doughtie menn muft have a fprighte
Dote yn the armour brace that Mychael bore, 20
Whan he wyth Satan kynge of helle dyd fyghte,
And earthe was drented yn a mere of gore ;
Orr, foone as theie dyd fee the worldjs lyghte,
Fate had wrott downe, thys mann ys borne to fyghte.

Ælle, I fayd, or els my mynde dyd faie, 25
Whie ys thy actyons left fo fpare yn ftorie ?
Were I toe difpone, there fhould lyvven aie
In erthe and hevenis rolles thie tale of glorie ;
Thie actes foe doughtie fhould for aie abyde,
And bie theyre tefte all after actes be tryde. 30

Next holie Wareburghus fylld mie mynde,
As fayre a fayncte as anie towne can boafte,

T 4

Or

Or bee the erthe wyth lyghte or merke ywrynde,
I fee hys ymage waulkeyng throwe the coafte :
Fitz Hardynge, Bithrickus, and twentie moe   35
Ynn vifyonn fore mie phantafie dyd goe.

Thus all mie wandrynge faytour thynkeynge ftrayde,
And eche dygne buylder dequac'd onn mie mynde,
Whan from the diftaunt ftreeme arofe a mayde,
Whofe gentle treffes mov'd not to the wynde ;   40
Lyche to the fylver moone yn froftie neete,
The damoifelle dyd come foe blythe and fweete.

Ne browded mantell of a fcarlette hue,
Ne fhoone pykes plaited o'er wyth ribbande geere,
Ne coftlie paraments of woden blue,   45
Noughte of a dreffe, but bewtie dyd fhee weere ;
Naked fhe was, and loked fwete of youthe,
All dyd bewryen that her name was Trout he.

The ethie ringletts of her notte-browne hayre
What ne a manne fhould fee dyd fwotelie hyde,   50
Whych on her milk-white bodykin fo fayre
Dyd fhowe lyke browne ftreemes fowlyng the white tyde,

Or.

Or veynes of brown hue yn a marble cuarr,
Whyche by the traveller ys kenn'd from farr.

Aftounded mickle there I fylente laie,   55
Still fcauncing wondrous at the walkynge fyghte;
Mie fenfes forgarde ne coulde reyn awaie;
But was ne forftraughte whan fhee dyd alyghte
Anie to mee, drefte up yn naked viewe,
Whych mote yn fome ewbrycious thoughtes abrewe. 60

But I ne dyd once thynke of wanton thoughte;
For well I mynded what bie vowe I hete,
And yn mie pockate han a crouchee broughte,
Whych yn the blofom woulde fuch fins anete;
I lok'd wyth eyne as pure as angelles doe,   65
And dyd the everie thoughte of foule efchewe.

Wyth fweet femblate and an angel's grace
Shee 'gan to lecture from her gentle brefte;
For Trouthis wordes ys her myndes face,
Falfe oratoryes fhe dyd aie detefte: 70
Sweetneffe was yn eche worde fhe dyd ywreene,
Tho fhe ftrove not to make that fweetneffe fheene.

Shee

Shee fayd; mie manner of appereynge here
Mie name and fleyghted myndbruch maie thee telle;
I'm Trouthe, that dyd defcende fromm heaven were, 75
Goulers and courtiers doe not kenne mee welle;
Thie inmofte thoughtes, thie labrynge brayne I fawe,
And from thie gentle dreeme will thee adawe.

Full manie champyons and menne of lore,
Paynĉters and carvellers have gaind good name, 80
But there's a Canynge, to encreafe the ftore,
A Canynge, who fhall buie uppe all theyre fame.
Take thou mie power, and fee yn chylde and manne
What troulie noblenefle yn Canynge ranne.

As when a bordelier onn ethie bedde, 85
Tyr'd wyth the laboures maynt of fweltrie daie,
Yn flepeis bofom laieth hys deft headde,
So, fenfes fonke to refte, mie boddie laie;
Eftfoons mie fprighte, from erthlie bandes untyde,
Immengde yn flanched ayre wyth Trouthe afyde. 90

Strayte was I carryd back to tymes of yore,
Whylft Canynge fwathed yet yn flefhlie bedde,

                And

And faw all actyons whych han been before,
And all the fcroll of Fate unravelled;
And when the fate-mark'd babe acoine to fyghte,   95
I faw hym eager gafpynge after lyghte.

In all hys fhepen gambols and chyldes plaie,
In everie merriemakeyng, fayre or wake,
I kenn'd a perpled lyghte of Wyfdom's raie;
He eate downe learnynge wyth the waftle cake.   100
As wife as anie of the eldermenne,
He'd wytte enowe toe make a mayre at tenne.

As the dulce downie barbe beganne to gre,
So was the well thyghte texture of hys lore;
Eche daie enhedeynge mockler for to bee,   105
Greete yn hys councel for the daies he bore.
All tongues, all carrols dyd unto hym fynge,
Wondryng at one foe wyfe, and yet foe yinge.

Encreafeynge yn the yeares of mortal lyfe,
And hafteynge to hys journie ynto heaven,   110
Hee thoughte ytt proper for to cheefe a wyfe,
And ufe the fexes for the purpofe gevene.

Hee

Hee then was yothe of comelie femelikeede,
And hee had made a mayden's herte to blede.

He had a fader, (Jefus reft hys foule!)   115
Who loved money, as hys charie joie;
Hee had a broder (happie manne be's dole!)
Yn mynde and boddie, hys owne fadre's boie;
What then could Canynge wiffen as a parte
To gyve to her whoe had made chop of hearte?   120

But landes and caftle tenures, golde and bighes,
And hoardes of fylver roufted yn the ent,
Canynge and hys fayre fweete dyd that defpyfe,
To change of troulie love was theyr content;
Theie lyv'd togeder yn a houfe adygne,   125
Of goode fendaument commilie and fyne.

But foone hys broder and hys fyre dyd die,
And lefte to Willyam ftates and renteynge rolies,
And at hys wyll hys broder Johne fupplie.
Hee gave a chauntrie to redeeme theyre foules;   130
And put hys broder ynto fyke a trade,
That he lorde mayor of Londonne towne was made.

2   Eftfoons

Eftſoons hys mornynge tournd to gloomie nyghte;
Hys dame, hys ſeconde ſelfe, gyve upp her brethe,
Seekeynge for eterne lyfe and endleſs lyghte,   135
And ſleed good Canynge; ſad myſtake of dethe!
Soe have I ſeen a flower ynn Sommer tyme
Trodde downe and broke and widder ynn ytts pryme.

Next Radcleeve chyrche (oh worke of hande of heav'n,
Whare Canynge ſheweth as an inſtrumente,)   140
Was to my biſmarde eyne-ſyghte newlie giv'n;
'Tis paſt to blazonne ytt to good contente.
You that woulde faygn the fetyve buyldynge ſee
Repayre to Radcleve, and contented bee.

I ſawe the myndbruch of hys nobille ſoule   145
Whan Edwarde meniced a ſeconde wyfe;
I ſaw what Pheryons yn hys mynde dyd rolle;
Nowe fyx'd fromm ſeconde dames a preeſte for lyfe.
Thys ys the manne of menne, the viſion ſpoke;
Then belle for even-ſonge mie ſenſes woke.   150

O N

ON HAPPIENESSE, by WILLIAM CANYNGE.

MAIE Selyneffe on erthes boundes bee hadde ?
Maie yt adyghte yn human fhape bee founde ?
Wote yee, ytt was wyth Edin's bower beftadde,
Or quite eraced from the fcaunce-layd grounde,
Whan from the fecret fontes the waterres dyd abounde ?
Does yt agrofed fhun the bodyed waulke,
Lyve to ytfelf and to yttes ecchoe taulke ?

All hayle, Contente, thou mayde of turtle-eyne,
As thie behoulders thynke thou arte iwreene,
To ope the dore to Selyneffe ys thyne,
And Chryftis glorie doth upponne thee fheene.
Doer of the foule thynge ne hath thee feene ;
In caves, ynn wodes, ynn woe, and dole diftreffe,
Whoere hath thee hath gotten Selyneffe.

ONN JOHNE A DALBENIE, by the fame.

JOHNE makes a jarre boute Lancafter and Yorke ;
Bee ftille, gode manne, and learne to mynde thie
wotke.

THE

THE GOULER'S REQUIEM, by the fame.

MIE boolie entes, adieu! ne moe the fyghte
    Of guilden merke fhall mete mie joieous eyne,
Ne moe the fylver noble fheenynge bryghte
Schall fyll mie honde with weight to fpeke ytt fyne;
Ne moe, ne moe, alafs! I call you myne: 5
Whydder muft you, ah! whydder muft I goe?
I kenn not either; oh mie emmers dygne,
To parte wyth you wyll wurcke mee myckle woe;
I mufte be gonne, botte whare I dare ne telle;
O ftorthe unto mie mynde! I goe to helle.   10

Soone as the morne dyd dyghte the roddie funne,
A fhade of theves eche ftreake of lyght dyd feeme;
Whann ynn the heavn full half hys courfe was runn,
Eche ftirryng nayghbour dyd mie harte afleme;
Thye lofs, or quycke or flepe, was aie mie dreme; 15
For thee, O gould, I dyd the lawe ycrafe;
For thee I gotten or bie wiles or breme;
Ynn thee I all mie joie and good dyd place;
Botte now to mee thie pleafaunce ys ne moe,
I kenne notte botte for thee I to the quede muft goe. 20

THE

THE ACCOUNTE OF W. CANYNGES FEAST.

THOROWE the halle the belle hán founde;
 Byelecoyle doe the Grave befeeme;
The ealdermenne doe fytte arounde,
Ande fnoffelle oppe the cheorte fteeme.
Lyche affes wylde ynne defarte wafte
Swotelye the morneynge ayre doe tafte,

Syke keene theie ate; the minftrels plaie,
The dynne of angelles doe theie keepe;
Heie ftylle the gueftes ha ne to faie,
Butte nodde yer thankes ande falle aflape.
Thus echone daie bee I to deene,
Gyf Rowley, Ifcamm, or Tyb. Gorges be ne feene.

T H E   E N D.

A GLO

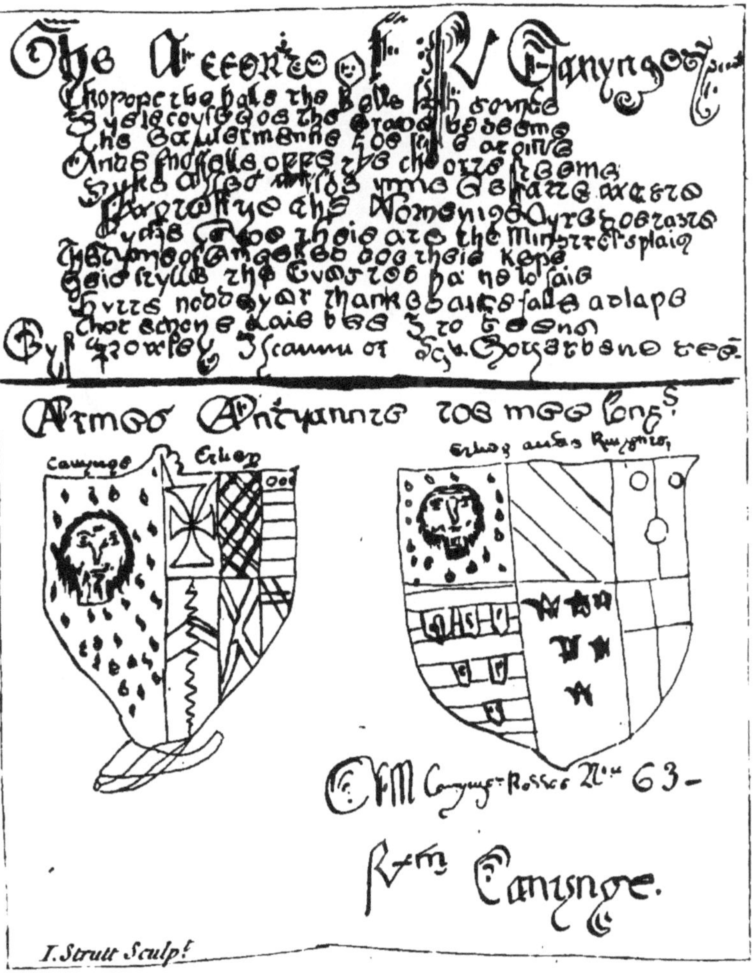

The Accompte of W. Canynge

(decorative gothic verse, largely illegible)

Armes Antyante toe mee longs

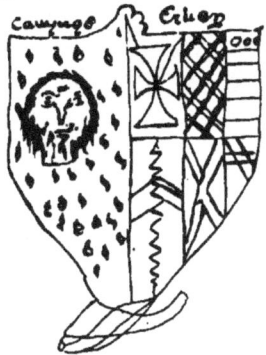

Canynges — Roses No. 63 —

Wm Canynge

A GLOSSARY of UNCOMMON WORDS
IN THIS VOLUME.

IN the following Glossary, the explanations of words by CHATTERTON, *at the bottom of the several pages, are drawn together, and digested alphabetically, with the letter* C. *after each of them. But it should be observed, that these explanations are not to be admitted but with great caution; a considerable number of them being (as far as the Editor can judge) unsupported by authority or analogy. The explanations of some other words, omitted by* CHATTERTON, *have been added by the Editor, where the meaning of the writer was sufficiently clear, and the word itself did not recede too far from the established usage; but he has been obliged to leave many others for the consideration of more learned or more sagacious interpreters.*

U   EXPLA-

EXPLANATION OF THE LETTERS OF REFERENCE.

The other references are made to the pages.

A GLOS-

A GLOSSARY.

ABESSIE, E. III. 89. *Humility.* C.

Aborne, T. 45. *Burnished.* C.

Abounde, H. 1. 55.

Aboune, G. 53. *Make ready.* C.

Abredynge, Æ. 334. *Upbraiding.* C.

Abrewe, p. 281. 60. as *Brew.*

Abrodden, E. I. 6. *Abruptly.* C.

Acale, G. 191. *Freeze.* C.

Accaie, Æ. 356. *Aswage.* C.

Achments, T. 153. *Atchievements.* C.

Acheke, G. 47. *Choke.* C.

Achevments, Æ. 65. *Services.* C.

Acome, p. 283. 95. as *Come.*

Acrool, El. 6. *Faintly.* C.

Adave, H. 2. 402.

Adawe, p. 282. 78. *Awake.*

Addawd, H. 2. 110.

Adente, Æ. 396. *Fastened.* C.

Adented, G. 32. *Fastened, annexed.* C.

Aderne, H. 2. 272. See *Derne, Dernie.*

Adigne. See *Adygne.*

Adrames, Ep. 27. *Churls.* C.

Adventaile, T. 13. *Armour.* C.

Adygne, Le. 46. *Nervous; worthy of praise.* C.

Affynd, H. 1. 132. *Related by marriage.*

Afleme, p. 287. 14. as *Fleme*; to drive away, to affright.

After la goure, H. 2. 353. should probably be *Astrelagour*; Astrologer.

Agrame, G. 93. *Grievance.* C.

Agreme, Æ. 356. *Torture.* C.— G. 5. *Grievance.* C.

Agrosed, p. 286. 6. as *Agrised*; terrified.

Agroted, Æ. 348. See *Groted.*

Agylted, Æ. 334. *Offended.* C.

Aidens, Æ. 222. *Aidance.*

Ake, E. II. 8. *Oak.* C.

Alans, H. 2. 124. *Hounds.*

Alatche, Æ. 117.

Aledge, G. 5. *Idly.* C.

Aleft, Æ. 50. *Left.*

All a boon, E. III. 41. *A manner of asking a favour.* C.

Alleyn, E. I. 52. *Only.* C.

Almer, Ch. 20. *Beggar.* C.

Aluste, H. 1. 88.

Alyne, T. 79. *Across his shoulders.* C.

Alyse,

Alyfe, Le. 29. *Allow.* C.

Amate, Æ. 58. *Deftroy.* C.

Amayld, E. II. 49. *Enameled.* C.

Ameded, Æ. 54. *Rewarded.*

Amenged, p. 278. 6. as *Menged*; mixed.

Amenufed, E. II. 5. *Diminifhed.* C.

Amield; T. 5. *Ornamented, ena-meled.* C.

Anente, Æ. 475. *Againft.* C.

Anere, Æ. 15. *Another.* C.

Anete, p. 281. 64.

Anie, p. 281. 59. as *Nie*; nigh.

Anlace, G. 57. *An ancient fword.* C.

Antecedent, Æ. 233. *Going before.*

Applings, E. I. 33. *Grafted trees.* C.

Arace, G. 156. *Diveft.* C.

Arift, Ch. 10. *Arofe.* C.

Arrowe-lede, H. 1. 74.

Afeaunce, E. III. 52. *Difdainfully.* C.

Afenglave, H. 1. 117.

Afkaunted, Le. 19.

Aflee, Æ. 504.

Affeled, E. III. 14. *Anfwered.* C.

Asfhrewed, Ch. 24. *Accurfed, un-fortunate.* C.

Affwaie, Æ. 352.

Aftedde, E. II. 11. *Scated.* C.

Aftenle, G. 47. *Aftonifh.* C.

Afterte, G. 137. *Neglected.* C.

Aftoun, E. II. 5. *Aftonifhed.* C.

Aftounde, M. 83. *Aftonifh.* C.

Afyde, p. 282. 90. perhaps *Aflyde*; afcended.

Athur, H. 2. 476. as *Thurgh*; thorough.

Attenes, Æ. 18. *At once.* C.

Attoure, T. 115. *Turn.* C.

Attoure, Æ. 322. *Around.*

Ave, H. 2. 645. for *Edu.* Fr. Water.

Atimere, Ch. 7. *A loofe robe, or mantle.* C.

Aumeres, E. III. 25. *Borders of gold and filver,* &c. C.

Auntire, H. 2. 133. as *Aven-ture*; adventure.

Autremete, Ch. 52. *A loofe white robe, worn by priefts.* C.

Awhaped, Æ. 400. *Aftonifhed.* C.

Aynewarde, Ch. 47. *Backwards.* C.

B.

Bankes, T. 3. *Benches.*

Barb'd hall, Æ. 219.

Barbed horfe, Æ. 27. *Covered with armour.*

Barén, Æ. 880, for *Barren.*

Barganette, E. III. 49. *A fong, or ballad.* C.

Bataunt, Ba. 276. 292.

Battayles, Æ. 707. *Boats, fhips.* Fr.

Batten,

Batten, G. 3. *Fatten.* C.

Battent, T. 52. *Loudly.* C.

Battently, G. 50. *Loud roaring.* C.

Battope, H. 1. 520. *Beat with flicks.* Fr.

Baubels, Ent. 7. *Jewels.* C.

Bawfin, Æ. 57. *Large.* C.

Bayre, E. II. 76. *Brow.* C.

Behefte, G. 60. *Command.* C.

Behight, H. 2. 365.

Behylte, Æ. 939. *Promifed.* C.

Belent, H. 2. 121.

Beme, Æ. 563. *Trumpet.*

Bemente, E. I. 45. *Lament.* C.

Benned. Æ. 1185. *Curfed, tormented.* C.

Benymmynge, P. G. 3. *Bereaving.* C.

Bercie, p. 278. 8.

Berne, Æ. 580. *Child.* C.

Berten, T. 58. *Venomous.* C.

Befeies, T. 124. *Becomes.* C.

Befprente, T. 132. *Scattered.* C.

Beftadde, p. 286. 3.

Beftanne, Æ. 411.

Befted, H. 2. 140.

Beftoiker, Æ. 91. *Deceiver.* C.

Beftreynts, H. 2. 644.

Bete, G. 85. *Bid.* C.

Betraffed, G. 7. *Deceived, impofed on.* C.

Betratte, Æ. 1031. *Betrayed.* C.

Betreinted, H. 2. 707.

Bevyle, E. II. 57. *Break. A herald term, fignifying a fpear broken in tilting.* C.

Bewrate, H. 2. 127.

Bewrecke, G. 101. *Revenge.* C.

Bewreen, Æ. 6. *Exprefs.* C.

Bewryen, Le. 42. *Declared, exprefs.* C.

Bewryne, G. 72. *Declare.* C.

Bewrynning, T. 128. *Declaring.* C.

Bighes, Æ. 371. *Jewels.* C.

Birlette, E. III. 24. *A hood, or covering for the back part of the head.* C.

Bifmarde, p. 285. 141.

Blake, Æ. 178, 407. *Naked.* C.

Blakied, E. III. 4. *Naked, original.* C.

Blanche, Æ. 369. *White, pure.*

Blaunchie, E. II. 50. *White.* C.

Blatauntlie, Æ. 108. *Loudly.* C.

Blente, E. III. 39. *Ceafed, dead.* C.

Blethe, T. 98. *Bleed.* C.

Blynge, Æ. 334. *Ceafe.* C.

Blyn, E. II. 40. *Ceafe, fland ftill.* C.

Boddekin, Æ. 265. *Body, fubftance.* C.

Boleynge, M. 17. *Swelling.* C.

Bollengers and Cottes, E. II. 33. *Different kinds of boats.* C.

Boolie, E. I. 46. *Beloved.* C.

Bordel, E. III. 2. *Cottage.* C.

Bordelier, Æ. 410. *Cottager.*

Borne, T. 13. Æ. 741. *Burnifh.* C.

Boun, E. II. 40. *Make ready.* C.

Bounde,

Bounde, T. 32. *Ready.* C.

Bourne, Æ. 483.

Bouting matche, p. 23. 2.

Bowke, T. 19.—Bowkie, G. 133. *Body.* C.

Brafteth, G. 123. *Burfteth.* C.

Brayd, G. 77. *Difplayed.* C.

Brayde, Æ. 1010.

Breme, fubft. G. 12. *Strength.* C.

———— adj. E. II. 6. *Strong.* C.

Brende, G. 50. *Burn, confume.* C.

Bretful, Ch. 19. *Filled with.* C.

Broched, H. 2. 345. *Pointed.*

Brondeous, E. II. 24. *Furious.* C.

Browded, G. 130. *Embroidered.* C.

Brynnyng, Æ. 680. *Declaring.* C.

Burled, M. 20. *Armed.* C.

Burlie bronde, G. 7. *Fury, anger.* C.

Byclecoyle, p. 288. 2. *Bel-acueil.* Fr. the name of a perfonage in the *Roman de la Rofe,* which Chaucer has rendered *Fair-welcoming.*

Byker, Æ. 246. *Battle.*

Bykrous, M. 37. *Warring.* C.

Byfmare, M. 95. *Bewildered, curious.* C.

Byfmarelie, Le. 26. *Curioufly.* C.

C.

Cale, Æ. 854. *Cold.*

Calke, G. 25. *Caft.* C.

Calked, E. I. 49. *Caft out.* C.

Caltyfning, G. 67. *Forbidding.* C.

Carnes, Æ. 1243. *Rocks, ftones.* Brit.

Caftle-ftede, G. 100. *A caftle.* C.

Caties, H. 2. 67. *Cates.*

Caytifned, Æ. 32. *Binding, enforcing.* C.

Celnefs, Æ. 882.

Chafe, Æ. 191. *Hot.* C.

Chaftes, G. 201. *Beats, ftamps.* C.

Champion, v. P. G. 12. *Challenge.* C.

Chaper, E. III. 48. *Dry, funburnt.* C.

Chapournette, Ch. 45. *A fmall round hat.* C.

Chefe, G. 11. *Heat, rafhnefs.* C.

Chelandree, Æ. 105. *Gold-finch.* C.

Cheorte, p. 288. 4.

Cherifaunce, Ent. 1. *Comfort.* C.

Cherifaunied, Æ. 839. perhaps *Chrifaunced.*

Cheves, Ch. 37. *Moves.* C.

Chevyfed, Ent. 2. *Preferved.* C.

Chirckynge, M. 23. *A confufed noife.* C.

Church-glebe-houfe, Ch. 24. *Grave.* C.

Cleme, E. II. 9. *Sound.* C.

Clergyon, P. G. 8. *Clerk, or clergyman.* C.

Clergyon'd, Ent. 13. *Taught.* C.

Clevis, H. 2. 46.

Cleyne,

Cleyne, Æ. 1102.

Clinie, H. 1. 431.

Cloude-agefted, p. 278. 9.

Clymmynge, Ch. 36. *Noify*. C.

Coiftrell, H. 2. 88.

Compheeres, M. 21. *Companions*. C.

Congeon, E. III. 89. *Dwarf*. C.

Contake, T. 87. *Difpute*. C.

Conteins, H. 1. 223. for *Contents*.

Conteke, E. II. 10. *Confufe*; contend with. C.

Contekions, Æ. 558. *Contentions*. C.

Cope, Ch. 50. *A cloke*. C.

Corven, Æ. 56. See *Ycorven*.

Cotte, E. II. 24. *Cut*.

Cottes, E. II. 33. See *Bollengers*.

Coupe, E. II. 7. *Cut*. C.

Couraciers, T. 74. *Horfe-courfers*. C.

Coyen, Æ. 125. *Coy*. q?

Cravent, E. III. 39. *Coward*. C.

Creand, Æ. 581. as *Recreand*.

Crine, Æ. 851. *Hair*. C.

Croched, H. 2. 521. perhaps *Broched*.

Croche, v. G. 26. *Crofs*. C.

Crokynge, Æ. 119. *Bending*.

Crofs-ftone, Æ. 1122. *Monument*. C.

Cuarr, p. 281. 53. *Quarry*. q?

Cullis-yatte, E. I. 50. *Portcullis-gate*. C.

Curriedowe, G. 176. *Flatterer*. C.

Cuyen kine, E. I. 35. *Tender cows*. C.

D.

Dareygne, G. 26. *Attempt, endeavour*. C.

Declynie, H. 1. 161. *Declination*. q?

Decorn, E. II. 14. *Carved*. C.

Deene, E. II. 69. *Glorious, worthy*. C.

Deere, E. III. 88. *Dire*. C.

Defs, M. 9. *Vapours, meteors*. C.

Defayte, G. 52. *Decay*. C.

Defte, Ch. 7. *Neat, ornamental*. C.

Deigned, E. III. 53. *Difdained*. C.

Delievretie, T. 44. *Activity*. C.

Demafing, H. 1. 276.

Dente, Æ. 886. See *Adente*.

Dented, Æ. 263. See *Adented*.

Denwere, G. 141. *Doubt*. C.— M. 13. *Tremour*. C.

Dequace, G. 56. *Mangle, deftroy*. C.

Dequaced, p. 280. 38.

Dere, Ep. 5. *Hurt, damage*. C.

Derkynnes, Æ. 229. *Young deer*. q?

Derne, Æ. 582.—H. 2. 532.

Dernie, E. I. 19. *Woeful, lamentable*. C. ——— M. 106. *Cruel*. C.

Deflavate, H. 2. 343.

Deflavatie, Æ. 1047. *Letchery*. C.

U 4

Detra-

Detratours, H. 2. 78.

Deyfde, Æ. 46. *Seated on a deis.*

Dheie; *They.*

Dhere, Æ. 192. *There.*

Dhereof; *Thereof.*

Difficile, Æ. 358. *Difficult.* C.

Dighte, Ch. 7. D *eſt, arrayed.* C.

Difpande, p. 276. *ult.* perhaps for *Difponed.*

Difpone, p. 279. 27. *Difpoſe.*

Diviniſtre, Æ. 141. *Divine.* C.

Dolce, Æ. 1187. *Soft, gentle.* C.

Dole, n. G. 137. *Lamentation.* C.

Dole, adj. p. 283. 13.

Dolte, Ep. 27. *Foolish.* C.

Donde, H. 1. 51.

Donore, H. 1. 5. This line ſhould probably be written thus; *O ſea-certeeming Dovor!*

Dortoure, Ch. 25. *A ſleeping room.* C.

Dote, p. 279. 20. perhaps as *Dighte.*

Doughtre mere, H. 2. 491. *D'outre mere.* Fr. From beyond ſea.

Dree, Æ. 983.

Dreite, Æ. 466. *Leaſt.* C.

Drented, G. 91. *Drained.* C.

Dreynted, Æ. 237. *Drowned.* C.

Dribblet, E. II. 48. *Small, inſignificant.* C.

Drites, G. 65. *Rights, liberties.* C.

Drocke, T. 40. *Drink.* C.

Droke, Æ. 461.

Droorie, Ep. 47. See Chatterton's note. *Druerie* is *Courtſhip, gallantry.*

Drooried, Æ. 127. *Courted.*

Dulce, p. 283. 103. as *Dolce.*

Dureſſed, E. I. 39. *Hardened.* C.

Dyd, H. 2. 9. ſhould probably be *Dyght.*

Dygne, T. 89. *Worthy.* C.

Dynning, E. I. 25. *Sounding.* C.

Dyfperpelleſt, Æ. 414. *Scattereſt.* C.

Dyfporte, E. I. 28. *Pleaſure.* C.

Dyfportifment, Æ. 250. as *Dyfporte.*

Dyfregate, Æ. 542.

E.

Edraw, H. 2. 52. for *Ydraw;* Draw.

Eft, E. II. 78. *Often.* C.

Eftſoones, E. III. 54. *Quickly.* C.

Ele, M. 74. *Help.* C.

Eletten, Æ. 448. *Enlighten.* C.

Eke, E. I. 27. *Alſo.* C.

Emblaunched, E. I. 36. *Whitened.* C.

Embodyde, E. I. 33. *Thick, ſtout.* C.

Embowre, G. 134. *Lodge.* C.

Emburled, E. II. 54. *Armed.* C.

Emmate, Æ. 34. *Leſſen, decreaſe.* C.

Emmers,

Emmers, p. 287. 7.

Emmertleynge, M. 72. *Glittering.* C.

Enalfe, G. 159. *Embrace.* C.

Encaled, Æ. 918. *Frozen, cold.* C.

Enchafed, M. 60. *Heated, enraged.* C.

Engyne, Æ. 381. *Torture.*

Enheedynge, p. 283. 105.

Enlowed, Æ. 606. *Flamed, fired.* C.

Enrone, Æ. 661.

Enfeme, Æ. 971. *To make feams in.* q ?

Enfeeming, Æ. 746. as *Seeming.*

Enfhoting, T. 174. *Shooting, darting.* C.

Enftrote, H. 2. 513.

Enfwote, Æ. 1175. *Sweeten.* q ?

Enfwolters, Æ. 629. *Swallows, fucks in.* C.

Enfyrke, p. 25. 10. *Encircle.*

Ent, E. III. 57. *A purfe or bag.* C.

Entendement, Æ. 261. *Underftanding.*

Enthoghteing, Æ. 704.

Entremed, p. 276. 4.

Entrykeynge, Æ. 304. as *Tricking.*

Entyn, P. G. 10. *Even.* C.

Eftande, H. 2. 281. for *Yftande;* Stand.

Eftells, E. II. 16. A corruption of *Eftoile.* Fr. A ftar. C.

Eftroughtld, Æ. 918.

Ethe, E. III. 59. *Eafe.* C.

Ethie, p. 280. 49. *Eafy.*

Evalle, E. III. 38. *Equal.* C.

Evefpeckt, T. 56. *Marked with evening dew.* C.

Ewbrice, Æ. 1085. *Adultery.* C.

Ewbrycious, p. 281. 60. *Lafcivious.*

Eyne-gears, p. 279. 13.

F.

Fage, Ep. 30. *Tale, jeft.* C.

Faifully, T. 147. *Faithfully.* C.

Faitour, Ch. 66. *A beggar, or vagabond.* C.

Faldftole, Æ. 61. *A folding ftool, or feat.* See Du Cange in v. *Faldiftorium.*

Fayre, Æ. 1204. 1224. *Clear, innocent.*

Feere, Æ. 965. *Fire.*

Feerie, E. II. 45. *Flaming.* C.

Fele, T. 27. *Feeble.* C.

Fellen, E. I. 10. *Fell* pa. t. fing. q ?

Fetelie, G. 24. *Nobly.* C.

Fetive, Ent. 7. as *Feftive.*

Fetivelie, Le. 42. *Elegantly.* C.

Fetivenefs, Æ. 400. as *Feftivenefs.*

Feygnes, E. III. 78. A corruption of *feints.* C.

Fbuir, G. 58. *Fury.* C.

Fie, T. 113. *Defy.* C.

Flaiten, H. 1. 84.

Flanched,

Flanched, H. 2. 252.

Flemed, T. 56. *Frighted.* C.

Flemie, p. 278. *ult.*

Flizze, G. 197. *Fly.* C.

Floe, H. 2. 54. *Arrow.*

Flott, Ch. 33. *Fly.* C.

Foile, E. III. 78. *Baffle.* C.

Fons, Fonnes, E. II. 14. *Devices.* C.

Forgard, Æ. 565. *Lose.* C.

Forletten, El. 19. *Forsaken.* C.

Forloyne, Æ. 722. *Retreat.* C.

Forreying, T. 114. *Destroying.* C.

Forslagen, Æ. 1076. *Slain.* C.

Forslege, Æ. 1106. *Slay.* C.

Forstraughte, p. 281. 58. *Distracted.*

Forstraughteyng, G. 34. *Distracting.* C.

Forswat, Ch. 50. *Sun-burnt.* C.

Forweltring, Æ. 618. *Blasting.* C.

Forwyned, E. III. 36. *Dried.* C.

Fremde, Æ. 430. *Strange.* C.

Fremded, Æ. 555. *Frighted.* C.

Freme, Æ. 267.

Fructile, Æ. 185. *Fruitful.*

G.

Gaberdine, T. 88. *A piece of armour.* C.

Gallard, Ch. 59. *Frighted.* C.

Gare, Ep. 7. *Cause.* C.

Gastnefs, Æ. 412. *Ghastliness.*

Gayne, Æ. 821. To gayne so *gayne* a pryze. *Gayne* has probably been repeated by mistake.

Geare, Æ. 299. *Apparel, accoutrement.*

Geafon, Ent. 7. *Rare.* C.—G. 120. *Extraordinary, strange.* C.

Geer, H. 2. 284. as *Gier.*

Geete, Æ. 736. as *Gite.*

Gemote, G. 94. *Assemble.* C.

Gemoted, E. II. 38. *United, assembled.* C.

Gerd, M. 7. *Broke, rent.* C.

Gies, C. 207. *Guides.* C.

Gier, H. 1. 527. *A turn, or twist.* C.

Gif, E. II. 39. *If.* C.

Gites, Æ. 2. *Robes, mantels.* C.

Glair, H. 2. 580.

Gledeynge, M. 22. *Livid.* C.

Glomb, G. 175. *Frown.* C.

Glommed, Ch. 22. *Clouded, dejected.* C.

Glytted, H. 2. 282.

Gorne, E. I. 36. *Garden.* C.

Gottes, Æ. 740. *Drops.*

Gouler, p. 282. 76.

Graiebarbes, Le. 25. *Greybeards.* C.

Grange, E. I. 34. *Liberty of pasture.* C.

Gratche, Æ. 115. *Apparel.* C.

Grave, p. 288. 2. *Chief magistrate, mayor.*

Gravots,

Gravots, E. I. 24. *Groves.* C.

Gree, E. I. 44. *Grow.* C.

Groffile, Æ. 547.

Groffifh, Æ. 257.

Groffynglie, Ep. 33. *Foolifhly.* C.

Gron, G. 90. *a fen, moor.* C.

Gronfer, E. II. 45. *A meteor,* from *gron* a fen, and *fir,* a corruption of fire. C.

Gronfyres, G. 200. *Meteors.* C.

Grore, H. 2. 27.

Groted, E. 337. *Swollen.* C.

Gule-depeincted, E. II. 13. *Red-painted.* C.

Gule-fteynct, G. 62. *Red-ftained.* C.

Gyttelles, Æ. 438. *Mantels.* C.

H.

Haile, E. III. 60. *Happy.* C.

Hailie, Æ. 148. 410. as *Haile.*

Halceld, M. 37. *Defeated.* C.

Hallie, T. 144. *Holy.* C.

Hallie, Æ. 33. *Wholly.*

Halline, Ch. 82. *Joy.* C.

Hancelled, G. 49. *Cut off, deftroyed.* C.

Han, Æ. 734. *Hath.* q?

Hanne, Æ. 409. *Had.* particip. q?—Æ. 685. *Had.* pa. t. fing. q?

Hantoned, Æ. 1094.

Harried, M. 82. *Toft.* C.

Hatched, p. 25. 1.

Haveth, E. I. 17. *Have.* 1ft perf. q?

Heafods, E. II. 7. *Heads.* C.

Heavenwere, G. 146. *Heavenward.* C.

Hecked, Æ. 394. *Wrapped clofely, covered.* C.

Heckled, M. 3. *Wrapped.* C.

Heie, E. II. 15. *They.* C.

Heiedeygnes, E. III. 77. *A country dance, ftill practifed in the North.* C.

Hele, n. G. 127. *Help.* C.

Hele, v. E. III. 16. *To help.* C.

Hem, T. 24. A contraction of *them.* C.

Hente, T. 175. *Grafp, hold.* C.

Hentyll, Æ. 1161.

Herfelle, Æ. 279. *Herfelf.*

Hefte, Æ. 1182.

Hilted, Hiltren, T. 47. 65. *Hidden.* C.

Hiltring, Ch. 13. *Hiding.* C.

Hoaftrie, E. I. 26. *Inn, or publick houfe.* C.

Holtred, Æ. 293.

Hommeur, Æ. 1190.

Hondepoint, Æ. 273.

Hopelen, Æ. 399.

Horrowe, M. 2. *Unfeemly, difagreeable.* C.

Horfe-millanar, Ch. 56. See C's note.

Houton, M. 92. *Hollow.* C.

Hulftred, M. 6. *Hidden, fecret.* C.

Hufcarles,

Huſcarles, Æ. 922. 1194. *Houſe-ſervants.*

Hyger, Æ. 627. The flowing of the tide in the Severn was antiently called the *Hygra.* Gul. Malmeſb. de Pontif. Ang. L. IV.

Hylle-fyre, Æ. 682. *A beacon.*

Hylte, T. 168. *Hid, ſecreted.* C.

——Æ. 1059. *Hide.* C.

I.

Jape, Ch. 74. *A ſhort ſurplice,* &c. C.

Jeſte, G. 195. *Hoiſted, raiſed.* C.

Ifrete, G. 2. *Devour, deſtroy.* C.

Ihantend, E. I. 40. *Accuſtomed.* C.

Jintle, H. 2. 82. for *Gentle.*

Impeſtering, E. I. 29. *Annoying.* C.

Inhild, El. 14. *Infuſe.* C.

Iſhad, Le. 37. *Broken.* C.

Jubb, E. III. 71. *A bottle.* C.

Iwreene, p. 286. 9.

K.

Ken, E. II. 6. *See, diſcover, know.* C.

Kennes, Ep. 28. *Knows.* C.

Keppend, Le. 44.

Kiſte, Ch. 25. *Coffin.* C.

Kivercled, E. III. 63. *The hidden or ſecret part.* C.

Knopped, M. 14. *Faſtened, chained, congealed.* C.

L.

Ladden, H. 1. 206.

Leathel, E. I. 42. *Deadly.* C.

Lechemanne, Æ. 31. *Phyſician.*

Leckedſt, H. 2. 342.

Lecturn, Le. 46. *Subject.* C.

Lecturnies, Æ. 109. *Lectures.* C.

Leden, El. 30. *Decreaſing.* C.

Ledanne, Æ. 1143.

Leege, G. 173. *Homage, obeyſance.* C.

Leegefolcke, G. 43. *Subjects.* C.

Lege, Ep. 3. *Law.* C.

Leggen, M. 92. *Leſſen, alloy.* C.

Leggende, M. 33. *Alloyed.* C.

Lemanne, Æ. 132. *Miſtreſs.*

Lemes, Æ. 42. *Lights, rays.* C.

Lemed, El. 7. *Gliſtened.* C.—— Æ. 606. *Lighted.* C.

Lere, Æ. 568. H. 2. 607. ſeems to be put for *Leather.*

Leſſel, El. 25. *A buſh or hedge.* C.

Lete, G. 60. *Still.* C.

Lethal, El. 21. *Deadly, or death-boding.* C.

Lethlen, Æ. 272. *Still, dead.* C.

Letten, Æ. 928. *Church-yard.* C.

Levynde, El. 18. *Blaſted.* C.

Levynne,

Levynne, M. 104. *Lightning.* C.

Levyn-mylted, Æ. 462. *Lightning-melted.* q?

Liefe, Æ. 217.

Liff, E. I. 7. *Leaf.*

Ligheth, Æ. 627.

Likand, H. 2. 187. *Liking.*

Limed, E. II. 7. ⎫ *Glaſſy, reflec-*
Limmed, M. 90. ⎭ *ting.* C.

Linge, Æ. 376. *Stay.* C.

Liſſed, T. 97. *Bounded.* C.

Lithie, Ep. 10. *Humble.* C.

Loaſte, Æ. 456. *Loſs.*

Logges, E. I. 55. *Cottages.* C.

Lordinge, T. 57. *Standing on their hind legs.* C.

Loverd's, E. III. 29. *Lord's.* C.

Low, G. 50. *Flame of fire.* C.

Lowes, T. 137. *Flames.* C.

Lowings, Ch. 35. *Flames.* C.

Lymmed, M. 33. *Poliſhed.* C.

Lynch, El. 37. *Bank.* C.

Lyoncel, E. II. 44. *Young lion.* C.

Lyped, El. 34.

Lyſſe, T. 2. *Sport, or play.* C.

Lyſſed, Æ. 53. *Bounded.* C.

M.

Mancas, G. 136. *Marks.* C.

Manchyn, H. 2. 232. *A ſleeve.* Fr.

Maynt, Meynte, E. II. 66. *Many, great numbers.* C.

Mee, Mees, E. I. 31. *Meadow.* C.

Meeded, Æ. 39. *Rewarded.*

Memuine, H, 2. 120.

Meniced, p. 285. 146. *Menaced.* q?

Mere, G. 58. *Lake.* C.

Merk-plante, T. 176. *Night-ſhade.* C.

Merke, T. 163. *Dark, gloomy.* C.

Mieſel, Æ. 551. *Myſelf.*

Miſkynette, El. 22. *A ſmall bag-pipe.* C.

Milt, Ch. 49. *Poor, needy.* C.

Mitches, El. 20. *Ruins.* C.

Mittee, E. II. 28. *Mighty.* C.

Mockler, p. 283. 105. *More.*

Moke, Ep. 5. *Much.* C.

Mokie, El. 29. *Black.* C.

Mole, Ch. 4. *Soft.* C.

Mollock, G. 90. *Wet, moiſt.* C.

Morglaien, M. 20. *The name of a ſword in ſome old Romances.*

Morthe, Æ. 307.

Morthynge, El. 4. *Murdering.* C.

Mote, E. I. 22. *Might.* C.

Motte, H. 2. 194. *Word, or motto.*

Myckle, Le. 16. *Much.* C.

Myndbruch, Æ. 401.

Mynſter, G. 75. *Monaſtery.* C.

Myſterk, M. 33. *Myſtic.* C.

N.

Ne, P. G. 6. *Not.* C.

Ne, p. 281. 58. *Nigh.*

Nedere.

Nedere, Ep. 11. *Adder.* C.

Neete, p. 280. 41. *Night.*

Neſh, T. 16. *Weak, tender.* C.

Nete, Æ. 399. *Night.*

Nete, T. 19. *Nothing.* C.

Nilling, Le. 16. *Unwilling.* C.

Nome-depeinted, E. II. 17. *Rebus'd ſhields*; a herald term, when the charge of the ſhield implies the name of the bearer. C.

Notte-browne, p. 280. 49. *Nutbrown.*

O.

Obaie, E. I. 41. *Abide.* C.

Offrendes, Æ. 51. *Preſents, offerings.* C.

Olyphauntes, H. 2. 629. *Elephants.*

Onknowlachynge, E. II. 26. *Not knowing.* C.

Onlight, Æ. 678.

Onliſt, Le. 45. *Boundleſs.* C.

Orreſts, G. 100. *Overſets.* C.

Ouchd, T. 80. See C's note.

Ouphante, Æ. 888. 929. *Ouphen, Elves.*

Ourt, H. 2. 588.

Ouzle, Æ. 104. *Black-bird.* C.

Owndes, G. 91. *Waves.* C.

P.

Pall, Ch. 31. Contraction from *appall,* to fright. C.

Paramente, Æ. 52. *Robes of ſcarlet.* C.—M. 36. *A princely robe.* C.

Paves, Pavyes, Æ. 433. *Shields.*

Peede, Ch. 5. *Pied.* C.

Pencte, Ch. 46. *Painted.* C.

Penne, Æ. 728. *Mountain.*

Percaſe, Le. 21. *Perchance.* C.

'Pere, E. I. 41. *Appear.* C.

Perpled, p. 283. 99. *Purple.* q?

Perſant, Æ. 561. *Piercing.*

Pete, Æ. 1001.

Pheeres, Æ. 46. *Fellows, equals.* C.

Pheon, H. 2. 282. in Heraldry, *the barbed head of a dart.*

Pheryons, p. 285. 147.

Picte, E. III. 91. *Picture.* C.

Pighte, T. 38. *Pitched, or bent down.* C.

Poyntel, Le. 44. *A pen.* C.

Prevyd, Æ. 23. *Hardy, valourous.* C.

Proto-ſlene, H. 2. 38. *Firſt-ſlain.*

Prowe, H. 1. 108.

Pynant, Le. 4. *Pining, meagre.*

Pyghte, M. 73. *Settled.* C.

Pyghteth, Ep. 15. *Plucks, or tortures.* C.

Quaced,

Q.

Quaced, T. 94. *Vanquished.* C.

Quaintiffed, T. 4. *Curiously de-vised.* C.

Quanfd, Æ. 241. *Stilled, Quenched.* C.

Queede, Æ. 284. 428. *The evil one; the Devil.*

R.

Receivure, G. 151. *Receipt.* C.

Recer, H. 1. 87. for *Racer.*

Recendize, Æ. 544.
Recrandize, Æ. 1193. } for *Recreandice; Coward-ice.*

Recreand, Æ. 508. *Coward.* C.

Reddour, Æ. 30. *Violence.* C.

Rede, Le. 18. *Wisdom.* C.

Reded, G. 79. *Counselled.* C.

Redeing, Æ. 227. *Advice.*

Regrate, Le. 7. *Esteem.* C.—M. 70. *Esteem, favour.* C.

Rele, n. Æ. 530. *Wave.* C.

Reles, v. E. II. 63. *Waves.* C.

Rennome, T. 28. *Honour, glory.* C.

Reyne, Reine, E. II. 25. *Run.* C.

Reyning, E. II. 39. *Running.* C.

Reytes, Æ. 900. *Water-flags.* C.

Ribaude, Ep. 9. *Rake, lewd person.* C.

Ribbande-geere, p. 280. 44. *Or-naments of ribbands.*

Rodded, Ch. 3. *Reddened.* C.

Rode, E. I. 59. *Complexion.* C.

Rodeing, Æ. 324. *Riding.*

Roder, Æ. 1065. *Rider, travel-ler.*

Roghling, T. 69. *Rolling.* C.

Roin, Æ. 325. *Ruin.*

Roiend, Æ. 578. *Ruin'd.*

Roiner, Æ. 325. *Ruiner.*

Rou, G. 10. *Horrid, grim.* C.

Rowncy, Le. 32. *Cart-horse.* C.

Rynde, Æ. 1192. *Ruin'd.*

S.

Sabalus, E. I. 22. *The Devil.* C.

Sabbatanners, Æ. 275.

Scalle, Æ. 703. *Shall.* C.

Scante, Æ. 1133. *Scarce.* C.

Scantillie, Æ. 1010. *Scarcely, spar-ingly.* C.

Scarpes, Æ. 52. *Scarfs.* C.

Scethe, T. 96. *Hurt or damage.* C.

Scille, E. III. 33. *Gather.* C.

Scillye, G. 207. *Closely.* C.

Scolles, Æ. 239. *Sholes.*

Scond, H. 1. 20. for *Alscond.*

Seck, H. 1. 461. for *Suck.*

Seeled, Ent. 11. *Closed.* C.

Seere, Æ. 1164. *Search.* C.

Selynefs, E. 1. 55. *Happiness.* C.

Semblate, p. 281. 67.

Seme, E. III. 32. *Seed.* C.

Semecope, Ch. 87. *A short under-cloke.* C.

Semm-

304 A GLOSSARY.

Semmlykeed, Æ. 298.

Semlykeene, Æ. 9. *Countenance.*
C.—G. 56. *Beauty, counte-nance.* C.

Sendaument, p. 284. 126.

Sete, Æ. 1689. *Seat.*

Shappe, T. 36. *Fate.* C.

Shap-scurged, Æ. 603. *Fate-scourged.* C.

Shemring, E. II. 14. *Glimmering.* C.

Shente, T. 157. *Broke, destroyed.* C.

Shepen, p. 283. 97.

Shepstere, E. I. 6. *Shepherd.* C.

Shoone-pykes, p. 280. 44. *Shoes with piked toes.* The length of the pikes was restrained to two inches, by 3 Edw. 4. c. 5.

Shrove, H. 2. 442.

Sletre, Æ. 539. *Slaughter.*

Slughornes, E. II. 9. *A musical instrument not unlike a hautboy.* C.—T. 31. *A kind of clarion.* C.

Smethe, T. 101. *Smoke.* C.

Smething, E. I. 1. *Smoking.* C.

Smore, H. 1. 412.

Smothe, Ch. 35. *Steam or vapours.* C.

Snett, T. 45. *Bent.* C.

Sothen, Æ. 227. *Sooth.* q?

Souten, H. 1. 252. for *Sought.* pa. t. sing. q?

Sparre, H. 1. 26. *A wooden bar.*

Spedde, H. 2. 535.

Spencer, T. 11. *Dispenser.* C.

Spere, Æ. 69.

Spyryng, Æ. 707. *Towering.*

Staie, H. 1. 198.

Starks, T. 73. *Stalks.*

Steeres, p. 25. 6. *Stairs.*

Stente, T. 134. *Stained.* C.

Steynced, Æ. 189.

Storthe, p. 287. 10.

Storven, Æ. 608. *Dead.* C.

Straughte, Æ. 59. *Stretched.* C.

Stret, Æ. 158. *Stretch.* C.

Strev, Æ. 358. *Strive.*

Stringe, G. 10. *Strong.* C.

Suffycyl, Æ. 62. 981.

Swarthe, Æ. 265.

Swarthcing, Æ. 295.

Swarthlefs, H. 2. 573.

Sweft-kervd, E. II. 20. *Short-liv'd.* C.

Swoltering, Æ. 444.

Swotie, E. II. 9. *Sweet.* C.

Swythe, Swythen, Swythyn; *Quickly.* C.

Syke, E. II. 6. *Such, so.* C.

T.

Takelse, T. 72. *Arrow.* C.

Teint, H. 1. 462. for *Tent.*

Tende, T. 113. *Attend, or wait.* C.

Tene,

Tene, Æ. 366. *Sorrow.*

Tentyflie, E. III. 48. *Carefully.* C.

Tere, Æ. 46. *Health.* C.

Thighte, p. 283. 104.

Thoughten, Æ. 172. 1136. for *Thought.* pa. t. fing. q?

Thyffen, E. II. 87. *Thefe,* or *thofe.* q?

Tochelod, Æ. 205.

Tore, Æ. 1020. *Torch.* C.

Trechit, H. 2. 93. for *Treget;* *Deceit.*

Treynted, Æ. 454.

Twyghte, E. II. 78. *Plucked, pulled.* C.

Twytte, E. I. 2. *Pluck, or pull.* C.

Tynge, Tyngue; *Tongue.*

U.

Val, T. 138. *Helm.* C.

Vernage, H. 2. 11. *Vernaccia.* Ital. a fort of rich wine.

Ugfomenefs, Æ. 507. *Terror.* C.

Ugfomme, E. II. 55. *Terribly.* C.—Æ. 303. *Terrible.* C.

Unaknell'd, H. 1. 288. *Without any knell rung for them.* q?

Unburied, Æ. 1186. *Unarmed.* C.

Uncted, M. 30. *Anointed.* C.

Undelievre, G. 27. *Unactive.* C.

Unenhantend, Æ. 636. *Unaccuftomed.* C.

Unefpryte, G. 27. *Unfpirited.* C.

Unhailie, Ch. 85. *Unhappy.* C.

Unliart, P. G. 4. *Unforgiving.* C.

Unlift, E. III. 86. *Unbounded.* C.

Unlored, Ep. 25. *Unlearned.* C.

Unlydgefull, Æ. 537.

Unplayte, G. 86.—Unplyte, Æ. 1238. *Explain.* C.

Unquaced, E. III. 90. *Unhurt.* C.

Unfprytes, Æ. 1212. *Un-fouls.* C.

Untentyff, G. 79. *Uncareful, neglected.* C.

Unthylle, T. 30. *Ufelefs.* C.

Unwere, E. III. 87. *Tempeft.* C.

Volunde, Æ. 73. *Memory, underftanding.* C.—G. 140. *Will.* C.

Uprifte, Æ. 928. *Rifen.* C.

Upryne, H. 2. 729.

Upfwalynge, Æ. 258. *Swelling.* C.

W.

Walfome, H. 2. 92. *Wlatfome; loathfome.*

Wanhope, G. 34. *Defpair.* C.

Wayld, Æ. 11. *Choice, felected.*

Waylinge, E. II. 68. *Decreafing.* C.

X   Wayne

Wayne, E. III. 31. *Car.* C.

Weere, Æ. 835. *Grief.* C.

Welked, E. III. 50. *Withered.* C.

Welkyn, Æ. 1055. *Heaven.* C.

Wifeegger, E. III. 8. *A philoso-pher.* C.

Wiffen, Æ. 685. *Wish.*

Wite, G. 176. *Reward.* C.

Withe, E. III. 36. A contraction of *Wither.* C.

Wolfome, Le. 5. See *Walfome.*

Wraytes. See *Reytes.*

Wrynn, T. 117. *Declare.* C.

Wurche, Æ. 500. *Work.* C.

Wychencref, Æ. 420. *Witchcraft.*

Wyere, E. II. 79. *Grief, trouble.* C.

Wympled, G. 207. *Mantled, co-vered.* C.

Wynnynge, Æ. 219.

Ycorne, Æ. 374.

Ycorven, T. 170. *To mould.* C.

Ycrafed, T. 132. *Broken.* C.

Yenne; *Then.*

Yer, E. II. 29. *Their.*

Yer, Æ. 152. *Your.*

Ygrove, H. 2. 444.

Yinder, Æ. 692. *Yonder.*

Yis; *This.*

Ylach'd, H. 2. 246.

Ynhyme, Ent. 5. *Interr.* C.

Ynutile, Æ. 198. *Useless.*

Yreaden, H. 2. 217.

Yroughte, H. 2. 328. for *Ywroughte.*

Yfped, M. 102. *Dispatched.* C.

Yfpende, T. 179. *Confider.* C.

Yftorven, E. I. 52. *Dead.* C.

Ytfel, E. I. 18. *Itself.*

Ywreen, E. II. 30. *Covered.* C.

Ywrinde, M. 100. *Hid, covered.* C.

Yyne, Æ. 540. *Thine.*

Y.

Yan, Æ. 72. *Than.*

Yaped, Ep. 30. *Laughable.* C.

Yatte, T. 9. *That.* C.

Yblente, Æ. 40. *Blinded.* C.

Ybroched, G. 97. *Horned.* C.

Z.

Zabalus, Æ. 428. as *Sabalus;* the Devil.

The following are not ERRATA *of the Printer, but such evident mistakes of the Transcriber as an Editor, perhaps, ought to have corrected, though, in the present case, it has been judged fitter barely to point them out in this manner to the Reader.*

P. 45.   6.   for *Canterlone*, r. *Canterloue*, or *Canteloxe*.

   72. ver. 49.   *ytts*, r. *yttself*.

   75.   1.   *cherisaunei 'tys*, r. *cherisaunce it ys*.

   80.   73.   *toe*, r. *doe*.

   100.   345.   r. to *be* dyghte.

   101.   367.   *feares*, r. *teares*.

   108.   442.   *Storven*, r. *Stroveu*.

   110.   486.   *be wreene*, r. *bewreen*.

   130.   770.   *sythe*, r. *syke*.

   135.   839.   *cherisaunied*, r. *cherisaunced*.

   149.   1008.   *Hallie*, r. *Hailie*.

   157.   1084.   *Bie* thankes, r. *Mie* thankes.

   167.   1197.   *slythe*, r. *swythe*.

   210.   O *sea! our teeming donore*, r. O *sea-oerteeming Donor!*

   215.   104.   r. horse *of* Tosselyn; or rather *Josselyn*.

   224.   300.   *men in women's*, r. *women in men's*.

   255.   353.   *After la goure*, r. *Aftrelagoure*.

   265.   548.   *vyctualle*, r. *vyctiynes*.

F I N I S.

APPENDIX;

CONTAINING

SOME OBSERVATIONS UPON THE

LANGUAGE OF THE POEMS

ATTRIBUTED TO ROWLEY;

TENDING TO PROVE,

THAT THEY WERE WRITTEN, NOT BY
ANY ANCIENT AUTHOR, BUT ENTIRELY
BY THOMAS CHATTERTON.

Tum levis haud ultra latebras jam quærit imago,
Sed fublime volans noçti fe immifcuit atræ.

VIRGIL, Æ. X.

Y

A P P E N D I X, &c.

WHEN thefe Poems were firft printed, it was thought beft to leave the queftion of their authenticity to the determination of the impartial Public. The Editor contented himfelf with intimating his opinion, [Pref. p. xii, xiii.] that the external evidence on both fides was fo defective as to deferve but little attention, and that the final decifion of the queftion muft depend upon the internal evidence. To fhew that this opinion was not thrown out in order to miflead the enquiries and judgements of the readers, I have here drawn together *fome obfervations upon* THE LANGUAGE * *of the poems attributed to Rowley,* which, I think, will be fufficient to prove, 1ft, that they were not written in the XV Century; and 2dly, that they were written entirely by Thomas Chatterton.

* I have chofen this *part* of the internal evidence, becaufe the arguments, which it furnifhes, are not only very decifive, but alfo lie within a moderate compafs. For the fame reafon of brevity, I have confined my obfervations to a *part* only of this *part,* viz. to *words,* confidered with refpect to their *fignifications* and *inflexions.* A complete examination of this fubject *in all its parts* would be a work of length.

The

The proof of the fecond propofition would in effect carry with it that of the firft; but, notwithftanding, I choofe to treat them feparately and to begin with the firft.

I fhall premife only one *poftulatum*, which is, that Poets of the fame age and country ufe the fame language, allowances being made for certain varieties, which may arife from the local fituation, the rank in life, the learning, the affectation of the writers, and from the different fubjects and forms of their compofitions *.

This being granted, I have nothing to do but to prove, that the language of the poems attributed to Rowley (when every proper allowance has been made) is totally different from that of the other Englifh writers of the XV Century, in many material particulars. It would be too tedious to go through them all; and therefore I fhall only take notice of fuch as can be referred to three general heads; the *firft* confifting of words

---

* Of thefe varieties all, except the firft, are more properly varieties of *ftyle* than of *language*. The *local fituation* of a writer may certainly produce a *provincial dialect*, which will often differ effentially from the language ufed at the fame time in other parts of the fame country. But this can only happen in the cafe of perfons of no education and to-tally illiterate; and fuch perfons feldom write. It is unneceffary how-ever to difcufs this point very accurately, as nobody, I believe, will contend, that the poems attributed to Rowley are written in any *provincial dialect*. If there fhould be a few words in them, which are now more common at Briftol than at London, it fhould be remembered that Chatterton was of Briftol.

not

not ufed by any other writer; the *fecond*, of words ufed by other writers, but in a different fenfe; and the *third*, of words inflected in a manner contrary to grammar and cuftom.

Under the *firft* head I would recommend the following words to the reader's confideration.

1. ABESSIE. E. III. 89.

Whyleft the congeon flowrette *abeffie* dyghte.

2. ABORNE. T. 45.

Snett oppe hys long ftrunge bowe and fheelde *aborne*.

3. ABREDYNGE. Æ. 334.

Agylted Ælla, thie *abredynge* blynge.

4. ACROOLE. El. 6.

Didde fpeke *acroole*, wythe languifhment of eyne.

5. ADAVE. H. 2. 402.

The fyneft dame the fun or moone *adave*.

6. ADENTE. Æ. 396. ADENTED. G. 32.

Ontoe thie vefte thy rodde fonne ys *adente*.

Adented prowefs to the gite of witte.

7. ADRAMES. Ep. 27.

Loughe loudlie dynneth from the dolte *adrames*.

8. ALATCHE. Æ. 117.

Leave me fwythe or I'lle *alatche*.

9. ALMER. Ch. 20.

Whoe from the hail-ftone coulde the *almer* flie?

      10. ALUSTE.

10. ALUSTE. H. 1. 88.

That Alured coulde not hymfelf *alufle.*

11. ALYNE. T. 79.

Wythe murther tyred he flynges hys bowe *alyne:*

12. ALYSE. Le. 29.—G. 180.

Somme dryblette fhare you fhoulde to that *alyfe.*

Fulle twentie mancas I wylle thee *alife.*

13. ANERE. Æ. 15.—Ep. 48.

And cann I lyve to fee herr wythe *anere?*

————————— Adieu untylle *anere.*

14. ANETE. p. 281. 64.

Whych yn the blofom woulde fuch fins *anete.*

15. APPLINGS. E. I. 33.

Mie tendre *applynges* and embodyde trees.

16. ARROW-LEDE. H. 1. 74.

Han by his foundynge *arrowe-lede* bene fleyne.

17. ASENGLAVE. H. 1. 117.

But Harold's *afenglave* ftopp'd it as it flewe.

18. ASLEE. Æ. 504.

That doeft *aflee* alonge ynn doled dyftreffe.

19. ASSWAIE. Æ. 352.

Botte thos to leave thee, Birtha, dothe *affwaie*

Moe torturynge peynes, &c.

20. ASTENDE. G. 47.

Acheke the mokie aire and heaven *aftende.*

I ftop

I ſtop here, not becauſe the other Letters of the alphabet would not afford a proportionable number of words which might be referred to this head, but becauſe I think theſe ſufficient for my purpoſe.   I proceed therefore to ſet down an equal number of words under the *ſecond* general head.

1. ABOUNDE. H. 1. 55.

His criſtede beaver dyd him ſmalle *abounde*.

The common ſenſe of *Abound*, a verb, is well known; but what can be the meaning of it here?

2. ALEDGE. G. 5.

Lette notte thie agreme blyn ne *aledge* ſtonde.

Aledge, or *Alege*, v. Fr. in Chaucer ſignifies *to alleviate*.   It is here uſed either as an adjective or as an adverb.   Chatterton interprets it to mean *idly*; upon what ground I cannot gueſs.

3. ALL A BOON. E. III. 41 —p. 23. l. 4.

All-a-boon, ſyr Prieſt, *all-a-boon*.

Thys ys the onelie *all-a-boone* I crave.

Here are three Engliſh words, the ſenſe of which, taken ſeparately, is clear.   As joined together in this paſſage they are quite unintelligible.

4. ALLEYN. E. I. 52.

Mie ſonne, mie ſonne *alleyn* yſtorven ys.

Granting *alleyn* to be rightly put for *alone*, no ancient writer, I apprehend, ever uſed ſuch a phraſe as this; any more than we ſhould now ſay—*my ſon alone* for *my only ſon*.

5. ASCAUNCE. E. III. 52.

Lokeynge *afcaunce* upon the naighboure greene.

The ufual fenfe of *afcaunce* in Chaucer, and other old writers, has been explained in a note on ver. 7327. of the Can-
terbury Tales. It is ufed in the fame fenfe by Gafcoigne.
The more modern adverb *afcaunce*, fignifying *fideways, obliquely,*
is derived from the Italian *a fchiancio,* and I doubt very much
whether it had been introduced into the Englifh language in
the time of the fuppofed Rowley.

6. ASTERTE. G. 137.

——————— You have theyr worthe *afterte.*

I defpair of finding any authorized fenfe of the word *afterte,*
that will fuit this paffage. It cannot, I think, fignifie *neglected
or paffed by,* as Chatterton has rendered it.

7. AUMERE. Æ. 398.—Ch. 7. AUMERES. E. III. 25.

Depyȼte wyth fkylled honde upponn thie wyde *aumere.*

And eke the grounde was dighte in its mofe defte *aumere.*

Wythe gelten *aumeres* ftronge ontolde.

The only place in which I remember to have met with this
word is in Chaucer's Romant of the Rofe, ver. 2271. and
there it undoubtedly fignifies *a purfe;* probably from the Fr.
Aumoniere. *Aumere of filk* is Chaucer's tranflation of *Bourfe de
foye.* In another place of the fame poem, ver. 2087. he ufes
aumener in the fame fenfe. The interpretations given of this
word by Chatterton will be confidered below.

8. BARBED.

8. BARBED. Æ. 27. 219.

Nott, whan from the *barbed* horfe, &c.

Mie lord fadre's *barbde* halle han ne wynnynge.

Let it be allowed, that *barbed horfe* was a proper expreffion, in the XV Century, for *a horfe covered with armour,* can any one conceive that *barbed hall* fignified *a hall in which armour was hung?* or what other fenfe can *barbde* have in this paffage?

9. BLAKE. Æ. 178. 407.

Whanne Autumpne *blake* and fonne-brente doe appere.

Blake ftondeth future doome, and joie doth mee alyfe.

Blake, in old Englifh, may fignifie either *black,* or *bleak.* Chatterton, in both thefe paffages, renders it *naked*; and, in the latter, fome fuch fignification feems abfolutely neceffary to make any fenfe.

10. BODYKIN. Æ. 265.

And for a *bodykyn* a *fwarthe* obteyne.

Bodekin is ufed by Chaucer more than once to fignifie *a bodkin* or *dagger.* I know not that it had any other fignification in his time. *Swarthe,* ufed as a noun, has no fenfe that I am acquainted with.

11. BORDEL. E. III. 2.—Æ. 147. **BORDELIER.** Æ. 410.

Goe ferche the logges and *bordels* of the hynde.

We wylle in a *bordelle* lyve.

Hailie the robber and the *bordelyer.*

Though

Though *bordel*, in very old French, fignifies a *cottage*, and *bordelier* a *cottager*, Chaucer ufes the firft word in no other fenfe than that of *brothel* or *bawdy-houfe*; and *bordeller* with him means the keeper of fuch a houfe. After this ufage of thefe words was fo eftablifhed, it is not eafy to believe that any later writer would hazard them in their primitive fenfe.

12. BYSMARE. M. 95.

Roaringe and rolleyng on yn courfe *byfmare*.

Bifmare, in Chaucer, fignifies *abufive fpeech*; nor do I believe that it ever had any other fignification.

13. CHAMPYON, v. PG. 12.

Wee better for to doe do *champyon* anie onne.

I do not believe that *champion* was ufed as a *verb* by any writer much earlier than Shakefpeare.

14. CONTAKE. T. 87. CONTEKE. E. II. 10.

———— I *contake* thie waie.

Conteke the dynnynge ayre and reche the fkies.

Conteke is ufed by Chaucer, as a *noun*, for *Contention*. I know no inftance of its being ufed as a *verb*.

15. DERNE. Æ. 582. DERNIE. E. I. 19. El. 8. M. 106.

Whan thou didft boafte foe moche of actyon *derne*.

Oh Raufe, comme lyfte and hear mie *dernie* tale.

O gentle Juga, heare mie *dernie* plainte.

He wrythde arounde yn drearie *dernie* payne.

Derne is a Saxon adj. fignifying *fecret, private*, in which fenfe it is ufed more than once by Chaucer, and in no other.

16. DROORIE.

16. DROORIE. Ep. 47.

Botte lette ne wordes, whiche *droorie* mote ne heare,
Bee placed in the fame ————.

The only fenfe that I know of *druerie* is *courtſhip, gallantry,* which will not fuit with this paffage.

17. FONNES. E. II. 14. Æ. 421. FONS. T. 4.

Decorn wyth *fonnes* rare ————.
On of the *fonnis* whych the clerche have made.
Quayntyffed *fons* depictedd on eche ſheelde.

A *fonne* in Chaucer fignifies a *fool*, and *fonnes—fools*; and Spenfer ufes *fon* in the fame fenfe; nor do I believe that it ever had any other meaning.

18. KNOPPED. M. 14.

Theyre myghte ys *knopped* ynne the froſte of fere.

Knopped is ufed by Chaucer to fignifie *faſtened* with a button, from *knoppe*, a button; but what poet, that knew the meaning of his words, would fay that any thing was *buttoned with froſt?*

19. LECTURN. Le. 46.

An onliſt *lecturn* and a fonge adygne.

I do not fee that *lecturn* can poffibly fignifie any thing but *a reading-deſk*, in which fenfe it is ufed by Chaucer.

20. LITHIE. Ep. 10.

Inne *lithie* muncke apperes the barronnes pryde.

If there be any fuch word as this, we ſhould naturally ex-
peƈt

pect it to follow the fignification of *lithe*; foft, limber : which will not fuit with this paffage.

I go on to the *third* general head of words inflected contrary to grammar and cuftom. In a language like ours, in which the inflections are fo few and fo fimple, it is not to be fuppofed that a writer, even of the loweft clafs, would commit very frequent offences of this fort. I fhall take notice of fome, which I think impoffible to have fallen from a genuine Rowley.

1. CLEVIS. H. 2. 46.
Fierce as a *clevis* from a rocke ytorne.

Clevis or *cleves* is the plural number of *Cleve*, a cliff. It is fo ufed by Chaucer. I cannot believe that it was ever ufed as a fingular noun.

EYNE. E. II. 79. T. 169. See alfo Æ. 681.
In everich *eyne* aredynge nete of wyere.
Wythe fyke an *eyne* fhee fwotelie hymm dydd view.

Eyne, a contraction of *eyen*, is the plural number of *eye*. It is not more probable that an ancient writer fhould have ufed the expreffions here quoted, than that any one now fhould fay—*In every eyes ;—With fuch an eyes.*

HEIE. E. II. 15. T. 123. Le. 5. 9. Ent. 2. Æ. 355.
Heie, the old plural of *He*, was obfolete, I apprehend, in the time of the fuppofed Rowley. At leaft it is very improbable that the fame writer, at any time, fhould ufe *heie* and *theie* indifferently, as in thefe poems.

5　　　　　　　　　　　　　　　　　　THYSSEN.

THYSSEN. E. II. 87.

Lette *thyssen* menne, who haveth fprite of love.

I cannot believe that *thyssen* was ever in ufe as the plural number of *this*. The termination feems to have been added, for the fake of the metre, by one who knew that many words formerly ended in *en*, but was quite ignorant of what particular forts they were. In the fame manner *coyen*. Æ. 125. and *fothen*. Æ. 227. are put for *coy* and *fothe*, contrary to all ufage or analogy.

And this leads me to the capital blunder, which runs through all thefe poems, and would alone be fufficient to deftroy their credit; I mean, the termination of *verbs in the fingular number in n* *. I will fet down a number of inftances, in which *han* is ufed for the prefent or paft time *fingular* of the v. *Have;* only premifing, that *han*, being an abbreviation of *haven*, is never ufed by any ancient writer except in the prefent time *plural* and the infinitive mode.

P. 26. v. 9. The Brytifh Merlyn oftenne *hanne*
The gyfte of infpyration.

* It is not furprizing that Chatterton fhould have been ignorant of a peculiarity of the Englifh language, which appears to have efcaped the obfervation of a profeffed editor of Chaucer. Mr. Urry has very frequently lengthened *verbs in the fingular number*, by adding *n* to them, without any authority, I am perfuaded, even from the errors of former Editions or MSS. It might feem invidious to point out living writers, of acknowledged learning, who have flipped into the fame miftake in their imitations of Chaucer and Spenfer.

Ba. 2.

Ba. 2. The featherd fongfter chaunticleer

   Han wounde hys bugle horne.

Æ. 685. Echone wylie wyfien h e *hanne* feene the daie.

   734. Bryghte fonne *han* ynne hys roddie robes byn dyghte.

   650. Whanne Eng'onde *han* her foemenn.

   1137. —— Mic ftede *han* notte mie love.

   1184 *Hanne* alle the fuirie of mysfortunes wylle

   Fallen onne mie benned headde I *hanne* been Ælla

   ftylle.

G. 20. *Hane* Englonde thenne a tongue butte notte a ftynge?

M. 61. A tye of love a dawter faire fhe *hanne.*

H. 1. 74. Ne doubting but the braveft in the londe

   Han by his foundynge arrowe-lede bene fleyne.

   182. Where he by chance *han* flayne a noble's fon.

   184. And in the battel he much goode *han* done.

   188. He of his boddie *han* kepte watch and ward.

   207. His chaunce in warr he ne before *han* tryde.

   281. The erlie felt de Torcies trecherous knyfe

   Han made his crymfon bloude and fpirits floe.

   319. O Hengift, *han* thy caufe bin good and true!

   321. The erlie was a manne of hie degree,

   And *han* that daie full manie Normannes fleine.

   337. But better *han* it bin to lett alone.

If more inftances fhould be wanted, fee H. 1. 396. 429.
455. H. 2. 316. 713.—p. 275. ver. 4.—p. 281. ver. 63.—
p. 288. ver. 1.

In

In the fame irregular manner the following verbs are ufed *fingularly*.

E. I. 10. Then *fellen* on the grounde and thus yfpoke.

H. 2. 675. Bewopen Alfwoulde *fellen* on his knee.

P. 287. ver. 17. For thee I *gotten* or bie wiles or breme.

H. 1. 252. He turned aboute and vilely *fouten* flie.

H. 2. 349. Fallyng he *fhooken* out his fmokyng braine.

H. 2. 344. His fprite—Ne *fhoulden* find a place in anie fonge.

Æ. 172. So Adam *thoughtenne* when ynn paradyfe——

1136. Tys now fulle morne; I *thoughten*, bie lafte nyghte—

Ch. 54. Full well it *fhewn*, he *thoughten* cofte no finne.

See alfo H. 2. 376. where *thoughten*, with the additional fyllable, not being quite long enough for the verfe, has had another fyllable added at the beginning.

Ne onne abafh'd *enthoughten* for to flee.

And (what is ftill more curious) we have a participle of the prefent tenfe formed from this fiƈtitious paft time, in Æ. 704.

Enthoughteyng for to fcape the *brondeynge* foe—

Which would not have been a bit more intelligible in the XV Century than it would be now. *Brondeynge* will be taken notice of below.

Many other inftances of the moft unwarrantable anomalies might be produced under this head; but I think I have faid enough to prove, that the language of thefe poems is totally different from that of the other Englifh writers of the XV Century;

tury; and confequently that they were not written in that century; which was my firft propofition. I fhall now endeavour to prove, from the fame internal evidence of the language, that they were written entirely by Thomas Chatterton.

For this purpofe it will only be neceffary to have recourfe to thofe interpretations of words by way of Gloffary, which were confeffedly written by him *. It will foon appear, if I am not much miftaken, that the author of the Gloffary was the author of the Poems.

Whoever will take the pains to examine thefe interpretations will find, that they are almoft all taken from SKINNER's *Etymologicon Linguæ Angiicanæ* †. In many cafes, where the

* This is a point fo material to the following argument, that, though it has never hitherto, I believe, been made a queftion, it ought not perhaps to be affumed without fome proof. It may be faid, that Chatterton was only the *tranfcriber* of the Gloffary as well as of the Poems. If to fuch an affertion we were to anfwer, that Chatterton always declared himfelf the *author* of the Gloffaries, we fhould be told perhaps, that with equal truth he always declared Rowley to have been the author of the Poems. But (not to infift upon the very different weight, which the fame teftimony might be allowed to have in the two cafes) it has happened luckily, that the Gloffary to the Poem, entitled " *Englyfh Metamorphofis*," [See p. 196.] was written down by Chatterton extemporally, without the affiftance of any book, at the defire and in the prefence of Mr. Barrett. Whoever will compare that Gloffary with the others, will have no doubt of their being all from the fame hand.

† Printed at London, MDCLXXI. The part, which Chatterton feems to have chiefly confulted, is that, which begins at Sign. U u u u, and is entitled " *Etymologicon vocum omnium antiquarum Anglicarum, quæ ufque a Wilhelmo Victore invaluerunt,* &c."

words

words are really ancient, the interpretations are perfectly right; and so far Chatterton can only be confidered in the light of a commentator, who avails himfelf of the beft affiftances to explane any genuine author. But in many other inftances, where the words are either not ancient or not ufed in their ancient fenfe, the interpretations are totally unfounded and fantaftical; and at the fame time the words cannot be altered or amended confiftently with any rules of criticifin, nor can the interpretations be varied without deftroying the fenfe of the paffage. In thefe cafes, I think, there is a juft ground for believing, that the words as well as their interpretations came from the hand of Chatterton, efpecially as they may be proved very often to have taken their rife either from blunders of Skinner himfelf, or from fuch miftakes and mifapprehenfions of his meaning as Chatterton, from hafte and ignorance, was very likely to fall into.

I will ftate firft fome inftances of words and interpretations which have evidently been derived from blunders of Skinner.

ALL A BOON. E. III. 41. See before, p. 315.

A manner of afking a favour, fays Chatterton.

Now let us hear Skinner.

" All a bone, exp. Preces, Supplex Libellus, Supplicatio, vel ut jam loquimur Petitio viro Principi exhibita, ni fallor ab AS. Bene, unde noftrum *Boon* additis particulis Fr. G. *A la.* Ch. Fab. Mercatoris fol. 30. p. 1. Col. 2."

The

The paſſage of Chaucer which is referred to, as an authority for this word, is the following, Canterb. Tales, ver. 9492.

"And alderfirſt he bade hem *all a bone*," i. e. he made a requeſt to them all. So that Skinner is entirely miſtaken in making one phraſe of theſe three words; and it is ſurely more probable that the author of the poems was miſled by him, than that a really ancient writer ſhould have been guilty of ſo egregious a blunder.

AUMERES. E. III. 25. is explained by Chatterton to mean *Borders of gold and ſilver*, &c.   And AUMERE in Æ. 398, and Ch. 7. ſeems to be uſed in the ſame ſenſe of *a border of a garment*.   And ſo Skinner has by miſtake explained the word, in that paſſage of Chaucer which has been mentioned above [See p. 316, where the true meaning of *Aumere* is given].

"Aumere ex contextu videtur *Fimbria* vel *Inſtita*, neſcio an a Teut. Umbher, Circum, Circa. q. d. Circuitus ſeu ambitus, Ch. f. 119. p. 1. C. 1."

BAWSIN. Æ. 57. *Large*. Chatterton. M. 101. *Huge, bulky*, Chatterton.

Without pretending to determine the preciſe meaning of *Bawſin*, I think I may venture to ſay that there is no older or better authority for rendering it *large*, than Skinner. "Bawſin, exp. *Magnus, Grandis*, &c."

BRONDEOUS. E. II. 24. *Furious*. Chatterton. BRONDED. H. 2. 568. BRONDEYNGE. Æ. 704. BURLIE BRONDE. G. 7. *Fury, anger*. Chatterton.   See alſo H. 2. 674.

All

All thefe ufes of *Bronde*, and its fuppofed derivatives, are taken from Skinner. " 𝕭𝖗𝖔𝖓𝖉𝖊, exp. *Furia*, &c." though in another place he explains 𝕭𝖚𝖗𝖑𝖞 𝖇𝖗𝖆𝖓𝖉 (I believe, rightly) to mean *Magnus enfis.* It fhould be obferved, that the phrafe *Burly brand*, if ufed in its true fenfe, would ftill have been liable to fufpicion, as it does not appear in any work, that I am acquainted with, prior to the *Teftament of Crefeide*, a Scottifh compofition, written many years after the time of the fuppofed Rowley.

BURLED. M. 20. *Armed*. Chatterton, So Skinner, " 𝕭𝖚𝖗𝖑𝖊𝖉, exp. *Armatus*, &c."

BYSMARE. M. 95. *Bewildered, curious*. Chatterton. BYS-MARELIE. Le. 26. *Curioufly*. Chatterton. See alfo p. 285. ver. 141. BISMARDE.

It is evident, I think, that all thefe words are originally derived from Skinner, who has very abfurdly explained 𝕭𝖎𝖘𝖒𝖆𝖗𝖊 to mean 𝕮𝖚𝖗𝖎𝖔𝖚𝖘𝖙𝖞. The true meaning has been ftated above, p. 318.

CALKE. G. 25. *Caft*. Chatterton. CALKED. E. I. 49. *Caft out, ejected*. Chatterton. This word appears to have been formed upon a mifapprehenfion of the following article in Skinner. " 𝕮𝖆𝖑𝖐𝖊𝖉, exp. 𝕮𝖆𝖘𝖙, credo 𝕮𝖆𝖘𝖙 𝖚𝖕." Chatterton did not attend to the difference between *cafting out* and *cafting up*, i. e. *cafting up figures in calculation*. That the latter was Skinner's meaning may be collected from his next article. " 𝕮𝖆𝖑𝖐𝖊𝖉 for 𝕮𝖆𝖑𝖈𝖚𝖑𝖆𝖙𝖊𝖉, Ch. the Frankeleynes tale." It is probable too, I

think,

think, that in both articles Skinner refers, by miftake, to a line of *the Frankelein's tale*, which in the common editions ftands thus :

" Ful fubtelly he had *calked* al this."

Where *calked* is a mere mifprint for *calculed*, the reading of the MSS. See the late Edit. ver. 11596.

It would be eafy to add many more inftances of words, *either not ancient or not ufed in their ancient fenfe*, which repeatedly occur in thefe poems, and muft be conftrued according to thofe fanciful fignifications which Skinner has afcribed to them. How that fhould have happened, unlefs either Skinner had read the Poems (which, I prefume, nobody can fuppofe,) or the author of the Poems had read Skinner, I cannot fee. It is againft all odds, that two men, living at the diftance of two hundred years one from the other, fhould accidentally agree in coining the fame words, and in affixing to them exactly the fame meaning.

I proceed to ftate fome inftances of words and interpretations which are evidently founded upon mifapprehenfions of paffages in Skinner.

ALYSE. Le. 29. G. 180. *Allow*. Chatterton. See before, p. 314.

Till I meet with this word, in this fenfe, in fome approved author, I fhall be of opinion that it has been formed from a miftaken reading of the following article in Skinner. " Alifd, Authori

Authori Dict. Angl. apud quem solum occurrit, exp. Allowed, ab A S. Alyfed, &c." In the Gothic types used by Skinner f might be easily mistaken for a long ſ.

Bestoiker. Æ. 91. *Deceiver.* Chatterton. See also Æ. 1064.

This word also seems plainly to have originated from a mistake in reading Skinner. " Beſwike, ab A S. Beſpican, Spicah, *Decipere,* Fallere, Prodere, Spica, Proditor, *Deceptor.*" Chatterton in his hurry read this as Beſtoike, and formed a noun from it accordingly.

Blake. Æ. 178. 407. *Naked.* Chatterton. Blakied. E. III. 4. *Naked, original.* Chatterton. See before, p. 317.

Skinner has the following article. " Blake *and* bare, videtur ex contextu prorsus *Nuda,* fort. q. d. Bleak *and* Bare, dum enim nudi sumus, eóque aeri expositi præ frigore pallescimus. Ch. fol. 184. p. 1. Col. 1."

Chatterton has caught hold of *Nuda,* which in Skinner is the exposition of *Bare,* as if it belonged to *Blake.*

Hancelled. G. 49. *Cut off, destroyed.* Chatterton. *Hancelled* from erthe these Normanne hyndes shalle bee.

Skinner has the same word, which he thus explains. " Hanceled, exp Cut of, credo dici proprie, vel primario saltem, tantum de prima portione seu segmento quod ad tentandam seu explorandam rem abscindimus, ut ubi dicimus, to Hanſell *a pasty or a gammon of bacon.*" Chatterton, who had

neither

neither inclination nor perhaps ability to make himſelf maſter of ſo long a piece of Latin, appears to have looked no further than the two Engliſh words at the beginning of this explanation; and underſtanding *Cut off* to mean *Deſtroyed,* he has uſed *Hancelled* in the ſame ſenſe.

SHAP. Æ. 34. G. 18. *Fate.* Chatterton. SHAP-SCURGED. Æ. 603. *Fate-ſcourged.* Chatterton.

Shap haveth nowe ymade hys woes for to emmate.

Stylle mormorynge atte yer *ſhap.*——

There ys ne houſe athrow thys *ſhap-ſcurged* iſle.

I never was able to conceive how *Shap* ſhould have been uſed in the Engliſh language to ſignifie *Fate,* till I obſerved the following article in Skinner. " **Shap,** *now is my* **ſhap,** nunc mihi *Fato* præſtitutum eſt (i. e.) *now is it* **ſhapen** *to me,* ab A S. Sceapan, &c." I ſuppoſe that the word *Fato,* in the Latin, led Chatterton to underſtand *now is my ſhap* to mean *now is my fate.*

The paſſage, to which Skinner refers, is in the Knight's tale of Chaucer, ver. 1227.

> *Now is me ſhape eternally to dwelle*
> Not only in purgatorie but in helle.

But in the Edit. of 1602, which Skinner appears to have made uſe of, it is written *Now is me ſhap.* The putting of *my* for *me* was probably a miſtake of the Printer, as Skinner's explanation ſhews that he read *me.*

I fancy

APPENDIX, &c. 331

I fancy the generality of readers will be satisfied by the fore-
going quotations, that the Author of these poems had not only
read Skinner, but has also misapprehended and misapplied
what he found in him. If more instances should be wanted, a
comparison of the words explained by Chatterton with the
same or similar words as explained by Skinner, will furnish
them in abundance *. I shall therefore conclude this Appendix with a short view of the preceding argument.

It

---

* I will state shortly some of those words, which have been cited
above, p. 313. as *either not ancient or not used in their ancient sense,* with
their corresponding articles in Skinner.

ABESSIE; *Humility.* C.—𝔄𝔟𝔢𝔰𝔰𝔢𝔡; —*Humiliatus.* Sk.

ABORNE; *Burnished,* C.—𝔅𝔬𝔯𝔫𝔢; *Burnish.* Sk. It was usual with
Chatterton to prefix *a* to words of all sorts, without any regard to cus-
tom or propriety. See in the Alphabetical Gloss. *Aboune, Abrewe,
Acome, Aderne, Adygne, Agrame, Agreme, Alest,* &c.

ABOUNDE. This word Chatterton has not interpreted, but the
context shews that it is used in the sense of *good.* So that I suspect it
was taken from the following article in Skinner. 𝔄𝔟𝔬𝔫𝔢.—a Fr. G.
Abonnir; *Bonum* facere.

ABREDYNGE; *Upbraiding.* C.—𝔄𝔟𝔯𝔢𝔡𝔢, exp. *Upbraid.* Sk.

ACROOL; *Faintly.* C.—𝔠𝔯𝔬𝔬𝔩, exp. *Murmurare.* Sk. See the remark upon ABORNE.

ADENTE, ADENTED; *Fastened, annexed.* C.—𝔄𝔡𝔢𝔫𝔱;—*Configere,
Conjungere.* Sk.

ALUSTE has no interpretation; but it is used in the sense of *raise.*
Perhaps it may have been derived from a mistaken reading of 𝔄𝔧𝔲𝔰𝔱,
which is explained by Skinner to mean *Tollere.* See the remarks upon
Alyse and *Bestoiker,* p. 328, 329.

DERNE,

It has been proved, that the poems attributed to Rowley were not written in the XV Century; and it follows of course, that they were written, at a subsequent period, by some impostor, who endeavoured to counterfeit an author of that century.

It has been proved, that this impostor lived since Skinner, and that the same person wrote the interpretations of words by way of Glossary, which are subjoined to most of the poems.

It has also been proved, that Chatterton wrote those interpretations of words.

Whether any thing further be necessary to prove, that the poems were entirely written by Chatterton, is left to the reader's judgement. If he should stick at the word *entirely*, which may possibly seem to carry the conclusion a little beyond the premisses, he is desired to reflect, that, the poems having been proved to be a forgery since the time of Skinner, and to have been written in great part by Chatterton, it is infinitely more

DERNE, DERNIE; *Woeful, lamentable, cruel.* C.—Derne; *Dirus, crudelis.* Sk.

DROORIE; *Modesty.* C.—Drury; *Modestia.* Sk.

FONS, FONNES; *Fancys, Devices.* C.—ffonnes; *Devises.* Sk.

KNOPPED; *Fastened, chained, congealed.* C.— Knopped; *Tied.* Sk.

LITHIE; *Humble.* C.—Lithy; *Humble.* Sk. But in truth I do not believe that there is any such word. Skinner probably found it in his edition of Chaucer's *Cuckow and Nightingale*, ver. 14. where the MSS. have LITHER *(wicked)*, which is undoubtedly the right reading.

probable

probable that the remainder was alſo written by him than by any other perſon. The great difficulty is to conceive that a youth, like Chatterton, ſhould ever have formed the plan of ſuch an impoſture, and ſhould have executed it with ſo much perſeverance and ingenuity; but if we allow (as I think we muſt) that he was the author of thoſe pieces to which he ſub-joined his interpretations, I can ſee no reaſon whatever for ſuppoſing that he had any aſſiſtance in the reſt. The internal evidence is ſtrong that they are all from one hand; and external evidence there is none, that I have been able to meet with, which ought to perſuade us, that a ſingle line, of verſe or proſe, purporting to be the work of ROWLEY, exiſted before the time of CHATTERTON.

www.ingramcontent.com/pod-product-compliance
Lightning Source LLC
Chambersburg PA
CBHW021104270326
41929CB00009B/732